Optimization Tools and Techniques for Enhanced Computational Efficiency

Hari Mohan Rai
Gachon University, South Korea

Abdul Razaque
Satbayev University, Kazakhstan

IGI Global
Scientific Publishing
Publishing Tomorrow's Research Today

Vice President of Editorial	Melissa Wagner
Managing Editor of Acquisitions	Mikaela Felty
Managing Editor of Book Development	Jocelynn Hessler
Production Manager	Mike Brehm
Cover Design	Phillip Shickler

Published in the United States of America by
IGI Global Scientific Publishing
701 East Chocolate Avenue
Hershey, PA, 17033, USA
Tel: 717-533-8845
Fax: 717-533-8661
Website: https://www.igi-global.com E-mail: cust@igi-global.com

Library of Congress Cataloging-in-Publication Data

LCCN: 2024053171 (CIP Data Pending)
ISBN13: 9798369368855
Isbn13Softcover: 9798369368862
EISBN13: 9798369368879

British Cataloguing in Publication Data
A Cataloguing in Publication record for this book is available from the British Library.

Table of Contents

Detailed Table of Contents

In today's quickly changing industrial sector, optimization strategies for mechanical applications are essential to improving product quality and preserving market competitiveness. In this chapter, several optimization techniques are discussed, including the gravitational search algorithms (GSA), analytic hierarchy process (AHP), Taguchi method (TM), artificial neural network (AFNN), response surface methodology (RSM), genetic algorithm (GA), firefly algorithm (FFA), fuzzy logic (FLA), and technique for order of preference by similarity to ideal solution (TOPSIS). Drilling, abrasive water jets (AWJ), milling, drive shafts, turning, and statistical properties for both general and high-speed mechanical applications of composite materials are some of the mechanical applications that employ these processes. Fiber composite structures are now the most appealing choice for mechanical engineering applications. Composite materials made of fiber-reinforced plastic polymer (FRP) have been used to build new buildings and restore existing, dilapidated traditional structures.

Evolutionary Algorithms (EAs) and Swarm Intelligence (SI)-based Optimization are powerful, nature-inspired methodologies used to solve complex optimization problems. EAs, including Genetic Algorithms and Evolution Strategies, simulate natural selection processes to iteratively improve solutions through selection, mutation, and crossover. On the other hand, SI-based techniques, such as Particle

Swarm Optimization and Ant Colony Optimization, draw from the collective behaviors of social organisms to effectively explore solution spaces. This chapter provides an overview of these approaches, examining their underlying principles, key algorithms, and applications in various fields. It also compares their strengths, discusses hybrid strategies that combine EAs and SI techniques, and explores future trends in optimization research.

Komal Singh, Pandit Deendayal Energy University, India
Nikhil Kumar Singh, Government Engineering College, Gandhinagar, India
Manish Khare, University of Allahabad, India

The internet plays a crucial role in modern society, with a vast number of individuals utilizing it for various purposes. Social media platforms are widely accessible to these users, allowing them to create posts and disseminate information online. Unfortunately, these platforms lack comprehensive user and content verification processes. Consequently, some users take advantage of this loophole to propagate false information. Such fake news can target individuals, societies, organizations, or political parties, and detecting them manually proves challenging for humans. Therefore, there is a pressing need for machine learning classifiers capable of automatically identifying fake news. Extensive research has explored the utilization of machine learning classifiers for fake news detection. This chapter examines six different machine learning techniques applied to six distinct approaches using the fake or real news dataset. The results indicate that the approach employing decision tree and SVM models achieves the highest accuracy compared to the other proposed machine learning classifiers.

Neha Verma, SGT University, India
Dheivanai Radhakrishnan, Dronacharya College of Engineering, India
Diya Ray, Dronacharya College of Engineering, India

The healthcare industry faces the challenge of balancing technological advancements with environmental sustainability. Emerging tools like digital twins and the metaverse hold promise for sustainable healthcare but remain underutilized. Digital twins replicate health data, while metaverse technologies (AR/VR) create interactive virtual environments, supporting eco-conscious practices. This study emphasizes energy-efficient virtual designs and algorithms to reduce environmental impact, human intervention, and resource use. Balancing innovation with data protection protocols, including encryption and decentralized storage, is essential. Eco-friendly production, ethical sourcing, and recycling further reduce the carbon footprint. User-friendly interfaces, accessibility features, and localized content can bridge digital gaps. For example, digital twins of healthcare professionals could enable virtual rounds, improving efficiency and reducing physical travel. These advancements, integrated with existing systems, enhance sustainability while minimizing environmental impact.

Lingala Thirupathi, Sreenidhi Institute of Science and Technology, India
B. Vasundara, Sreenidhi Institute of Science and Technology, India
Pallavi Rajan, Sreenidhi Institute of Science and Technology, India
Tejaswi Arella, Sreenidhi Institute of Science and Technology, India

Artificial intelligence (AI) and machine learning (ML) have revolutionized various industries and domains, enabling data-driven decision-making and automated problem-solving. However, the optimization of AI and ML models remains a critical challenge, as it directly impacts their performance, accuracy, and efficiency. It explores the optimization tools and techniques employed in AI and ML, focusing on their current state, limitations, and future directions. Through a comprehensive literature review, and analysis of industry practices, this chapter delves into the optimization landscape, covering topics such as hyperparameter tuning, model compression, federated learning, and quantum computing. Additionally, it investigates emerging trends and cutting-edge techniques that hold the potential to shape the future of AI and ML optimization. By examining the synergies between optimization methodologies and AI/ML algorithms, this research aims to provide a holistic understanding of the optimization landscape and its implications for advancing AI and ML capabilities.

David Samuel Azariya S., Sona College of Technology, India
V. Mohanraj, Sona College of Technology, India
V. Sathiyamoorthi, Government Polytechnic College, India
Jayapandian Natarajan, Christ University, India
Chinthakunta Manjunath, Christ University, India

The rapid growth of internet of things (IoT) devices necessitates efficient power management to curb escalating energy consumption. This chapter proposes a novel solution by employing deep learning techniques to optimize energy use in IoT sensors. The authors review existing IoT sensor energy consumption challenges and conventional power management limitations. Drawing on deep learning's successes, they develop an architecture trained on curated sensor data. Practical implications span industries, scalability, and generalizability to diverse IoT setups. Economic insights highlight potential cost savings and benefits. In conclusion, the innovative deep learning-based approach addresses IoT energy challenges, offering a promising solution that optimizes usage and could reshape IoT device efficiency. This work opens avenues for hybrid strategies, merging deep learning with other techniques, further advancing energy efficient IoT systems.

Yashika Goyal, Dr. A.P.J. Abdul Kalam Technical University, India
Hari Mohan Rai, Gachon University, South Korea
Aditya Pal, Dronacharya Group of Institutions, India

To efficiently handle finances and enhance quality of life, optimizing financial planning is crucial. Challenges like inaccurate data and delayed processing hinder current financial planners. Advanced machine learning is vital for automating and optimizing financial planning, ensuring accurate advice on savings, goal-setting, investments, and tax efficiency. Human errors risk stability. 'FinGenius: An Automatic Financial Planner' tackles these issues with tailored recommendations for budgeting, retirement planning, and investments, including sustainable funds. It integrates predictive analytics, real-time data processing, multilingual support, and robust security measures. Utilizing machine learning models like CNN, RNN, and K-means clustering, it achieves superior performance in financial data analysis, benchmarked against historical S&P stock data. Integration with APIs and cloud platforms (AWS, GCP) enhances utility and accuracy (F1 score: 0.88). This research underscores the role of technology in improving user experience, ensuring data security, and optimizing financial management.

Siddharth Rana, Dronacharya Group of Institutions, India
Hari Mohan Rai, International Information Technologies University, Kazakhstan

This chapter explores the theoretical foundations along with the vast implications of time travel from the theory of relativity to the concepts of higher dimensions. Derived from the Einstein's words embedded within the concept of relativity, this chapter provides a profound overlook upon the space-time continuum, allowing forward time-travel, while studying the multiple theoretical possibilities of backward time-travelling. This chapter provides a visualizations of the object approaching the speed of light and embarking beyond, unlocking the un-explored branches of the cosmos. Multiple visualization aspects to contemplate the lived-past and to-be-lived future have been visualized, connecting dots to every possibility of the entire cosmos. A unique aspect to understand the flow of the 4th dimension—time—has been overlooked from the 5th dimension, providing a complete access over the 4th dimension, unfolding all-past and all-future simultaneously, while going beyond the conventional scope of human thinking. It addresses multiple aspects of time aiming to understand cosmos.

Quantum computing is a novel kind of computation that solves very complicated problems rapidly by applying concepts from basic physics. Concepts like quantum mechanical computing and quantum algorithms are included in the field of quantum computing study. Researchers have imagined quantum computing as a revolutionary idea among emerging technologies in terms of concepts, methods, and techniques. These are cross-pollinated. Hence, quantum computing becomes more and more multidisciplinary. Quantum computing leverages quantum mechanical phenomena like superposition and quantum interference to deal with some kinds of problems more precisely than conventional computing. Because of its unique characteristics, which set it apart from conventional computers in terms of functionality and operation, quantum computing has grown in popularity. There are possibilities of creating hybrid models, namely approaches for large-scale mixed-integer programming issues, that effectively combine the strengths of quality control techniques with deterministic algorithms to handle combinatorial challenges.

Preface

Optimization techniques have emerged as a cornerstone of contemporary research and development, exerting a profound influence across a broad spectrum of engineering and technology domains. These methods represent the culmination of cutting-edge ideas and groundbreaking innovations, harnessing the computational prowess of modern computing systems to tackle intricate and multifaceted challenges. The field of optimization has rapidly evolved into a dynamic and multidisciplinary arena of exploration, drawing insights and expertise from diverse technical disciplines to drive innovation and efficiency.

At its core, optimization serves as a critical bridge between the realms of industry and academia. Its primary objective is to enhance processes, minimize resource consumption, and accelerate the introduction of new products and technologies to the market. By employing sophisticated computational algorithms and mathematical modeling, optimization techniques enable researchers and engineers to fine-tune parameters and variables to achieve optimal outcomes. This systematic approach has the potential to revolutionize industries by unlocking novel solutions to complex problems and driving operational excellence.

The realm of optimization encompasses a wide array of methodologies, including but not limited to linear programming, nonlinear optimization, integer programming, dynamic programming, genetic algorithms, simulated annealing, and particle swarm optimization. These techniques leverage mathematical principles and computational simulations to explore vast solution spaces, enabling the identification of optimal configurations and strategies.

The primary objective of this publication, titled *Optimization Tools and Techniques for Enhanced Computational Efficiency*, is to offer a nuanced understanding of optimization tools and techniques, their current trends, and their wide-ranging applications in engineering and technology. By examining the theoretical underpinnings, methodological advancements, and practical implementations of optimization methodologies, this publication seeks to provide readers with actionable insights and innovative approaches to problem-solving. Furthermore, it aims to foster interdisciplinary collaboration, knowledge exchange, and the development of novel solutions to complex challenges by engaging researchers, practitioners, educators, and students across various domains. Through a detailed exploration of optimization methodologies and their real-world impact, this publication endeavors to contribute to the advancement of knowledge, stimulate further research, and inspire transformative innovations in engineering and technology.

This book is aimed at professionals, researchers, and academics across various fields of study, including Computer Science and Information Technology, Education, Environmental, Agricultural, and Physical Sciences, Medical, Healthcare, and Life Sciences, Security and Forensics, as well as Science and Engineering. Specifically, individuals interested in optimization techniques and their applications within these domains will find valuable insights and practical implementations discussed in this publication. Graduate students, educators, and industry practitioners seeking to deepen their understanding of optimization methodologies and their real-world impact will also benefit from the content provided in this book.

ORGANIZATION OF THE BOOK

Chapter 1: A Study of Optimization Techniques Used in Composite Materials for Mechanical Applications

This chapter examines the critical role of optimization techniques in enhancing the performance and quality of mechanical applications within the rapidly evolving industrial sector. It explores a variety of optimization methods, including Gravitational Search Algorithms (GSA), Analytic Hierarchy Process (AHP), Taguchi Method (TM), Artificial Neural Network (ANN), Response Surface Methodology (RSM), and more. These techniques are applied across mechanical applications such as drilling, milling, and high-speed operations of fiber-reinforced plastic polymers (FRPs). With a focus on both developing new structures and rehabilitating old ones, the chapter demonstrates how composite materials have become essential for innovative mechanical engineering applications.

Chapter 2: Evolutionary Algorithms for Optimization and Swarm Intelligence-Based Optimization

This chapter introduces Evolutionary Algorithms (EAs) and Swarm Intelligence (SI)-based optimization techniques, drawing inspiration from natural systems to address complex challenges. It reviews foundational approaches, including Genetic Algorithms, Evolution Strategies, Particle Swarm Optimization, and Ant Colony

Optimization. Highlighting their strengths, hybrid applications, and future trends, the chapter delves into the efficacy of these algorithms across domains, emphasizing their ability to explore solution spaces effectively.

Chapter 3: Fake News Detection using Machine Learning Classifiers

Social media platforms have become breeding grounds for misinformation, necessitating advanced technological solutions. This chapter explores the use of machine learning classifiers to detect fake news, presenting an in-depth analysis of six techniques applied to the "Fake or Real News" dataset. Among these, Decision Tree and SVM models exhibit the highest accuracy. By automating detection, the chapter addresses the critical challenge of combating misinformation across digital platforms.

Chapter 4: Greening Digital Healthcare: Balancing Act for a Sustainable Future

This chapter addresses the healthcare sector's dual goals of technological advancement and environmental sustainability. It examines emerging tools like digital twins and the metaverse for creating eco-friendly practices. Emphasizing energy-efficient algorithms, reduced human intervention, and ethical sourcing, the chapter offers actionable strategies to reduce healthcare's carbon footprint. It also highlights the integration of these technologies with existing systems to enhance efficiency while prioritizing data protection and accessibility.

Chapter 5: Optimization Tools and Techniques for AI and ML: Exploring Future Directions and Emerging Trends

This chapter provides a comprehensive exploration of optimization methodologies in AI and ML, including hyperparameter tuning, model compression, federated learning, and quantum computing. Through a detailed review of current limitations and emerging trends, the chapter highlights the synergies between optimization tools and AI/ML algorithms. It emphasizes the critical need for advancements that will shape the future of AI and ML optimization.

Chapter 6: Optimizing Energy Consumption in IoT Sensors Through Deep Learning-Based Power Management

As IoT devices proliferate, energy consumption management has become critical. This chapter proposes a deep learning-based architecture to optimize energy use in IoT sensors. By addressing limitations in conventional power management strategies, the chapter highlights the scalability and cost-saving potential of its approach. Practical applications across industries and the promise of hybrid strategies underscore the transformative potential of deep learning in IoT systems.

Chapter 7: Optimizing Financial Planning Through Advanced Machine Learning Techniques

Financial planning faces challenges like data inaccuracies and delayed processing, which hinder its effectiveness. This chapter presents a solution through the development of "FinGenius," an automated financial planning tool leveraging advanced machine learning techniques such as CNNs and RNNs. Offering personalized recommendations and real-time data analysis, the tool ensures accuracy, security, and improved financial management.

Chapter 8: Optimizing Theoretical Foundations and Implications of Time Travel: From Relativity to Higher Dimensions and Beyond

Exploring the realm of time travel, this chapter connects the Theory of Relativity with higher-dimensional concepts. It examines the possibilities of traversing the space-time continuum and accessing the fourth dimension from a fifth-dimensional perspective. By pushing the boundaries of conventional human understanding, the chapter delves into the theoretical and practical implications of time travel within the broader context of cosmic exploration.

Chapter 9: Quantum Computing for Optimization and its Applications

This chapter introduces quantum computing as a revolutionary tool for solving complex optimization problems. It explores the unique characteristics of quantum algorithms, such as superposition and quantum interference, that enable precise solutions beyond the capabilities of classical computing. The chapter discusses potential hybrid models for large-scale combinatorial challenges, highlighting quantum computing's multidisciplinary applications and transformative potential across industries.

CONCLUSION

In conclusion, this edited reference book serves as a comprehensive exploration of the diverse optimization techniques and transformative innovations shaping industries today. From advanced composite materials to evolutionary algorithms, machine learning applications, sustainable healthcare, and the burgeoning fields of quantum computing and time travel, the chapters collectively reflect the dynamic interplay between technological advancements and practical applications. By bringing together the insights and expertise of researchers and practitioners, this volume aims to inspire further exploration, foster interdisciplinary collaboration, and equip readers with the knowledge to address the complex challenges of the modern era. We hope this work serves not only as a valuable academic resource but also as a catalyst for innovation and progress across fields.

Hari Mohan Rai
Gachon University, South Korea

Abdul Razaque
Satbayev University, Kazakhstan

Chapter 1
A Study of Optimization Techniques Used in Composite Materials for Mechanical Applications

Sagar Dnyandev Patil
https://orcid.org/0000-0003-0283-4853
Sharad Institute of Technology College of Engineering, Yadrav Ichalkaranji, India

Prafulla Ratnakar Hatte
MIT Academy of Engineering, Alandi, India

ABSTRACT

In today's quickly changing industrial sector, optimization strategies for mechanical applications are essential to improving product quality and preserving market competitiveness. In this chapter, several optimization techniques are discussed, including the gravitational search algorithms (GSA), analytic hierarchy process (AHP), Taguchi method (TM), artificial neural network (AFNN), response surface methodology (RSM), genetic algorithm (GA), firefly algorithm (FFA), fuzzy logic (FLA), and technique for order of preference by similarity to ideal solution (TOPSIS). Drilling, abrasive water jets (AWJ), milling, drive shafts, turning, and statistical properties for both general and high-speed mechanical applications of composite materials are some of the mechanical applications that employ these processes. Fiber composite structures are now the most appealing choice for mechanical engineering applications. Composite materials made of fiber-reinforced plastic polymer (FRP) have been used to build new buildings and restore existing, dilapidated traditional structures.

DOI: 10.4018/979-8-3693-6885-5.ch001

1. INTRODUCTION

The process of machining involves utilizing power-driven machine tools to remove material from a workpiece. Work materials, process parameter settings, and the tools utilized all affect the efficiency of the method and the quality of the result. Selecting crucial process parameters that provide desirable responses with an acceptable degree of variation can result in a considerable improvement in process efficiency. Many optimization strategies for metal-cutting operations are covered by Mukherjee and Ray (2006). Within the materials community, Metal Matrix Composites (MMC) has attracted increased attention during the last three decades (Muguthu et al. 2015). Hardness, Strong specific strength, stiffness at room temperature and higher temperatures, strong fatigue and creep resistance, strength-to-weight ratio and wear resistance are just a few of the many advantages that MMC offers in terms of mechanical qualities. The aeronautics industry uses MMC for a variety of applications, making its high-speed CNC machining important. The rising demand for productivity, quality, and cost reduction has made High-Speed Milling (HSM) the favored method in contemporary years (Pare et al.2015).

This review is founded on several optimization techniques, including the Taguchi method, genetic algorithms, artificial neural networks, Response surface methodology, Taguchi method, genetic search algorithms, Firefly algorithm, Genetic algorithms, and fuzzy logic. These techniques are used during composite material machining processes like turning, drilling, milling, and abrasive water jet (AWJ).

2. DIFFERENT OPTIMIZATION TECHNIQUES USED BY THE RESEARCHER TO DEAL WITH VARIOUS APPLICATIONS IN COMPOSITE STRUCTURES

In the late 1940s, Dr. Genichi Taguchi created the Taguchi method, a novel approach to experimentation that makes use of an altered and standardized version of the Design of Experiments (DOE). The Taguchi method's application has received increased attention in the literature, and it is now widely used in many different domains, including process optimization, mechanical component design, and production systems. The Taguchi method's parameter design makes use of primary effects, orthogonal arrays (OA), analysis of variance (ANOVA), and signal-to-noise (S/N) ratios. (Fie et al.2013)

A branch of statistics known as response surface methodology (RSM) uses model fitting of an interest response in addition to the design and analysis of experiments. Finding the operating conditions on a set of control (or input) variables that produce the best response is one of the primary goals of response system management (RSM). (Khuri 2011)

Artificial neural network (ANN) is an arithmetic model that is modeled after biological neural networks, in which the neurons calculate output values based on inputs. It uses a non-linear parallel processing approach to learn from mistakes and prior experiences. The fundamental computing unit, the neuron, computes from several inputs and outputs a single value that is compared to a threshold value to activate (fire). ANNs can assist in making inferences from case observations and handle the problems of interpretation and prediction (Puri et al. 2016).

To calculate the gap between the two various types of solutions, Hwang and Yoon (1981) developed the TOPSIS technique. Alternatives that are furthest from the ideal negative solution and closest to the perfect positive solution are calculated using the data. Perfect negative solutions extend the cost and minimize profit criteria, whereas perfect positive solutions maximize gain criteria and minimize cost criteria (J Kumar and Varma 2020). The TOPSIS method applies to the resolution of multi-objective optimization problems and the optimization of process parameters in any machining process (C. Divya et al. 2019). One method that draws inspiration from nature and can be used to address optimization challenges is the Gravitational Search method (GSA). Laws of motion and gravity inspire GSA. The population-based strategy, which takes into account varying masses, is where the algorithm falls under. The masses are communicating with each other based on the force of gravity to pinpoint the ideal spot inside the search space (Sabri et al. 2013). In addition to being normative, fuzzy optimization addresses transitional and information deficit uncertainty as a mathematical model (Lodwick and Untiedt 2012). Utilizing a common selection process akin to biological evolution, a genetic algorithm (GA) is a technique for handling optimization issues, both constrained and unconstrained. As stated by Papanicolaou et al. (2016) one popular approach to handling multi-criteria decision-making problems is the analytic hierarchy process (AHP), which was first presented by Lai (2019).

Based on the gregarious flashing behavior of fireflies, the Firefly Algorithm (FA) is an algorithm inspired by nature. The algorithm's primary benefit is that it relies mostly on genuine random numbers. It also appears to be more effective multi-objective optimization because it is based on the global communication of the swarming particles, or fireflies. According to this algorithm, fireflies use their flashing light to attract potential prey, find mates, and defend themselves against predators. The fireflies will disperse to more attractive and brighter areas in response to the flashing light intensity that corresponds with the problem's objective function, which is taken into consideration to produce effective and ideal solutions (Girish Dutta 2019).

3. LITERATURE SURVEY

Tools, Depth of cut, Cutting speed, and Feed are taken into consideration as input parameters when Muguthu et al. (2015) utilize the Taguchi technique to discover the optimal cutting variables during the turning operation of Al2224/SiCp (48% wt) MMC. Response factors include surface roughness, tool wear, and particular power utilization. The results show that it is challenging to optimize two machinability characters of Al2124/SiCp (45%wt) MMC at the same time.

Gravitational Search Algorithms (GSA) are utilized by Pare et al. (2015) to optimize the cutting feed, step-over ratio, speed, and depth of cut for end milling control parameters aimed at minimizing surface roughness. The work material used is Al_2O_3 + SiC MMC. Equations for both linear and non-linear regression show an empirical link between the independent and dependent variables. It is determined that GSA outperforms the Genetic algorithm, simulated annealing, and TLBO approaches in terms of surface roughness. Response surface methodology (RSM), as proposed by Kumar et al. (2018), is a suggestion for improving the abrasive water jet grinding process parameter. Using a high-velocity stream of finely-grained abrasive particles, abrasive water jet machining (AWJM) evacuates material from the surface. Using stir-casting aluminum composite specimens reinforced with 2, 4, 6, 8, and 10% tungsten carbide, investigations were conducted. Surface roughness and Material Removal Rage (MRR) are considered the output responses, whereas Transverse speed, Standoff distance, and % WC are used as input parameters. To investigate the impact of AWJM, a second-order polynomial response is created. The influencing input parameter is found using ANOVA. Both single- and multi-objective responses are handled by RSM. Ultimately, the model created by RSM is verified through the application of the ANOVA approach. It is discovered that the generated model has a 95% confidence level. Taguchi's approach for AWJ Machining process parameter optimization was presented by Sasikumar et al. (2018). It looks into the best way to optimize the abrasive water jet machining process parameters for hybrid aluminum 7075 metal matrix composites that have 5%, 10%, or 15% TiC and B4C reinforcement. The kerf features, such as kerf angle, kerf top breadth, and surface roughness, were investigated for variety of abrasive water jet machining process variables, such as water jet pressure, standoff distance, and jet traversal speed. The input parameters' contribution is calculated using an ANOVA. Based on a confirmation test, the difference between the expected and actual numbers has an error of less than 5%. To maximize the machining parameters and produce the least amount of cutting force, Kumar and Sait (2017) discovered the genetic algorithm (GA). A determination of the impact of cutting parameters on carbon fiber-reinforced polymer (CFRP) pipe is attempted. The turning process took into account input factors such as feed, speed, and cut depth. Experiment trials are created using Taguchi's Design of Experiments (DOE). The machining process has been modeled using an ANN and the back propagation neural network algorithm. The final result demonstrated that the observed and experimental values had the least amount of error, proving that ANN and GA can be used to predict and optimize the machining variables for bidirectional CFRP composite pipes.

In Gowda et al. (2015), the Taguchi technique which is predicated on a robust design was used to optimize drilling parameters. Experiments were carried out utilizing different percentages of Si3N4 in epoxy Si3N4 composite materials, with an HSS tool for different drill bit diameters and cutting conditions. The drill bit diameter, speed, feed, percentage of Si3N4, and machining time are the control process characteristics that are taken into account. For the experiments, surface roughness, circularity, and cylindricity are the output variables that are measured. Following the experiment's conclusion, it was determined that the optimized parameters had produced satisfactory outcomes. It is possible to obtain a good surface finish, circularity, and cylindricity by using optimized settings. The significance of environmentally friendly lubricants and the detrimental effects of traditional coolants on human health, the environment, and product quality are covered by Jamil et al. (2019). The input machining parameters for turning aluminum-6061 T6 composite include feed, depth of cut, cutting speed, and Electrostatic Minimum Quantity Lubrication (EMQL) flow rate. The output machining variables include material tool life, surface roughness, removal rate, and power consumption. Genetic algorithms were studied by Davim and António (2001) to optimize feed and cutting velocity during drilling and turning operations. The A356/21/SiCp-T6 composite work material is used in this experiment to test the effects of cutting force, tool wear, and surface polish. It has been discovered that discrete parameters based on a population of cutting condition values acquired from time-scale dependent tests can be effectively optimized using genetic algorithms.

In their proposal for a hybrid module for optimization, Kumar and Verma (2020) noted that the TOPSISAHP hybrid MCDM approach's computational efforts are less complicated to calculate than those of other conventional optimization techniques. Thus, it may have anything to do with machining scenarios when it's necessary to optimize a variety of competing reactions. The purpose of milling GO-doped Epoxy/ CFRP composites is to maximize the response MRR, cutting force, and roughness by optimizing the input parameters feed rate, spindle speed, depth of cut and GO weight percent (GO).

The TOPSIS-Fuzzy logic hybrid was used by Tamiloli et al. (2019) to optimize the cutting parameters during the milling of Al-SiC fly ash MMC. Feed, cut depth, and speed were the control parameters; cutting force and roughness were the reaction parameters. Fuzzy logic is used to identify the ideal parameters, and the TOPSIS method was utilized to reduce the multi-objective problem to a mono-objective problem. To optimize the input parameters for speed, feed, and depth of cut during the end milling of aluminum alloy 6061, Srinivasan et al. (2020) investigated TOPSIS-Grey Relational Analysis (GRA). Response is defined as the cutting force in the x, y, and z axes. Using Taguchi's L9 OA, the experimental design was completed. The outcomes demonstrated that both optimization techniques produced output characteristics in a similar sequence and with good agreement.

Girish Gautam and Dhananjay Mishra (2019) investigated through experimentation, the effects of five distinct process variables like lamp current, air pressure, pulse frequency, cutting speed and pulse width and on kerf deviation, kerf width, and kerf taper were determined. Additionally, a multi-objective optimization method is based on the firefly algorithm (FA). A method has been put into place to optimize every assessed kerf quality attribute at the same time. The final step was to conduct validation experiments to verify the premeditated optimal solutions. During the evaluation, kerf quality characteristics showed an overall enhancement of 27.75%, with individual improvements in kerf width, kerf deviation, and kerf taper of 27.78%, 29.68%, and 22.80%, respectively.

Numerous studies have examined the impact of a single design parameter, according to this thorough literature assessment. However, a small amount of effort has been made to optimize mechanical abilities by taking into account the combined influence of design characteristics including the thickness of the composite laminate, the variety of resins used, and the stacking sequence and angle (Sagar D Patil et al. 2020-2024).

4. CASE STUDY: MULTI-OBJECTIVE OPTIMIZATION OF MACHINING VARIABLES FOR COMPOSITE MATERIALS BASED ON FIREFLY ALGORITHM

Recently, a field of study called "swarm intelligence" was identified, which looks at social insect behavior and applies its concepts to human problem-solving. Simple agents that interact with their environment and each other according to predetermined, basic principles comprise swarm-based systems. Global behavior becomes intelligent even when individual particles are unaware of their nature. The flickering patterns and habits of fireflies serve as the model for firefly algorithms. With about 1900 species in their population, fireflies are members of the Coleoptera order and family of beetles, Lampyridae. The insects that emit light on them. Certain photogenic organs that are situated very near to the body's surface and hidden behind a translucent cuticle window cause them to create repetitive flashes.

This brief, rhythmic flash aids in firefly attraction, communication, and warning.

Yang (2010) created the FA algorithm, which was called after the biochemical and social characteristics of actual fireflies. For the fundamental formulation of FA, he has taken into consideration three ideal rules.

1. Because fireflies are unisex, they are drawn to one another regardless of sex.
2. Fireflies' brightness determines how beautiful they are; when two fireflies become farther apart, their attractiveness decreases. There is a proportionality relationship between the brightness of flies and their attractiveness.
3. The objective function controls how brilliant a firefly is.

Taking into account that all artificial fireflies are unisex, FA is one of the most recent metaheuristic algorithms based on the light-emitting characteristic of fireflies. Based on their respective attractions, fireflies will be drawn to one another. In this case, the beauty of any two fireflies is correlated with their brightness. More fireflies will approach a firefly with more light. The fireflies' brilliance diminishes in tandem with their increasing separation. If there aren't any fireflies left, they will travel on their own. Fireflies fly in swarms to brighter, more appealing places based on the intensity of their flashing light. To find effective, optimal solutions, this idea can be linked to the objective function of a variety of problems. This is the FA procedure flowchart explained in Figure 2.

4.1 Pseudocodes of Firefly Algorithm

The present position of ith firefly, the desirability of another attractive firefly, and the randomization constraint α and the random integer εi are the three terms involved in updating the firefly's position. Figure 1 displays the FA's pseudocodes that will be used in this study.

Figure 1. Pseudocodes of firefly algorithm

Objective function $f(\mathbf{x})$, $\mathbf{x} = (x_1, ..., x_d)^T$
Generate initial population of fireflies $\mathbf{x}_i$ $(i = 1, 2, ..., n)$
Light intensity I_i *at* $\mathbf{x}_i$ *is determined by* $f(\mathbf{x}_i)$
Define light absorption coefficient γ
while *(t <MaxGeneration)*
for $i = 1 : n$ *all n fireflies*
  for $j = 1 : i$ *all n fireflies*
    if $(I_j > I_i)$, *Move firefly i towards j in d-dimension;* **end if**
    Attractiveness varies with distance r via $\exp[-\gamma r]$
    Evaluate new solutions and update light intensity
  end for j
end for i
Rank the fireflies and find the current best
end while
Postprocess results and visualization

Figure 2. Firefly algorithm flowchart

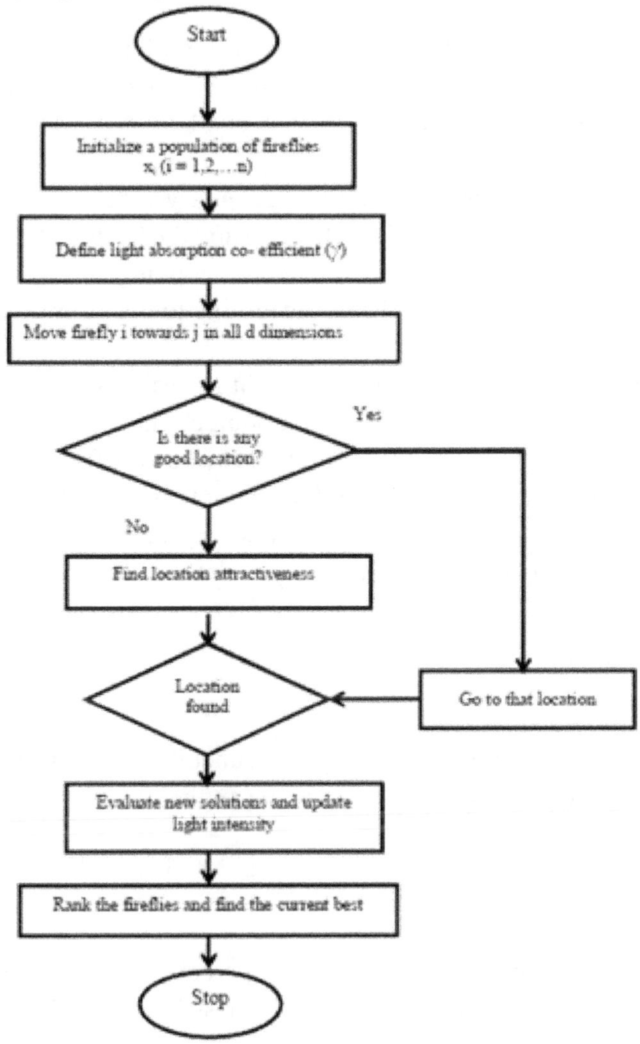

4.2 Attractiveness of Fireflies

The phrasing of appeal and the adjustment of light intensity are two major issues in the firefly algorithm. To keep things simple, we can always assume that the brightness of a firefly, which is related to the encoded objective function, is what affects its attractiveness.

For maximum optimization issues, the elementary case involves selecting the brightness I of a firefly at a provided location x using the formula $I(x) \alpha f(x)$. But β's attractiveness is relative; one should estimate it by looking at it or by comparing it to the other firefly. As such, it will change according to the r_{ij}, or distance, between firefly i and firefly j.

The inverse square law governs how the light intensity I(r) changes in its most basic form. I(r) is equal to I_s/r^2, where Is is the source's intensity. The light intensity (I) of a provided medium with a steady light absorption coefficient (γ) varies with distance (r). $I = I_0 e^{-\gamma r}$, where I_0 is the initial light intensity, is the formula for this. The following Gaussian form can be used to approximate the combined impact of absorption and the inverse square law to prevent the singularity at r = 0 in the calculation I_s/r^2.

$$I(r) = I_0 e^{-\gamma r^2} \tag{1}$$

There are situations where we could require a function that reduces monotonically but more slowly. The following estimate can be applied in this situation.

$$I(r) = \frac{I_0}{1 + \gamma r^2} \tag{2}$$

Since the light intensity that nearby fireflies perceive determines how appealing a firefly is, we can now determine the attractiveness β of a firefly by

$$\beta(r) = \beta_0 e^{-\gamma r^2} \tag{3}$$

where the attraction at r = 0 is denoted by β_0. The above function can easily be substituted with $\beta = \beta_{0/}1+\eta r^2$, over which the attractiveness varies substantially from β_0 to $\beta_0 e^{-1}$, since it is frequently quicker to calculate $1/(1+r^2)$ than an exponential function.

Any monotonically declining function, like the following generalized version, can be used as the actual form of the attractiveness function β(r) in the implementation.

5. COMPARISON OF FA WITH OTHER ALGORITHMS

PSO methods have been shown in numerous experiments to perform better at addressing many optimization issues than conventional algorithms, including genetic algorithms (GA).

This is partly because the best estimates now available have better and faster convergence to optimality due to their broadcasting ability. A thorough discussion of a generic methodology for assessing the statistical accomplishment of transformative algorithms has been provided by Shilane *et al.* (2008). Many researchers have now evaluated the Firefly Algorithms against PSO and genetic algorithms for a range of common test functions. With a mutation probability of pm = 0.06 and a crossover probability of 0.95, Many researchers have employed the normal version of genetic algorithms, devoid of elitism.

Many researchers have also utilized the normal version of the particle swarm optimization without the inertia correction, using learning parameters $\alpha \approx \beta \approx 2$. Many researchers have tested a range of population sizes, from n = 16 to 201, and discovered that n = 15 to 50 works well for the majority of situations. As a result, for comparison, Many researchers have kept the population size of n = 30 constants across all of our simulations.

6. CONCLUSION OF CASE STUDY

Here many researchers have studied a novel firefly algorithm and examined how it differs and is comparable to other optimization techniques in this study. These algorithms were then put into practice and contrasted. Many simulation results for determining the global optimality of different test functions indicate that the new firefly algorithm is more successful and efficient than other techniques, while particle swarm frequently beats conventional algorithms like genetic algorithms.

Future research will look into this further as it suggests that FA may be more effective at addressing NP-hard problems.

Although the fundamental firefly method is incredibly efficient, many researchers can observe that as the optima gets closer, the solutions are still changing. By progressively lowering the randomness, the quality of the answer can be raised. Moreover, multi-objective optimization issues can be solved with a relatively simple modification of the Firefly Algorithm. Furthermore, using firefly algorithms in conjunction with other algorithms could be a fascinating topic for future study.

REFERENCES

Aniket, , Patil, & Patil. (2023). Analyzing the effect of Process Parameters on Amaranth Popping and Puffing in the Lahi Machine using the Taguchi Method. *Journal of Physics: Conference Series*, 2601012013.

Davim, J. P., & Conceição António, C. A. (2001). Optimisation of cutting conditions in machining of aluminium matrix composites using a numerical and experimental model. *Journal of Materials Processing Technology*, 112(1), 78–82. DOI: 10.1016/S0924-0136(01)00551-9

Divya, Raju, & Singaravel. (2019). A Review of TOPSIS Method for Multi Criteria.

Fei, N. C., Mehat, N. M., & Kamaruddin, S. (2013). Practical Applications of Taguchi Method for Optimization of Processing Parameters for Plastic Injection Moulding: A Retrospective Review. ISRN Indust. Eng., 1–11.

Gautam, G. D., & Mishra, D. R. (2019). Firefly algorithm based optimization of kerf quality characteristics in pulsed Nd:YAG laser cutting of basalt fiber reinforced composite. *Composites. Part B, Engineering*, 176, 107340. DOI: 10.1016/j.compositesb.2019.107340

Gautam, G. D., & Mishra, D. R. (2019). Evaluation of geometrical quality characteristics in pulsed Nd: YAG laser cutting of Kevlar-29/basalt fiber reinforced hybrid composite using grey relational analysis based on genetic algorithm. *FME Trans.*, 47(3), 560–575. DOI: 10.5937/fmet1903560G

Gowda, B. M. U., Ravindra, H. V., Prakash, G. V. N., Nishanth, P., & Ugrasen, G. (2015). Optimization of Process Parameters in Drilling of Epoxy Si3N4. *Materials Today: Proceedings*, 2(4–5), 2852–2861. DOI: 10.1016/j.matpr.2015.07.300

Jamil, Khan, He, Li, Zhao, & Sarfraz. (2019). Multi-response optimisation of machining aluminium-6061 under eco-friendly electrostatic minimum quantity lubrication environment. Int. J. Mach. Mach. Mater., 21(5– 6), 459–479.

Kumar, J., & Verma, R. (2020). Experimental investigations and multiple criteria optimization during milling of Graphene Oxide (GO) doped epoxy/CFRP composites using TOPSIS-AHP hybrid module. *FME Transactions*, 48(3), 628–635. DOI: 10.5937/fme2003628K

Kumar, K. R., Sreebalaji, V. S., & Pridhar, T. (2018). Characterization and optimization of abrasive water jet machining parameters of aluminium/tungsten carbide composites. *Measurement*, 117, 57–66. DOI: 10.1016/j.measurement.2017.11.059

Kumar, K. V., & Sait, A. N. (2017). Modelling and optimisation of machining parameters for composite pipes using artificial neural network and genetic algorithm. *International Journal on Interactive Design and Manufacturing*, 11(2), 435–443. DOI: 10.1007/s12008-014-0253-0

Lai, C. M. (2019). Integrating simplified swarm optimization with AHP for solving capacitated military logistic depot location problem. *Applied Soft Computing*, 78, 1–12. DOI: 10.1016/j.asoc.2019.02.016

Lodwick, W. A., & Untiedt, E. A. (2012). *Fuzzy Optimization. In Computational Complexity*. Springer New York.

Muguthu, Dong, & Ikua. (2015). Optimization of machining parameters influencing machinability of Al2124SiCp (45% wt) metal matrix composite. J. Compos. Mater.

Mukherjee, I., & Ray, P. K. (2006). A review of optimization techniques in metal cutting processes. *Computers & Industrial Engineering*, 50(1–2), 15–34. DOI: 10.1016/j.cie.2005.10.001

Papanicolaou & Papantoniou. (2016). Optimum design of textile-reinforced concrete as integrated formwork in slabs. Textile Fibre Compos. Civil Eng., 245–274.

Pare, V., Agnihotri, G., & Krishna, C. (2015). Selection of optimum process parameters in high speed CNC end-milling of composite materials using meta heuristic techniques–a comparative study. *Strojniški vestnik-J.Mechanical Engineering (New York, N.Y.)*, 61(3), 176–186.

Patil, S. D., & Bhalerao, Y. (2019). Optimization of dynamic properties of hybrid composite shaft with newly developed resin (N.D.R.E.) using grey relational analysis. *International Journal of Structural Integrity*, 11(2), 248–263. DOI: 10.1108/IJSI-07-2019-0073

Patil, S. D., & Bhalerao, Y. (2020). Multi-objective optimization of carbon/glass hybrid composites with newly developed resin (N.D.R.E.) using gray relational analysis. *Multidiscipline Modeling in Materials and Structures*, 16(6), 1709–1729. DOI: 10.1108/MMMS-08-2019-0141

Patil, S. D., Bhalerao, Y., & Takale, A. (2020). Optimization of design variables for carbon/glass hybrid composites laminates using Taguchi Technique. *World Journal of Engineering*, 17(2), 309–323. DOI: 10.1108/WJE-10-2019-0290

Patil, S. D., Hatte, P., Khan, S. N., Desai, A. A., & Yadav, P. H. (2023). Analyzing the Design Parameters and Their Influence on the Tensile Strength of Composite Layers using Taguchi Technique. *Materials Today: Proceedings*, 77, 640–646. DOI: 10.1016/j.matpr.2022.11.276

Puri, M., Solanki, A., Padawer, T., Tipparaju, S. M., Moreno, W. A., & Pathak, Y. (2016). *Introduction to Artificial Neural Network (ANN) as a Predictive Tool for Drug Design, Discovery, Delivery, and Disposition. In Artificial Neural Network for Drug Design, Delivery and Disposition*. Elsevier.

Sabri, N. M., Puteh, M., & Mahmood, M. R. (2013). An overview of Gravitational Search Algorithm utilization in optimization problems. 2013 IEEE 3rd International Conference on System Engineering and Technology, 61–66. DOI: 10.1109/ICSEngT.2013.6650144

Sagar D Patil, D.S.Chavan and M.V Kavade, (2012). Investigation of Composite Torsion Shaft for Static Structural Analysis using Finite Element Analysis. *International Journal of Engineering Research & Technology (Ahmedabad)*, 1(7), 1–5.

Sagar D Patil, D.S.Chavan, M.V.Kavade , (2012). Investigation of Composite Torsion Shaft for Torsional Buckling Analysis using Finite Element Analysis. *IOSR Journal of Mechanical and Civil Engineering*, 4(3), 26–31. DOI: 10.9790/1684-0432631

Sagar Dnyandev Patil, Khot, & Hatte. (2024). Multi-objective Optimization and Development of Mathematical Model for Process Parameters of Amaranth Grains using Regression Analysis. Research Square.

Sasikumar, K., Arulshri, K., Ponappa, K., & Uthayakumar, M. (2018). A study on kerf characteristics of hybrid aluminium 7075 metal matrix composites machined using abrasive water jet machining technology. *Proceedings of the Institution of Mechanical Engineers. Part B, Journal of Engineering Manufacture*, 232(4), 690–704. DOI: 10.1177/0954405416654085

Shilane, D., Martikainen, J., Dudoit, S., & Ovaska, S. J. (2008). A general framework for statistical performance comparison of evolutionary computation algorithms. Information Sciences. *International Journal (Toronto, Ont.)*, 178, 2870–2879.

Srinivasan, Thirumurugaveerakumar, Raffic, & Babu. (2020). Mono and Multi Response Optimization of End Milling Parameters for AA6061 by Taguchi Based GRA and TOPSIS Methodology. J. Xidian Univers., 14(6).

Srinivasan, S., Thirumurugaveerakumar, S., Nagarajan, N., Mohammed Raffic, N., & Ganesh Babu, K. (2013). A review of optimization techniques in machining of composite Materials. *Materials Today: Proceedings*.

Tamiloli, N., Venkatesan, J., Murali, G., Kodali, S. P., Sampath Kumar, T., & Arunkumar, M. P. (2019). Optimization of end milling on Al–SiC-fly ash metal matrix composite using Topsis and fuzzy logic. *SN Applied Sciences*, 1(10), 1204. DOI: 10.1007/s42452-019-1191-z

Yang, X.-S. (2010). Nature-inspried metaheuristic algorithms (2nd ed.). Academic Press.

Chapter 2
Evolutionary Algorithms for Optimization and Swarm Intelligence-Based Optimization

Rajeshwari Sissodia
https://orcid.org/0000-0002-9978-0187
Galgotias University, India

ManMohan Singh Rauthan
Hemwati Nandan Bahuguna Garhwal University, India

Varun Barthwal
https://orcid.org/0000-0002-5289-9471
Hemwati Nandan Bahuguna Garhwal University, India

Vinay Dwivedi
Galgotias University, India

ABSTRACT

Evolutionary Algorithms (EAs) and Swarm Intelligence (SI)-based Optimization are powerful, nature-inspired methodologies used to solve complex optimization problems. EAs, including Genetic Algorithms and Evolution Strategies, simulate natural selection processes to iteratively improve solutions through selection, mutation, and crossover. On the other hand, SI-based techniques, such as Particle Swarm Optimization and Ant Colony Optimization, draw from the collective behaviors of social organisms to effectively explore solution spaces. This chapter provides an overview of these approaches, examining their underlying principles,

DOI: 10.4018/979-8-3693-6885-5.ch002

key algorithms, and applications in various fields. It also compares their strengths, discusses hybrid strategies that combine EAs and SI techniques, and explores future trends in optimization research.

1. INTRODUCTION

Optimization is a fundamental aspect of problem-solving in a wide array of scientific, engineering, and business disciplines. It involves finding the best possible solution to a problem within a defined set of constraints. By systematically exploring potential solutions, optimization techniques help to maximize or minimize an objective function, such as cost, efficiency, or performance. This chapter delves into two prominent classes of optimization techniques: evolutionary algorithms (EAs) and swarm intelligence-based optimization.

Optimization techniques can be broadly classified into deterministic, stochastic, and heuristic or metaheuristic methods. Deterministic optimization methods, such as linear programming and dynamic programming, provide exact solutions to problems assuming complete and precise information. Stochastic optimization methods, like simulated annealing and genetic algorithms, incorporate randomness and are useful for tackling problems with uncertainty or incomplete information. Heuristic and metaheuristic methods, including tabu search, ant colony optimization, and evolutionary strategies, offer approximate solutions to complex problems by efficiently exploring the solution space.

Optimization plays a crucial role in various fields by enhancing performance, reducing costs, and improving decision-making processes. In engineering, optimization is used to design efficient structures, systems, and processes by fine-tuning parameters like material usage and energy consumption. In economics and finance, it aids in optimizing investment portfolios, pricing strategies, and resource allocation to maximize profits and minimize risks. Logistics and supply chain management benefit from optimization in routing, scheduling, and inventory management, leading to more efficient supply chains. Healthcare applications include optimizing treatment plans, resource allocation, and medical decision-making to improve patient outcomes and operational efficiency. In artificial intelligence and machine learning, optimization is essential for tuning hyperparameters, selecting features, and enhancing model performance and accuracy.

This chapter aims to provide a comprehensive understanding of evolutionary algorithms and swarm intelligence-based optimization techniques. It will cover fundamental concepts, various types of algorithms, their applications, and a comparative analysis. The structure of the chapter includes an in-depth exploration of evolutionary algorithms, followed by a detailed discussion on swarm intelligence-based optimization. It will then offer a comparative analysis of these methods, highlight hybrid approaches, discuss advanced topics such as parameter tuning and multi-objective optimization, and conclude with future trends and research directions. This structure ensures a thorough coverage of the topic, providing readers with both theoretical insights and practical knowledge about evolutionary algorithms and swarm intelligence-based optimization.

1.1 Overview of Optimization Techniques

Optimization techniques are mathematical methods used to find the best possible solution or decision for a given problem under a set of constraints. These techniques are crucial in various disciplines, including engineering, economics, computer science, and operations research. They aim to maximize or minimize an objective function by systematically selecting input values from within an allowed set and computing the value of the function. Key types of optimization techniques include:

- **Deterministic Optimization**: Methods such as linear programming, integer programming, and dynamic programming, which assume that all information about the problem is known and fixed.
- **Stochastic Optimization**: Techniques like simulated annealing, genetic algorithms, and particle swarm optimization that incorporate randomness and are particularly useful when the problem includes uncertainty or incomplete information.
- **Heuristic and Metaheuristic Methods**: Approaches like tabu search, ant colony optimization, and evolutionary strategies that provide approximate solutions to complex problems by exploring the solution space efficiently.

1.2 Importance of Optimization in Various Fields

Optimization plays a vital role in numerous fields due to its ability to enhance performance, reduce costs, and improve decision-making processes. Some notable applications include:

- **Engineering**: Designing efficient structures, systems, and processes by optimizing parameters such as material usage, energy consumption, and operational efficiency.
- **Economics and Finance**: Optimizing investment portfolios, pricing strategies, and resource allocation to maximize profits and minimize risks.

- **Logistics and Supply Chain Management**: Improving routing, scheduling, and inventory management to enhance the efficiency and effectiveness of supply chains.
- **Healthcare**: Optimizing treatment plans, resource allocation, and medical decision-making to improve patient outcomes and operational efficiency.
- **Artificial Intelligence and Machine Learning**: Tuning hyperparameters, feature selection, and model optimization to achieve better performance and accuracy in predictive models and algorithms.

1.3 Scope and Structure of the Chapter

This chapter aims to provide a comprehensive understanding of evolutionary algorithms and swarm intelligence-based optimization techniques. It will cover the fundamental concepts, various types of algorithms, their applications, and comparative analysis. The chapter is structured as follows:

- **Section 2**: An in-depth exploration of Evolutionary Algorithms (EAs), including their key concepts, types, and applications.
- **Section 3**: A detailed discussion on Swarm Intelligence-Based Optimization, covering the main types of algorithms, their concepts, and applications.
- **Section 4**: Comparative analysis of EAs and swarm intelligence-based algorithms, highlighting their strengths, weaknesses, and performance metrics.
- **Section 5**: Examination of hybrid approaches that combine EAs and swarm intelligence techniques, including examples and case studies.
- **Section 6**: Advanced topics such as parameter tuning, multi-objective optimization, and implementations in dynamic environments.
- **Section 7**: Future trends and research directions in the field of optimization algorithms.
- **Section 8**: Conclusion summarizing the key points discussed in the chapter.
- **References**: A comprehensive list of academic references and resources.
- **Appendices**: Additional materials for further study.

This structure ensures a thorough coverage of the topic, providing readers with both theoretical insights and practical knowledge about evolutionary algorithms and swarm intelligence-based optimization.

2. LITERATURE REVIEW

Deb, K. (2019): Deb's research has been pivotal in the domain of evolutionary algorithms, particularly focusing on large-scale multi-objective optimization problems. His work emphasizes the development of efficient algorithms that can handle complex engineering design challenges, balancing between exploration and exploitation to find optimal solutions.

Zhang, J. & Li, X. (2020): Zhang and Li have made significant contributions by exploring adaptive parameter control strategies within evolutionary algorithms. Their research aims to dynamically adjust algorithm parameters based on the problem environment, enhancing the algorithms' robustness and performance across different optimization tasks.

Kennedy, J. & Eberhart, R. (2021): Known for their foundational work on Particle Swarm Optimization (PSO), Kennedy and Eberhart continue to advance swarm intelligence algorithms. Their recent studies focus on hybrid approaches that integrate PSO with other optimization techniques, aiming to improve convergence rates and solution quality in diverse optimization scenarios.

Yang, X.-S. (2022): Yang's research in nature-inspired optimization algorithms, such as the Firefly Algorithm and Bat Algorithm, explores innovative approaches to solving complex optimization problems. His work emphasizes algorithmic enhancements and applications in diverse fields, including engineering design and data mining.

Dorigo, M. (2023): Dorigo is renowned for his contributions to Ant Colony Optimization (ACO), which mimics the foraging behavior of ants to solve optimization problems. His recent work focuses on advancing ACO algorithms to handle dynamic environments and multi-objective optimization challenges, expanding their applicability in real-world scenarios.

Talbi, E.-G. (2019): Talbi's research has significantly contributed to parallel and distributed metaheuristics for optimization. His work explores algorithms that leverage high-performance computing environments to solve large-scale optimization problems efficiently, addressing computational challenges and enhancing scalability.

Coello Coello, C. A. (2020): Coello Coello's work centers on evolutionary multi-objective optimization techniques. He has pioneered advancements in algorithms that aim to optimize multiple conflicting objectives simultaneously, providing decision-makers with a diverse set of Pareto-optimal solutions to choose from in complex decision-making scenarios.

Blum, C. (2021): Blum's research focuses on hybrid metaheuristics that integrate different optimization techniques. His studies explore novel combinations of algorithms to leverage their complementary strengths, aiming to improve the efficiency and effectiveness of optimization processes in various domains.

Li, Y., et al. (2022): Li and collaborators have investigated swarm intelligence-based algorithms for solving complex scheduling problems. Their research emphasizes the application of swarm algorithms, such as Particle Swarm Optimization (PSO) and Ant Colony Optimization (ACO), in optimizing resource allocation and scheduling tasks in dynamic environments.

Engelbrecht, A. P. (2023): Engelbrecht's work contributes to advancing Particle Swarm Optimization (PSO) algorithms and their applications in engineering and robotics. His research explores algorithmic enhancements to improve PSO's performance in complex optimization tasks, including parameter tuning and adaptive strategies.

Glover, F. (2019): Glover's contributions focus on metaheuristic optimization algorithms, particularly tabu search. His research aims to develop algorithms that efficiently explore solution spaces by preventing revisiting previously searched solutions, enhancing the algorithm's ability to find optimal solutions in combinatorial optimization problems.

Yang, X.-S. & Deb, S. (2020): Yang and Deb collaborated on hybrid optimization techniques that integrate evolutionary algorithms and swarm intelligence methods. Their research explores innovative approaches to optimize algorithm performance by combining strengths from both paradigms, aiming for enhanced solution quality and convergence rates.

Shi, Y. (2021): Shi's research has advanced the field of differential evolution, focusing on its applications in solving constrained optimization problems. His work explores algorithmic improvements and applications in various domains, aiming to develop efficient optimization techniques that can handle complex constraints effectively.

Tanabe, R., & Fukunaga, A. (2022): Tanabe and Fukunaga have developed novel variants of evolutionary algorithms and explored their applications in diverse optimization problems. Their research emphasizes algorithmic innovations to enhance performance, robustness, and applicability across different domains, including engineering and computational biology.

Voss, S., et al. (2023): Voss and collaborators have investigated the use of metaheuristic optimization techniques in renewable energy optimization and resource allocation. Their research focuses on developing algorithms that can efficiently optimize resource allocation and energy management, addressing sustainability challenges in energy systems.

These authors and their respective works highlight the diverse advancements and applications in optimization algorithms, showcasing innovations in algorithm design, efficiency improvements, and applications across various fields from 2019 to 2024.

3. EVOLUTIONARY ALGORITHMS (EAs)

3.1 Introduction to Evolutionary Algorithms

Definition and Historical Background

Evolutionary Algorithms (EAs) are a class of optimization techniques inspired by the principles of natural selection and genetics. These algorithms simulate the process of natural evolution to find optimal or near-optimal solutions to complex problems. The concept of EAs dates back to the 1960s, with the development of early models like Genetic Algorithms by John Holland, Evolution Strategies by Ingo Rechenberg, and Evolutionary Programming by Lawrence J. Fogel. These foundational works laid the groundwork for modern EAs, which have since been refined and extended to tackle a wide range of optimization problems.

Biological Inspiration

EAs draw their inspiration from biological evolution, particularly the mechanisms of selection, crossover, and mutation observed in nature. In biological systems, individuals with advantageous traits are more likely to survive and reproduce, passing their traits to the next generation. Over time, this process leads to the emergence of highly adapted organisms. EAs mimic this process by evolving a population of candidate solutions through iterative application of selection, crossover, and mutation operations, guided by a fitness function that measures the quality of each solution.

3.2 Key Concepts in Evolutionary Algorithms

Population

The population in an EA is a set of candidate solutions to the optimization problem. Each candidate solution, often represented as a chromosome or individual, is evaluated based on a fitness function. The population evolves over successive generations, with new populations being formed through the application of selection, crossover, and mutation operations.

Selection

Selection is the process of choosing individuals from the current population to participate in the creation of the next generation. The selection process is typically biased towards individuals with higher fitness values, ensuring that better solutions are more likely to be passed on to future generations. Common selection methods include roulette wheel selection, tournament selection, and rank-based selection.

Crossover (Recombination)

Crossover, or recombination, is a genetic operator used to combine the genetic information of two parent individuals to produce one or more offspring. The crossover process introduces new genetic variations into the population, promoting diversity and allowing the algorithm to explore new regions of the solution space. There are various crossover techniques, such as single-point crossover, multi-point crossover, and uniform crossover.

Mutation

Mutation is a genetic operator that introduces random changes to an individual's genetic representation. It serves to maintain genetic diversity within the population and helps prevent premature convergence to suboptimal solutions. Mutation rates are typically kept low to ensure that the search process remains focused around high-quality solutions while still allowing for occasional exploration of new areas in the solution space.

Fitness Function

The fitness function is a crucial component of EAs, as it quantifies the quality or suitability of each candidate solution. The fitness function provides a measure of how well a solution satisfies the optimization criteria, guiding the selection process and influencing the direction of the evolutionary search. The design of an appropriate fitness function is critical to the success of an EA.

3.3 Types of Evolutionary Algorithms

Genetic Algorithms (GAs)

Genetic Algorithms are the most widely known type of EAs, introduced by John Holland in the 1970s. GAs represent candidate solutions as fixed-length strings, often binary, and apply genetic operators such as selection, crossover, and mutation to evolve the population. GAs are highly versatile and have been applied to a wide range of optimization problems, from engineering design to machine learning.

Genetic Programming (GP)

Genetic Programming, developed by John Koza, extends the principles of GAs to evolve computer programs or symbolic expressions. Instead of fixed-length strings, GP individuals are represented as tree structures, with nodes representing functions and terminals representing variables or constants. GP has been successfully used for tasks such as symbolic regression, automated program synthesis, and machine learning model development.

Evolution Strategies (ES)

Evolution Strategies, pioneered by Ingo Rechenberg and Hans-Paul Schwefel, focus on the optimization of real-valued parameters. ES employs self-adaptive mutation strategies, where the mutation rates themselves evolve over time. This allows ES to effectively search continuous parameter spaces and has proven effective in engineering optimization and continuous function optimization problems.

Differential Evolution (DE)

Differential Evolution, introduced by Rainer Storn and Kenneth Price, is a population-based optimization algorithm specifically designed for continuous optimization problems. DE relies on the differential mutation operator, which perturbs candidate solutions by adding weighted differences between randomly selected individuals. DE is known for its simplicity, robustness, and effectiveness in solving a variety of real-valued optimization problems.

Evolutionary Programming (EP)

Evolutionary Programming, developed by Lawrence J. Fogel, focuses on the evolution of finite state machines and other representations for solving optimization problems. EP emphasizes the mutation operator and typically does not use crossover. It has been applied to areas such as machine learning, control systems, and optimization of complex systems.

3.4 Applications of Evolutionary Algorithms

Engineering Design

In engineering, EAs are used to optimize the design of structures, systems, and components. Applications include structural optimization, aerodynamic design, electronic circuit design, and control system tuning. EAs help engineers find optimal configurations that meet performance requirements while minimizing cost, weight, or other constraints.

Machine Learning and Data Mining

EAs are employed in machine learning for tasks such as feature selection, hyperparameter tuning, and model optimization. They are also used in data mining for clustering, classification, and regression tasks. EAs can efficiently search large and complex parameter spaces to identify high-performing models and feature sets.

Robotics

In robotics, EAs are used to evolve control algorithms, sensor configurations, and robot morphologies. They enable the development of adaptive and autonomous robots capable of performing complex tasks in dynamic environments. Applications include robot path planning, swarm robotics, and evolutionary robotics.

Economics and Finance

EAs are applied in economics and finance to optimize investment portfolios, trading strategies, and resource allocation. They help in identifying profitable trading rules, managing risk, and optimizing financial models. EAs provide robust solutions in environments characterized by uncertainty and complex interactions.

By leveraging the principles of natural evolution, evolutionary algorithms offer powerful and flexible optimization techniques applicable across diverse domains. Their ability to handle complex, multimodal, and dynamic optimization problems makes them invaluable tools for researchers and practitioners.

4. SWARM INTELLIGENCE-BASED OPTIMIZATION

4.1 Introduction to Swarm Intelligence

Definition and Historical Background

Swarm intelligence refers to the collective behavior of decentralized, self-organized systems, typically made up of simple agents interacting with each other and their environment. The term was first introduced by Gerardo Beni and Jing Wang in 1989 in the context of cellular robotic systems. Swarm intelligence algorithms are inspired by the behavior of natural swarms, such as flocks of birds, schools of fish, and colonies of ants, which exhibit complex, coordinated behavior without a central control mechanism.

Biological Inspiration

Swarm intelligence is rooted in the study of social insects and other animal groups that operate collectively to solve complex tasks. For instance, ants find the shortest path to food sources using pheromone trails, while birds in a flock coordinate their movements to avoid predators and efficiently find resources. These natural behaviors are characterized by simple rules, local interactions, and the emergence of global patterns, providing a rich source of inspiration for optimization algorithms.

4.2 Key Concepts in Swarm Intelligence

Agents and Individuals

In swarm intelligence, the basic unit of computation is the agent or individual. Each agent represents a potential solution to the optimization problem and operates based on simple rules. Agents are typically autonomous, meaning they make decisions based on local information and interactions with other agents and the environment. The collective behavior of these agents leads to the emergence of optimal or near-optimal solutions.

Cooperation and Competition

Swarm intelligence relies on both cooperative and competitive interactions among agents. Cooperation involves agents working together to achieve a common goal, such as sharing information about good solutions or collectively exploring the solution space. Competition, on the other hand, involves agents vying for limited resources or trying to outperform each other. The balance between cooperation and competition is crucial for the effectiveness of swarm-based algorithms.

Emergent Behavior

Emergent behavior refers to complex patterns and solutions that arise from the simple interactions of individual agents. This behavior is not explicitly programmed but emerges from the collective dynamics of the swarm. Emergent behavior enables swarm intelligence algorithms to adapt to changing environments, find robust solutions, and efficiently explore large and complex solution spaces.

4.3 Types of Swarm Intelligence-Based Algorithms

Particle Swarm Optimization (PSO)

Particle Swarm Optimization (PSO) was developed by James Kennedy and Russell Eberhart in 1995. Inspired by the social behavior of birds flocking and fish schooling, PSO involves a population of particles (agents) that move through the solution space. Each particle adjusts its position based on its own experience and the experience of its neighbors, with the goal of finding the optimal solution. PSO is known for its simplicity, ease of implementation, and ability to handle continuous optimization problems.

Ant Colony Optimization (ACO)

Ant Colony Optimization (ACO) was introduced by Marco Dorigo in the early 1990s, inspired by the foraging behavior of ants. In ACO, artificial ants traverse a graph representing the solution space, depositing and following pheromone trails to find the shortest paths. The pheromone levels guide the search process, with higher pheromone concentrations attracting more ants. ACO is particularly effective for combinatorial optimization problems such as the traveling salesman problem and network routing.

Artificial Bee Colony (ABC)

Artificial Bee Colony (ABC) algorithm, proposed by Dervis Karaboga in 2005, mimics the foraging behavior of honey bees. The algorithm involves three types of bees: employed bees, onlooker bees, and scout bees. Employed bees explore food sources and share information with onlooker bees, who then choose food sources based on this information. Scout bees search for new food sources randomly. ABC is effective for numerical optimization problems and is known for its robustness and simplicity.

Firefly Algorithm

The Firefly Algorithm, developed by Xin-She Yang in 2008, is inspired by the flashing behavior of fireflies. In this algorithm, fireflies are attracted to each other based on their brightness, which is associated with the quality of the solution. The attractiveness decreases with distance, and fireflies move towards brighter (better) solutions. The Firefly Algorithm is useful for multimodal optimization problems and is appreciated for its ability to escape local optima.

Bat Algorithm

The Bat Algorithm, also proposed by Xin-She Yang in 2010, is inspired by the echolocation behavior of bats. Bats emit ultrasonic pulses and use the echoes to navigate and find prey. In the Bat Algorithm, virtual bats move through the solution space using velocity updates based on their frequency and loudness parameters. The algorithm combines local search with global search capabilities, making it suitable for a wide range of optimization problems.

4.4 Applications of Swarm Intelligence-Based Algorithms

Network Optimization

Swarm intelligence algorithms are widely used in network optimization, including routing, load balancing, and resource allocation. For instance, ACO has been applied to optimize routing protocols in wireless sensor networks, where ants find efficient paths for data transmission. PSO has been used for optimizing network design and traffic management, improving the performance and reliability of communication networks.

Scheduling Problems

Scheduling problems, such as job scheduling, task allocation, and project management, benefit from swarm intelligence-based optimization. Algorithms like PSO and ABC have been employed to find optimal schedules that minimize completion time, resource usage, and costs. These algorithms handle the complexity and constraints of scheduling problems effectively, providing robust and efficient solutions.

Control Systems

Swarm intelligence is applied in control systems for tuning controllers, optimizing control strategies, and improving system performance. PSO, for example, has been used to optimize the parameters of PID controllers, enhancing the stability and response of dynamic systems. Swarm-based algorithms provide adaptive and flexible solutions for complex control problems in robotics, industrial automation, and aerospace engineering.

Image and Signal Processing

In image and signal processing, swarm intelligence algorithms are used for tasks such as image segmentation, feature extraction, and signal denoising. The Firefly Algorithm, for instance, has been applied to image thresholding, where it identifies optimal thresholds for segmenting images. ACO and PSO have been used for edge detection, pattern recognition, and signal filtering, improving the accuracy and efficiency of processing techniques.

Swarm intelligence-based optimization offers powerful and versatile tools for solving complex problems across various domains. By harnessing the collective behavior of simple agents, these algorithms provide robust, adaptive, and efficient solutions, making them valuable assets in both theoretical research and practical applications.

5. COMPARATIVE ANALYSIS

5.1 Strengths and Weaknesses of Evolutionary Algorithms

Strengths:

- **Versatility:** EAs can be applied to a wide range of optimization problems, including those that are non-linear, non-convex, and multi-modal.
- **Global Search Capability:** EAs are effective in exploring the entire solution space, reducing the risk of getting trapped in local optima.
- **Adaptability:** EAs can adapt to changes in the problem environment and constraints, making them suitable for dynamic optimization problems.
- **Parallelism:** The population-based nature of EAs allows for parallel processing, which can significantly speed up the search process.

Weaknesses:

- **Computational Cost:** EAs can be computationally expensive, particularly for problems requiring large populations and many generations to converge.
- **Parameter Sensitivity:** The performance of EAs is highly dependent on the choice of parameters, such as population size, mutation rate, and crossover rate. Improper tuning can lead to suboptimal performance.
- **Premature Convergence:** EAs can sometimes converge prematurely to suboptimal solutions, especially if there is insufficient diversity in the population.
- **Fitness Function Design:** The effectiveness of EAs relies on a well-designed fitness function. Poor fitness functions can mislead the search process.

5.2 Strengths and Weaknesses of Swarm Intelligence-Based Algorithms

Strengths:

- **Simple Implementation:** Swarm intelligence algorithms are generally simple to implement and understand.
- **Robustness:** These algorithms are robust and can handle noisy and dynamic environments effectively.
- **Scalability:** Swarm intelligence algorithms can easily scale to large problem sizes by increasing the number of agents.
- **Flexibility:** They are flexible and can be adapted to a variety of optimization problems without significant modifications.

Weaknesses:

- **Local Optima:** Swarm intelligence algorithms may struggle with problems that have many local optima, as agents can become trapped.
- **Parameter Tuning:** Like EAs, the performance of swarm intelligence algorithms is sensitive to the choice of parameters (e.g., cognitive and social coefficients in PSO).
- **Convergence Speed:** Some swarm intelligence algorithms can have slow convergence rates, especially for high-dimensional problems.
- **Over-reliance on Randomness:** The reliance on random processes can sometimes lead to inefficient exploration of the solution space.

5.3 Criteria for Selecting an Optimization Algorithm

Problem Characteristics: The nature of the optimization problem, including its dimensionality, constraints, and objective function properties, influences the choice of algorithm. For example, combinatorial problems might be better suited for ACO, while continuous problems might favor PSO or DE.

Solution Quality Requirements: The required precision and quality of the solution determine the suitability of an algorithm. Some problems may require exact solutions, while others can tolerate approximate solutions.

Computational Resources: The availability of computational resources, such as processing power and memory, impacts the choice of algorithm. EAs and swarm intelligence algorithms with parallel processing capabilities can leverage high-performance computing environments.

Algorithm Complexity: The complexity of implementing and tuning the algorithm is a practical consideration. Simple algorithms like PSO might be preferred in scenarios where ease of implementation is critical.

Scalability and Flexibility: The ability of the algorithm to scale with problem size and adapt to changes is essential for dynamic and large-scale optimization problems.

5.4 Performance Metrics for Optimization Algorithms

Convergence Speed: The rate at which an algorithm approaches the optimal solution. Faster convergence is generally desirable but must be balanced with the risk of premature convergence.

Solution Quality: The accuracy and optimality of the final solution obtained by the algorithm. High-quality solutions are essential for critical applications.

Computational Efficiency: The computational resources required by the algorithm, including time and memory. Efficient algorithms are necessary for real-time and large-scale applications.

Robustness: The ability of the algorithm to perform well across a variety of problem instances and under different conditions, including noisy and dynamic environments.

Scalability: The capability of the algorithm to handle increasing problem sizes and complexities without significant degradation in performance.

6. HYBRID APPROACHES

6.1 Combining Evolutionary Algorithms and Swarm Intelligence

Hybrid approaches leverage the strengths of both EAs and swarm intelligence algorithms to overcome their individual limitations and enhance overall performance. These combinations can provide improved convergence rates, solution quality, and robustness by integrating complementary mechanisms from each type of algorithm. For instance, the global search capability of EAs can be combined with the local search efficiency of swarm intelligence methods to achieve a more balanced and effective search process.

6.2 Examples of Hybrid Algorithms

Genetic Swarm Optimization (GSO): Genetic Swarm Optimization combines the principles of Genetic Algorithms (GAs) and Particle Swarm Optimization (PSO). In GSO, the population of solutions is evolved using both genetic operators (selection, crossover, mutation) and PSO operations (velocity and position updates). This hybrid approach aims to exploit the global exploration capability of GAs and the fast convergence of PSO, resulting in a more efficient search process that can effectively balance exploration and exploitation.

Hybrid Particle Swarm Optimization (HPSO): Hybrid Particle Swarm Optimization integrates PSO with other optimization techniques, such as Differential Evolution (DE) or Evolution Strategies (ES). In HPSO, the PSO algorithm is enhanced with additional operators from the secondary algorithm to improve diversity and avoid premature convergence. For example, DE operators can be used to perturb particle positions, introducing new variations and helping the swarm escape local optima. This hybridization enhances the overall search capability and robustness of the algorithm.

6.3 Benefits and Challenges of Hybrid Approaches

Benefits:

- **Enhanced Performance:** Hybrid algorithms often achieve better performance in terms of convergence speed, solution quality, and robustness by combining complementary strengths of different optimization techniques.
- **Improved Diversity:** By integrating multiple mechanisms, hybrid approaches can maintain higher diversity in the population, reducing the risk of premature convergence.

- **Adaptability:** Hybrid algorithms can be tailored to specific problem characteristics and requirements, providing more flexible and effective solutions.
- **Balanced Search:** The combination of global and local search capabilities allows hybrid algorithms to balance exploration and exploitation more effectively, leading to improved optimization results.

Challenges:

- **Increased Complexity:** Designing and implementing hybrid algorithms can be more complex than using single algorithms. The integration of different techniques requires careful tuning and management of additional parameters.
- **Parameter Sensitivity:** Hybrid approaches may introduce new parameters that need to be optimized, increasing the overall parameter sensitivity and the effort required for parameter tuning.
- **Computational Overhead:** The combination of multiple algorithms can result in higher computational overhead, particularly if the hybrid approach involves significant interactions between the components.
- **Balancing Components:** Ensuring that the different components of the hybrid algorithm work synergistically and do not interfere with each other is a key challenge. Proper balancing of the contributions from each component is essential for achieving optimal performance.

Hybrid approaches represent a powerful strategy for addressing complex optimization problems by leveraging the strengths of multiple optimization techniques. By carefully designing and tuning these hybrid algorithms, researchers and practitioners can achieve superior performance and robustness in a wide range of applications.

7. ADVANCED TOPICS

7.1 Parameter Tuning and Control

Parameter Tuning: Parameter tuning involves finding the optimal values for the parameters that control the behavior of an optimization algorithm. In evolutionary algorithms (EAs) and swarm intelligence (SI) algorithms, parameters such as population size, mutation rate, crossover rate, and learning coefficients play a crucial role in the algorithm's performance. Traditional methods for parameter tuning include grid search and random search. More advanced techniques involve adaptive and self-adaptive methods, where parameters are dynamically adjusted during the optimization process. For example, in self-adaptive differential evolution, mutation and crossover rates are encoded in individuals and evolve over time.

Parameter Control: Parameter control differs from parameter tuning in that it involves changing parameter values dynamically during the run of the algorithm. There are three main strategies for parameter control:

- **Deterministic Control:** Parameters change according to a predetermined schedule, such as decreasing the mutation rate linearly over time.
- **Adaptive Control:** Parameters are adjusted based on feedback from the optimization process. For example, if the population diversity decreases, the mutation rate might be increased to introduce more variation.
- **Self-adaptive Control:** Parameters are encoded within the individuals and evolve alongside the solution, allowing the algorithm to automatically find optimal parameter settings.

Effective parameter tuning and control can significantly enhance the performance and robustness of optimization algorithms, enabling them to adapt to different problem landscapes.

7.2 Multi-Objective Optimization

Multi-objective Optimization: Many real-world problems involve optimizing multiple conflicting objectives simultaneously, such as maximizing performance while minimizing cost. Multi-objective optimization (MOO) aims to find a set of trade-off solutions, known as Pareto-optimal solutions, where no single solution can be considered superior without degrading another objective.

Techniques:

- **Pareto-based Methods:** These methods, such as Non-dominated Sorting Genetic Algorithm II (NSGA-II) and Strength Pareto Evolutionary Algorithm (SPEA2), use Pareto dominance to rank solutions and maintain a diverse set of Pareto-optimal solutions.
- **Scalarization Methods:** These methods convert the multi-objective problem into a single-objective problem by combining objectives using weighted sums or utility functions. Adjusting weights generates different trade-off solutions.
- **Indicator-based Methods:** These methods use performance indicators, such as hypervolume, to guide the search process towards well-distributed Pareto fronts.

MOO techniques provide valuable insights into the trade-offs between different objectives, enabling decision-makers to choose solutions that best meet their needs.

7.3 Dynamic and Noisy Environments

Dynamic Environments: In dynamic environments, the optimization problem changes over time due to variations in constraints, objectives, or problem landscapes. Algorithms need to adapt to these changes to maintain optimal performance. Techniques for handling dynamic environments include:

- **Memory-based Approaches:** Storing previous solutions and using them as references when the environment changes.
- **Diversity Maintenance:** Ensuring diversity in the population to adapt quickly to new optima.
- **Prediction Methods:** Using models to predict changes and guide the search process proactively.

Noisy Environments: In noisy environments, the evaluation of solutions is subject to random variations or measurement errors. This noise can mislead the optimization process. Techniques for handling noise include:

- **Re-sampling:** Evaluating solutions multiple times and using the average fitness to reduce noise impact.
- **Robust Optimization:** Focusing on solutions that perform well under various noise conditions.
- **Filtering Methods:** Applying statistical filters to smooth out noise from fitness evaluations.

Handling dynamic and noisy environments is crucial for the robustness and applicability of optimization algorithms in real-world scenarios.

7.4 Parallel and Distributed Implementations

Parallel Implementations: Parallel implementations involve executing multiple operations simultaneously to speed up the optimization process. Techniques include:

- **Master-Slave Models:** The master node handles the main algorithm, distributing tasks (e.g., fitness evaluations) to slave nodes.

- **Island Models:** The population is divided into subpopulations (islands), each evolving independently with occasional migration of individuals between islands.
- **Fine-Grained Models:** Each individual or small group of individuals is assigned to a separate processor, enabling high degrees of parallelism.

Distributed Implementations: Distributed implementations leverage distributed computing resources, such as clusters or cloud computing, to handle large-scale optimization problems. Techniques include:

- **MapReduce Framework:** Dividing the optimization tasks into map and reduce functions for distributed processing.
- **Peer-to-Peer Networks:** Decentralized systems where each node performs optimization tasks and exchanges information with other nodes.

Parallel and distributed implementations significantly enhance the scalability and efficiency of optimization algorithms, making them suitable for large-scale and computationally intensive problems.

8. FUTURE TRENDS AND RESEARCH DIRECTIONS

8.1 Emerging Trends in Evolutionary Algorithms

Adaptive and Self-adaptive EAs: Research is focusing on developing EAs that can adapt their parameters and strategies in real-time, enhancing their performance and flexibility across different problems.

Machine Learning Integration: Combining EAs with machine learning techniques to create intelligent optimization systems that can learn from data and improve their search strategies over time.

Hybrid EAs: Developing hybrid algorithms that integrate multiple EAs or combine EAs with other optimization techniques to leverage their complementary strengths.

8.2 Emerging Trends in Swarm Intelligence

Multi-swarm Systems: Using multiple interacting swarms to improve diversity and search capabilities, enhancing the algorithm's ability to find global optima.

Bio-inspired Variants: Exploring new bio-inspired models, such as those based on social insects, animal herding, and plant root growth, to develop novel swarm intelligence algorithms.

Intelligent Agents: Enhancing agents with learning capabilities and adaptive behaviors, allowing them to autonomously adjust their strategies based on the problem environment.

8.3 Interdisciplinary Applications

Healthcare: Applying optimization algorithms to medical diagnosis, treatment planning, and bioinformatics, improving patient outcomes and healthcare efficiency.

Environmental Science: Using optimization techniques for resource management, climate modeling, and ecosystem conservation, addressing critical environmental challenges.

Industry 4.0: Integrating optimization algorithms into smart manufacturing, logistics, and supply chain management to enhance productivity and sustainability.

8.4 Open Research Problems

Scalability: Developing algorithms that can efficiently handle extremely large-scale optimization problems with millions of variables and constraints.

Robustness: Enhancing the robustness of optimization algorithms to cope with highly dynamic and uncertain environments, ensuring consistent performance.

Explainability: Improving the interpretability and transparency of optimization algorithms, enabling users to understand and trust the solutions provided.

Energy Efficiency: Creating energy-efficient optimization algorithms, particularly for use in mobile and embedded systems, where computational resources are limited.

9. CONCLUSION

Optimization algorithms have profoundly impacted numerous fields, providing powerful tools to solve complex, real-world problems. Evolutionary algorithms (EAs) and swarm intelligence-based algorithms (SI) stand out for their ability to tackle diverse and challenging optimization tasks through mechanisms inspired by natural and biological processes. The strengths of these algorithms lie in their flexibility, adaptability, and robustness, which enable them to find optimal or near-optimal solutions in various applications, from engineering design and machine learning to network optimization and robotics.

9.1 Evolutionary Algorithms (EAs)

EAs, inspired by the principles of natural evolution, have proven their efficacy in exploring vast and complex solution spaces. Their mechanisms, such as selection, crossover, and mutation, facilitate the generation of diverse populations and the evolution of high-quality solutions over generations. The adaptability of EAs makes them suitable for dynamic and multi-objective optimization problems, where multiple conflicting objectives must be balanced. However, challenges such as computational cost, parameter sensitivity, and the risk of premature convergence necessitate continuous advancements in parameter tuning, self-adaptive techniques, and hybrid approaches to maintain their effectiveness and efficiency.

9.2 Swarm Intelligence-Based Algorithms (SI)

SI algorithms draw inspiration from the collective behavior of social organisms like ants, bees, and birds. These algorithms excel in distributed problem-solving and are characterized by their simplicity, robustness, and ability to handle noisy and dynamic environments. The emergent behavior arising from the interactions of simple agents enables SI algorithms to find high-quality solutions through cooperation and competition. While they offer significant advantages, such as ease of implementation and scalability, they also face challenges related to parameter tuning, convergence speed, and susceptibility to local optima.

9.3 Comparative Analysis and Hybrid Approaches

A comparative analysis of EAs and SI algorithms highlights their respective strengths and weaknesses, guiding the selection of appropriate algorithms based on problem characteristics, computational resources, and solution quality requirements. Hybrid approaches, which combine elements of EAs and SI, offer promising solutions by leveraging the complementary strengths of both methods. These hybrids, such as Genetic Swarm Optimization (GSO) and Hybrid Particle Swarm Optimization (HPSO), enhance performance, maintain diversity, and provide balanced search capabilities, addressing the limitations of individual algorithms.

9.4 Advanced Topics and Future Directions

Advanced topics in optimization, including parameter tuning, multi-objective optimization, and handling dynamic and noisy environments, continue to drive research and development. Parallel and distributed implementations further extend the scalability and efficiency of these algorithms, enabling their application to large-scale and computationally intensive problems. Emerging trends in adaptive algorithms, machine learning integration, and bio-inspired models promise to enhance the intelligence and adaptability of optimization techniques.

Interdisciplinary applications in healthcare, environmental science, and Industry 4.0 demonstrate the far-reaching impact of optimization algorithms. By addressing open research problems related to scalability, robustness, explainability, and energy efficiency, the optimization community can develop more advanced and reliable solutions.

In conclusion, optimization algorithms, particularly EAs and SI-based methods, have revolutionized the way complex problems are approached and solved. Their ongoing evolution, driven by advancements in hybrid techniques, adaptive mechanisms, and interdisciplinary applications, ensures their continued relevance and effectiveness. By addressing current challenges and exploring emerging trends, researchers and practitioners can unlock the full potential of these algorithms, paving the way for innovative solutions that meet the growing demands of a rapidly changing world. The future of optimization holds exciting prospects, promising significant advancements and broader impacts across diverse domains.

REFERENCES

Blum, C. (2021). *Hybrid metaheuristics in optimization: Combining different techniques*. Springer Nature Switzerland AG. DOI: 10.1007/978-3-030-60152-2

Coello Coello, C. A. (2020). *Evolutionary multi-objective optimization techniques and applications*. Springer Nature Switzerland AG. DOI: 10.1007/978-3-030-52173-8

Deb, K. (2019). An efficient evolutionary algorithm for large-scale multi-objective optimization. *Journal of Optimization Theory and Applications*. Advance online publication. DOI: 10.1007/s10957-019-01670-2

Dorigo, M. (2023). Ant colony optimization for dynamic and multi-objective optimization. *Artificial Intelligence Review*. Advance online publication. DOI: 10.1007/s10462-022-10141-0

Engelbrecht, A. P. (2023). *Particle swarm optimization in engineering and robotics*. Springer Nature Switzerland AG. DOI: 10.1007/978-3-030-75967-9

Glover, F. (2019). *Metaheuristic optimization algorithms: Tabu search*. Springer Nature Switzerland AG. DOI: 10.1007/978-3-030-65338-6

Kennedy, J., & Eberhart, R. (2021). Particle swarm optimization and its hybrid approaches in optimization. *IEEE Transactions on Evolutionary Computation*, 25(6), 1095–1105. DOI: 10.1109/TEVC.2020.3007312

Li, Y. (2022). Swarm intelligence-based algorithms for complex scheduling problems. *IEEE Transactions on Systems, Man, and Cybernetics. Systems*. Advance online publication. DOI: 10.1109/TSMC.2021.3124661

Shi, Y. (2021). *Differential evolution in constrained optimization problems*. Springer Nature Switzerland AG. DOI: 10.1007/978-3-030-74906-8

Talbi, E.-G. (2019). *Parallel and distributed metaheuristics for optimization*. Wiley-ISTE., DOI: 10.1002/9781119508653

Tanabe, R., & Fukunaga, A. (2022). *Novel variants of evolutionary algorithms and their applications*. Springer Nature Switzerland AG. DOI: 10.1007/978-3-030-87985-7

Voss, S. (2023). *Metaheuristics in renewable energy optimization and resource allocation*. Springer Nature Switzerland AG. DOI: 10.1007/978-3-030-90171-9

Yang, X.-S. (2022). *Nature-inspired optimization algorithms: Firefly algorithm and bat algorithm*. Springer Nature Switzerland AG. DOI: 10.1007/978-3-030-19719-3

Yang, X.-S., & Deb, S. (2020). *Hybrid optimization techniques integrating evolutionary and swarm algorithms*. Wiley. DOI: 10.1002/9781119644097

Zhang, J., & Li, X. (2020). Adaptive parameter control strategies in evolutionary algorithms. *Evolutionary Computation*, 28(3), 437–460. DOI: 10.1162/evco_a_00259 PMID: 31120773

Chapter 3
Fake News Detection Using Machine Learning Classifiers

Komal Singh
Pandit Deendayal Energy University, India

Nikhil Kumar Singh
https://orcid.org/0000-0002-8668-1569
Government Engineering College, Gandhinagar, India

Manish Khare
University of Allahabad, India

ABSTRACT

The internet plays a crucial role in modern society, with a vast number of individuals utilizing it for various purposes. Social media platforms are widely accessible to these users, allowing them to create posts and disseminate information online. Unfortunately, these platforms lack comprehensive user and content verification processes. Consequently, some users take advantage of this loophole to propagate false information. Such fake news can target individuals, societies, organizations, or political parties, and detecting them manually proves challenging for humans. Therefore, there is a pressing need for machine learning classifiers capable of automatically identifying fake news. Extensive research has explored the utilization of machine learning classifiers for fake news detection. This chapter examines six different machine learning techniques applied to six distinct approaches using the fake or real news dataset. The results indicate that the approach employing decision tree and SVM models achieves the highest accuracy compared to the other proposed machine learning classifiers.

DOI: 10.4018/979-8-3693-6885-5.ch003

1. INTRODUCTION

The Internet serves as a crucial primary source of information for many users. It offers access to an extensive range of content across various topics and domains. Users can explore websites, read articles, watch videos, and participate in online discussions to gather knowledge and stay informed about current events (Donepudi, 2020). Social media platforms, such as Facebook and Twitter, have emerged as popular channels for connecting with others and consuming news and media content. These platforms provide several advantages in facilitating quick and convenient access to news:

- **Ease of use and accessibility:** Social media platforms are designed to be highly user-friendly, enabling individuals to navigate, browse, and consume news content with ease. These platforms are accessible on various devices, including smartphones, tablets, and computers, allowing users to stay connected and informed, even while on the move.
- **Wide range of content:** Social media platforms host a diverse range of content, including news articles, videos, images, and infographics. Users can access a variety of sources and viewpoints, allowing for a more comprehensive understanding of different perspectives on current events.
- **Real-time updates:** Social media platforms enable real-time updates and notifications, ensuring that users receive timely news and updates on the topics and accounts they follow. This provides an instant and up-to-date source of information.
- **User engagement and interaction:** One key advantage of social media platforms is the ability for users to engage with content by posting comments, sharing their thoughts, and reacting to posts. This fosters a sense of community and allows for discussions and exchanges of ideas.

However, it's important to note that there are some considerations and challenges when relying solely on social media platforms for news consumption:

- **Credibility and reliability:** Not all information shared on social media platforms is accurate or verified. These platforms can easily become channels for the spread of misinformation, rumors, and fake news. Therefore, users must remain vigilant and critically assess the credibility of the content and the reliability of its sources.
- **Filter bubbles and echo chambers:** Social media algorithms often personalize content based on users' preferences and past behavior, which can lead to the formation of filter bubbles and echo chambers. This means that users

may primarily see content that aligns with their existing beliefs and opinions, limiting exposure to diverse perspectives.

- **Lack of context and depth:** Social media platforms typically provide concise and brief snippets of news, which may lack the depth and context necessary for a comprehensive understanding of complex issues. Users may need to seek additional sources and conduct further research to obtain a more complete picture.
- **Privacy and data concerns:** Social media platforms collect and analyze user data for targeted advertising and content personalization. Users should be aware of the privacy implications and take necessary precautions to protect their personal information.

While social media platforms offer convenience and engagement in accessing news and media, users should approach them with a critical mindset. It is essential to verify information from reliable sources and actively seek diverse perspectives to ensure a well-rounded and accurate understanding of current events. These advantages continue to attract users to such platforms (Donepudi, Banu, Khan, Neogy, & Ahmed, 2020).

Social media platforms have become fertile ground for the spread of fake news due to their wide reach and ease of sharing information. Cybercriminals and malicious actors take advantage of these platforms to disseminate false information and manipulate public opinion. Here are some key points related to the spread of fake news on social media:

- **Ease of dissemination:** Social media platforms offer a convenient and fast way for individuals to create and share content, including false or misleading information. The viral nature of these platforms enables misinformation to spread quickly, reaching a vast audience in a short amount of time.
- **Difficulty in controlling the spread:** Controlling the spread of fake news on social media platforms is indeed a challenging task. The openness and freedom of these platforms make it difficult to regulate or monitor the content being shared. Identifying and removing fake news can be a complex and time-consuming process.
- **Lack of discrimination:** Social media platforms generally have limited mechanisms in place to differentiate between genuine and fake content. Fake news creators can exploit this lack of discrimination to promote their deceptive narratives, making it harder for users to distinguish between reliable and unreliable sources.
- **Impact on society and individuals:** The spread of fake news on social media can have significant societal and political consequences. It can undermine

trust in institutions, manipulate public opinion, and create social divisions. Individuals may unknowingly believe and share false information, leading to the perpetuation of misinformation.

Addressing the spread of fake news on social media is a multifaceted challenge that requires a combination of efforts from platform operators, users, and policymakers. Some potential strategies to combat fake news include:

- **Strengthening platform policies:** Social media platforms can adopt stricter guidelines and policies to reduce the spread of fake news. Measures may include enhanced content moderation, robust fact-checking mechanisms, and algorithms designed to detect and flag potentially misleading information.
- **Promoting media literacy:** Educating users about the dangers of fake news and providing them with the necessary tools to critically evaluate information can help reduce its impact. This includes promoting media literacy skills such as fact-checking, source verification, and critical thinking.
- **Collaborating with fact-checkers and experts:** Partnering with reputable fact-checking organizations and subject matter experts can enhance the accuracy and reliability of information on social media platforms. This collaboration can help identify and debunk fake news more effectively.
- **Encouraging responsible sharing:** Users play a crucial role in combating the spread of fake news. Encouraging responsible sharing practices, such as verifying information before sharing, reporting suspicious content, and being mindful of the potential impact of their actions, can contribute to a more informed and trustworthy social media environment.

The spread of fake news on social media platforms is a significant concern. It requires collective efforts from platform operators, users, and society as a whole to mitigate its impact and foster a more reliable and trustworthy information ecosystem.

In 2018, Zubiaga et al. (Zubiaga, Aker, Bontcheva, Liakata, & Procter, 2018) highlighted the challenges of controlling the spread of fake news on social media. Anyone registered on these platforms can disseminate messages, and individuals can create webpages specifically to generate and spread fake news. These platforms often lack the ability to distinguish between genuine and fake advertisers, enabling anyone to broadcast misleading information targeting specific individuals or institutions. Such fake news can tarnish the reputation of individuals, politicians, or entire communities. Reports indicate that the dissemination of false information can significantly influence human perceptions (Levin, 2017). To protect the reputation and integrity of organizations, political parties, or individuals, controlling the spread of fake news is essential. Often, such misinformation is used as propaganda against political entities or organizations. Artificial intelligence (AI) and machine learning (ML) techniques offer promising solutions for addressing this issue. Machine learning approaches, including supervised, unsupervised, and reinforcement learning algorithms, enable systems to learn and perform various tasks effectively (Donepudi, 2019).

Machine Learning based approaches must first be trained using data called training data. After training machine learning techniques are used for performing various tasks based on the problem and goals. Machine learning is used in different departments to do different jobs. Oftentimes, these learning approaches are used for predictive purposes and to extract the hidden facts. These online platforms are very user friendly to access the news or any other data or information. On the other side these platforms provide an opportunity to cyber criminals in spreading the false news. This misleading news is proved to be dangerous to the society or humans. Users read such news and start believing without knowing the fact. It is very difficult to identify the fake news and is very challenging task (Shu, Sliva, Wang, Tang, & Liu, 2017). If fake news isn't identified earlier then it will spread from person to person and everyone start believing on it. In 2016 US elections (Dewey, 2016) decision making was based on people's opinions which was largely affected by fake news decision making.

Many researchers are continuously doing research to investigate fake news. Researchers used different techniques to detect fake news. The use of Machine Learning has proven beneficial in this regard. Researchers in (Wang, 2017) said that it is very difficult and challenging to detect the fake news and have used machine learning to detect the fake news. Researchers in (Zhou, Zafarani, Shu, & Liu, 2019) identified that fake news are increasing with time and its utmost important to identify the fake news.

1.1 Objective

- Investigate and analyze existing fake news using machine learning procedures.
- Apply a pre-processing and decommissioning process to remove false positives for estimates.
- Use machine learning techniques to generate fake news to predict whether news stories are true or fake.
- Calculate and analyze methods for existing systems using non-standard functions such as accuracy, confusion matrix, precision, regression.

1.2 Motivation

The increased use of the internet has made it easier to spread fake news. Various social media platforms enable the rapid dissemination of false information to a large audience. With the sharing features of these platforms, news or information can spread quickly. Fake news not only affects individuals but also organizations and businesses (Donepudi, Ahmed, & Saha, 2020). Therefore, it is crucial to verify the authenticity of information. Machine learning can play a key role in detecting fake news in an automated manner (Khan, Khondaker, Afroz, Uddin, & Iqbal, 2021; Della Vedova et al., 2018).

Those who know all the stories of the topic can only know that the news is fake. Different researchers are trying to find the best machine learning to detect fake news (Kurasinski & Mihailescu, 2020). The accuracy of the classifier must be determined because if it does not detect fake news, will be dangerous for the society and the people. The accuracy of the classification depends on the training of this classifier. A properly trained model can give more accuracy.

This paper is organized into 7 sections. Section 2 explains about the background of fake news, Machine learning classifiers are discussed in section 3. Related works are discussed in section 4 and proposed approaches are in section 5. Section 6 contains implementation and results and finally section 7 concludes the paper.

2. BACKGROUND OF FAKE NEWS

Fake news often contains grammatical errors and is emotionally charged. It frequently aims to influence the reader's opinion on specific issues, and its content is not always accurate. Fake news often employs short messages, such as slogans or clickbait, and tends to present information that seems "too good to be true." Additionally, the sources of such information are often unreliable (Kumar, Kumar, Singh, & Pachauri, 2021). The definition of fake news has two key aspects: authenticity and intent. Authenticity refers to the fact that fake news is verifiable misinformation; for example, conspiracy theories do not qualify as fake news because it is difficult to definitively prove whether they are true or false. Intent, on the other hand, refers to the deliberate aim to mislead the reader. Next, it is important to identify the features that can be used to classify fake news. Analyzing the content of fake news reveals that it typically consists of four primary elements:

1. **Source:** Where the news came from, who wrote it, and which source believed or not.
2. **Headline:** A brief summary of the news in order to attract the reader.

3. **Text:** The actual content of the news.
4. **Image/Video:** Usually text is enriched with visual information such as images, video or audio.

Features can be extracted from the above four main components. Main features of the above components are linguistic-based and visual-based. As mentioned earlier, fake news is used to impress consumers, and to do this they often use specific language to attract readers. On the other hand, non-fake news often uses a list of different languages, which are more formal. This is a linguistic-based feature in which lexical features like word count, word frequency or special words can be added.

2.1 Characteristics of Fake News

Fake news articles often exhibit certain characteristics that can help identify them. These characteristics include:

- **Grammatical errors:** Fake news articles often contain spelling and grammatical mistakes, indicating a lack of quality control and credibility.
- **Emotional language:** Fake news articles tend to use emotionally charged language to evoke strong reactions from readers, appealing to their emotions rather than presenting factual information.
- **Bias and opinionated content:** Fake news articles often have a biased perspective and present subjective opinions as facts. They may attempt to manipulate the reader's opinion on specific issues rather than providing objective information.
- **Inaccurate information:** Fake news articles frequently contain false or misleading information that is not backed by reliable sources or evidence. They may distort facts or present outright fabrications.
- **Use of clickbait and sensationalism:** Fake news articles often employ attention-grabbing headlines or clickbait tactics to lure readers into clicking and sharing the content without verifying its accuracy. They aim to generate high engagement and virality.
- **Unrealistic claims:** Fake news articles often make exaggerated or sensational claims that are too good to be true. They may promise miraculous results, incredible stories, or unrealistic scenarios to capture the reader's attention.
- **Unreliable sources:** Fake news articles often cite dubious or nonexistent sources, making it difficult to verify the accuracy of the information presented. They may reference anonymous experts or use misleading quotations.

By being aware of these common characteristics, readers can develop a critical mindset and evaluate the credibility and reliability of news articles before accepting them as true. Fact- checking, verifying sources, and cross-referencing information with reputable news outlets can help identify and combat the spread of fake news.

2.2 Types of Fake News

According to the literature, there are five types of fake news. The first form of fake news is deliberate misinformation, which is false information spread in predetermined way to deceive users. Another form of fake news could be clickbait (Chen, Conroy, & Rubin, 2015) (Shu, Sliva, Wang, Tang, & Liu, 2017) that lures readers to click on fake news they see on the internet. Users who set up fake websites earn huge income and clicking on these websites lead to attacks.

Articles written by critics such as "The Onion" (Wei & Wan, 2017) are often repeated and tell the news as if the published stories are true. Articles of Parody or satirical (Rubin, Conroy, Chen, & Cornwell, 2016) uses vulgarity, nonsense, and exaggeration to comment on current events and upset readers. False headline of the fake news is intentionally published to intrigue readers. Article titles from such news may not coincide with the content of the news. News headline can be read as one way, which presents something different contents as a fact. Such fake news is untrue at worst and misleading at best. Hoax is another type of misinformation that deliberately misleads readers by causing harm and material loss to users.

3. MACHINE LEARNING CLASSIFIERS

Some of the popular machines learning classifiers for fake news detection are listed below: –

3.1 Support Vector Machine

The Support Vector Machine (SVM) is indeed a widely used classification approach in machine learning, particularly for supervised learning tasks with labeled datasets. It has been applied to various domains, including fake news detection. Singh et al. (Singh, Dasgupta, Sonagra, Raman, & Ghosh, 2017) conducted a study in 2017 where they compared the performance of different machine learning classifiers for fake news detection. In their research, they found that SVM outperformed other classifiers in terms of its ability to accurately identify fake news. SVM operates by finding an optimal hyper plane that separates data points of different classes with a maximum margin. It aims to create a decision boundary that maximally separates the true and false news instances in the dataset. By finding this optimal boundary, SVM can make predictions on new, unseen data points and classify them as either true or false news.

The performance superiority of SVM in fake news detection, as concluded by Singh et al. (Singh, Dasgupta, Sonagra, Raman, & Ghosh, 2017) highlights its effectiveness in handling this classification task. However, it is important to note that the performance of SVM, or any classifier for that matter, may depend on various factors such as the dataset used, feature selection, and hyper parameter tuning. Overall, SVM has demonstrated its capability in fake news detection, and Singh et al.'s study (Singh, Dasgupta, Sonagra, Raman, & Ghosh, 2017) provides evidence supporting its superior performance compared to other machine learning classifiers in this specific context.

3.2 Naive Bayes

Naive Bayes is also one of the classification approaches which is used by many researchers to classify authentic and fake news (Granik & Mesyura, 2017). Naive Bayes is indeed another popular classification approach used in fake news detection. Many researchers have utilized the Naive Bayes machine learning technique to classify between authentic and fake news articles.

In a study conducted by Pratiwi et al. (Pratiwi, Asmara, & Rahutomo, 2017) in 2017, they employed the Naive Bayes classifier for detecting fake news. Naive Bayes is a probabilistic classifier that is based on the application of Bayes' theorem with the assumption of independence among features. Despite its simplicity, Naive Bayes has been proven to be effective in various text classification tasks, including fake news detection.

The Naive Bayes classifier works by calculating the probability of a given article belonging to a certain class (e.g., authentic or fake) based on the probabilities of observing different features within the article. By considering the joint probabilities of these features, Naive Bayes can make predictions on new, unseen articles and assign them to the appropriate class. Naive Bayes is a widely used classification approach for fake news detection, and the study by Pratiwi et al. (Pratiwi, Asmara, & Rahutomo, 2017) provides evidence of its effectiveness in accurately classifying between authentic and fake news articles.

3.3 Logistic Regression

Logistic Regression is a machine learning classifier commonly used for categorical value prediction, including binary classification tasks such as predicting true or false labels. In the context of fake news detection, Logistic Regression has been applied by researchers to determine the authenticity of news articles. In a study conducted by Kaur et. al. (Kaur, Kumar, & Kumaraguru, 2020) in 2020, they employed Logistic Regression as a classifier to identify whether a given news article is true or false. Logistic Regression is a linear classifier that models the relationship between input features and the probability of a binary outcome. It estimates the probability that an instance belongs to a certain class by applying a logistic function to a linear combination of the input features.

However, it's important to note that the performance of Logistic Regression, as with any classifier, can be influenced by factors such as the quality and representativeness of the training data, feature selection, and the tuning of hyper parameters. Logistic Regression is a machine learning classifier suitable for binary classification tasks, including determining the authenticity of news articles. The study by Kaur et. al. (Kaur, Kumar, & Kumaraguru, 2020) showcases its application in identifying whether a given news article is true or false.

3.4 Random Forests

Random Forest Classifier is a machine learning algorithm that utilizes an ensemble of decision trees to make predictions. Each decision tree in the random forest independently classifies an input, and the final prediction is determined by aggregating the votes or predictions from all the trees. In the context of fake news detection, Random Forest Classifier has been employed by researchers, including the study conducted by Ni et al. (Ni, Guo, Li, & Jiang, 2020) in 2020. They used multiple classifiers, including Random Forest, to detect fake news.

The Random Forest algorithm works by constructing a multitude of decision trees, where each tree is trained on a random subset of the data and features. During prediction, each decision tree independently assigns a class label to the input instance, and the final prediction is determined by the majority vote or the average prediction of all the trees.

Random Forest Classifier has several advantages, including its ability to handle high- dimensional data, capture complex relationships, and mitigate over fitting. It is particularly effective when dealing with diverse features and datasets with noise or missing values. It's important to note that the performance of Random Forest Classifier can be influenced by factors such as the number of trees in the forest, the depth of the trees, and the selection of input features. Random Forest Classifier is a machine learning algorithm used for fake news detection. The study by Ni et al. (Ni, Guo, Li, & Jiang, 2020) showcases the utilization of Random Forest, along with other classifiers, to identify and classify fake news articles.

3.5 Recurrent Neural Network

Recurrent Neural Networks (RNN) have been applied in the classification of fake news. RNN is a type of neural network that is particularly effective in handling sequential data, such as text. In the study conducted by Jadhav and Thepade (Jadhav & Thepade, 2019) in 2019, they utilized the RNN approach to classify news articles as either true or false. RNNs are well-suited for tasks that involve analyzing and understanding sequences of data, making them a suitable choice for analyzing textual information in fake news detection. It's important to note that RNNs, particularly variants such as Long Short-Term Memory (LSTM) and Gated Recurrent Unit (GRU), have shown promising results in various natural language processing tasks. However, their performance can be influenced by factors such as the availability and quality of training data, the architecture of the RNN model, and the choice of hyper parameters.

Recurrent Neural Networks (RNN) have been utilized in the classification of fake news, as demonstrated by the study conducted by Jadhav and Thepade (Jadhav & Thepade, 2019). By leveraging the sequential nature of text data, RNNs can capture the contextual information necessary to distinguish between true and false news articles.

3.6 Neural Networks

Neural Networks are widely used in various classification tasks, including the detection of fake news. Neural Networks are a type of machine learning algorithm inspired by the structure and functioning of the human brain. They consist of interconnected nodes, called neurons, organized in layers.

In the study conducted by Kaliyaret et al. (Kaliyar, Goswami, Narang, & Sinha, 2020) in 2020, they employed Neural Networks to detect fake news. Neural Networks have the ability to learn complex patterns and relationships in data by adjusting the weights and biases of the connections between neurons during the training process. This allows them to capture intricate features and make accurate predictions.

In the context of fake news detection, Neural Networks can be trained on labeled data, where the input features are the textual content of news articles, and the output is a binary classification indicating whether the news is true or false. The Neural Network learns to extract relevant features from the text and make predictions based on those features. It's important to note that the performance of Neural Networks in fake news detection can be influenced by factors such as the architecture of the network, the amount and quality of training data, and the choice of hyperparameters. Additionally, techniques such as regularization and optimization algorithms can be applied to enhance the performance and generalization of Neural Networks.

Neural Networks have been successfully employed in the detection of fake news, as demonstrated by the study conducted by Kaliyaret et al. (Kaliyar, Goswami, Narang, & Sinha, 2020). By leveraging their ability to learn complex patterns in data, Neural Networks can effectively analyze the textual content of news articles and classify them as true or false.

3.7 K-Nearest Neighbor

K-Nearest Neighbor (KNN) algorithm is a supervised machine learning algorithm that can be used for classification tasks. KNN is a non-parametric method that stores labeled instances in a training dataset and classifies new instances based on their similarity to the labeled instances.

In the study conducted by Kesarwani et al. (Kesarwani, Chauhan, & Nair, 2020) in 2020, KNN was employed to detect fake news on social media. The KNN algorithm works by calculating the distance between the new instance and the labeled instances in the training dataset. The k-nearest neighbors, determined based on the calculated distances; vote to determine the class label of the new instance. KNN is particularly useful when there is no underlying assumption about the distribution of the data, as it does not make any assumptions about the underlying data distribution. It can handle both numerical and categorical data and can be applied to various classification tasks.

To use KNN for fake news detection, the textual content of news articles can be transformed into numerical feature vectors using techniques such as TF-IDF or word embeddings. The distance metric, such as Euclidean distance or cosine similarity, can be used to measure the similarity between the feature vectors. K-Nearest Neighbor (KNN) is a supervised machine learning algorithm that has been used in the detection of fake news, as demonstrated by the study conducted by Kesarwani et al. (Kesarwani, Chauhan, & Nair, 2020). By calculating the similarity between new instances and labeled instances in the training dataset, KNN can classify news articles as true or fake based on their similarities to previously labeled instances.

3.8 Decision Tree

A Decision Tree is a supervised machine learning algorithm that can be effectively used for detecting fake news. It is a tree-like model in which the dataset is divided into smaller subsets based on specific features. The algorithm recursively selects the most relevant features to make decisions and constructs a tree structure.

This tree can then be used for classification purposes, helping to identify whether the news is fake or genuine.

In the study conducted by Kotteti et al. (Kotteti, Dong, Li, & Qian, 2018) in 2018, various machine learning classifiers, including Decision Trees, were used to detect fake news. Decision Trees are effective for this task as they can handle both nominal and continuous features. By recursively splitting the dataset based on different features, the Decision Tree algorithm can create rules to classify instances as true or fake news.

The process of building a Decision Tree involves selecting the most informative features at each split point, based on criteria such as Gini impurity or information gain. The tree is grown until a stopping criterion is met, such as a maximum depth or a minimum number of instances in each leaf node. Once the Decision Tree is constructed, it can be used to classify new instances by following the decision path from the root to a leaf node. Each internal node represents a decision based on a feature, and each leaf node represents a class label.

Decision Trees offer several advantages, such as interpretability and the ability to handle both numerical and categorical features. However, they can be prone to overfitting, particularly when the tree becomes too deep or complex. Techniques like pruning or the use of ensemble methods, such as Random Forests, can help mitigate overfitting and enhance the performance of Decision Trees. Decision Trees, as a supervised machine learning algorithm, have been effectively applied in detecting fake news, as demonstrated in the study by Kotteti et al. (Kotteti, Dong, Li, & Qian, 2018). By recursively splitting the dataset based on informative features, Decision Trees generate decision rules that classify news articles as either true or fake, based on their characteristics.

4. LITERATURE REVIEW

Detecting fake news is a challenging task for humans due to the increasing complexity and sophistication of misinformation. However, machine learning techniques have shown great potential in addressing this issue. By leveraging large datasets and automated pattern recognition, machine learning classifiers can assist in determining the authenticity of news articles. Researchers have utilized various machine learning algorithms and classifiers to tackle the fake news detection problem. These classifiers analyze features extracted from news articles, such as linguistic patterns, sentiment analysis, source credibility, and contextual information, to predict the veracity of the content. Common machine learning classifiers employed in fake news detection include decision trees, support vector machines, and neural networks.

While machine learning classifiers provide valuable tools for detecting fake news, they are not foolproof. The evolving nature of misinformation and the use of adversarial techniques to deceive classifiers pose significant challenges. To address these limitations, researchers must continually refine and enhance these models by incorporating new data, adopting ensemble methods, and exploring hybrid approaches that integrate machine learning with techniques like natural language processing and network analysis.

Machine learning classifiers represent a promising solution for fake news detection, leveraging the power of automated pattern recognition and large datasets. However, ongoing research and development are essential to improve their effectiveness and robustness in the dynamic landscape of misinformation.

In 2020, Wang et. al. (Wang, Wang, Fan, Liu, & Tang, 2020) conducted a study on addressing the class imbalance problem. Their approach involved a simultaneous exploration of both local and global data information. The rationale behind this approach was two-fold: (i) leveraging the local data distribution to generate minority samples with detailed information, and (ii) utilizing the global data distribution to guide the generation process and prevent the creation of outliers or samples that overlap with the majority classes. To accomplish this, they proposed a novel framework called GL-GAN. GL- GAN combined the use of the SMOTE method to explore the local distribution within a learned latent space and employed a GAN (Generative Adversarial Network) to capture the global information. This integration allowed for the generation of synthetic minority samples, even in highly imbalanced scenarios. Through extensive experiments conducted on various real-world datasets, the researchers demonstrated the effectiveness of the GL-GAN framework. It successfully produced realistic and discriminative minority samples, leading to improved classification performance when utilized alongside different classifiers in the context of imbalanced training data.

In 2018, Asaad et. al. (Al Asaad & Erascu, 2018) introduced machine learning techniques, specifically supervised learning, for the purpose of detecting fake news. Their approach involved utilizing a dataset containing both fake and real news articles to train a machine learning model using the Scikit- learn library in Python. To extract features from the dataset, they employed text representation models such as Bag-of-Words, Term Frequency-Inverse Document Frequency (TF-IDF), and Bigram frequency. These models enabled the conversion of textual data into numerical representations that could be processed by the machine learning algorithms. The researchers conducted experiments using two classification approaches: probabilistic classification and linear classification. They applied these approaches to classify the title and content of the news articles into categories of clickbait/non-clickbait and fake/real, respectively. The experimental results revealed that the linear classification approach performed the best when using the TF-IDF model for content classification. In the context of title classification, the Bi-gram frequency model yielded the lowest accuracy compared to the Bag-of-Words and TF-IDF models.

In 2017, Ahmed et. al. (Ahmed, Traore, & Saad, 2018) presented a novel n-gram model aimed at automatically detecting fake content, with a specific emphasis on fake reviews and fake news. Their research involved studying and comparing two distinct techniques for feature extraction, as well as six different machine learning classification techniques. To evaluate the effectiveness of their approach, the researchers conducted experiments using both existing public datasets and a newly introduced dataset specifically created for fake news. The results obtained from these experiments demonstrated highly promising and improved performance in comparison to existing state-of-the- art methods. By introducing their new n-gram model and exploring various feature extraction techniques and machine learning classification approaches, They made significant strides in the field of automatic detection of fake content. Their findings showed enhanced accuracy and effectiveness in identifying fake reviews and fake news, as evidenced by their experimental evaluations on both established and novel datasets.

In 2019, Abdullah-All-Tanviret. al. (Abdullah-All-Tanvir, Mahir, Akhter, & Huq, 2019) used machine learning classifiers to detect fake news. As tested by the researchers, the SVM and Naive Bayes classifiers are best for detecting fake news. These two classifiers outperform over other classifiers in terms of the accuracy they provide. Classifier with higher accuracy is considered as relatively better classifier. A more accurate classification would help identify more fake news.

In 220, Kudarvalli and Fiaidhi (Kudarvalli & Fiaidhi, 2020) said that there is a need for investigation of fake news as people spread fake news on social media to deceive people. Fake news should be necessarily identified so that people or organizations do not lose their reputation due to such misleading news (Rahman et al., 2020). They used many machine learning algorithms and also found that Logistic Regression is a better classifier as it provides greater accuracy.

In 2018 Aphiwongsophon and Chongstitvatana (Aphiwongsophon & Chongstitvatana, 2018) analysed that social media generates huge no of posts. Anyone can sign up to these platforms and post anything. This post contains false information against people or businesses. Detecting this fake news is an important and difficult task. To do this, the researchers Aphiwongsophon and Chongstitvatana uses three different machine learning methods, Naive Bayes, Neural Networks and Support Vector Machines. Naive Bayes gives an accuracy of 96.08%. On the other hand, other two methods, Neural Network and SVM, give 90.90%

According to Ahmed et. al. Get. (Ahmed, Traore, & Saad, 2017), fake news has a significant impact on the politics of a society. Fake news on social media platforms can change people perceptions. People change their minds based on fake news without any valid proof. There is a need for a method that can identify such information. To do this, the researchers used machine learning classifiers. Different classifiers used by researchers are K-neighbors, support vector machine, logistic regression, linear support vector machine, pruning tree, stochastic gradient descent. The results show that the linear SVM provides good accuracy in detecting fake news.

Ahmed et al. (Ahmed, Traore, & Saad, 2017) highlighted the significant impact of fake news on the political landscape of a society, particularly through social media platforms. They emphasized that fake news has the potential to alter people's perceptions and influence their decision-making, even in the absence of credible evidence. Recognizing the need to identify such misinformation, the researchers turned to machine learning classifiers as a potential solution. In their study, Ahmed et al. (Ahmed, Traore, & Saad, 2017) employed various machine learning classifiers to detect fake news. These classifiers included K-nearest neighbors, support vector machine, logistic regression, linear support vector machine, pruning tree, and stochastic gradient descent. By leveraging these classifiers, the researchers aimed to develop a method capable of accurately identifying fake news.

In 2019, Reis et al. (Reis, Correia, Murai, Veloso, & Benevenuto, 2019) used machine learning classifiers to detect fake news. They used various features to train the classifiers. Classifiers training are an important part of work because a trained classifier can deliver more accurate results.

According to Granik and Mesyura (Granik & Mesyura, 2017), artificial intelligence can detect fake news better. They used the Naive Bayesian classifier to detect fake news in Facebook posts. This classifier gave them 74% accuracy, but they claim to improve the accuracy. In this article, the researchers also discussed various different ways to improve the accuracy.

In 2022, N. Leela Siva Rama Krishna and M. Adimoolam (Krishna & Adimoolam, 2022) conducted a study comparing a Decision Tree (DT) algorithm and Support Vector Machines (SVM) for detecting fake news based on textual properties found that the DT algorithm achieved higher accuracy at 97.67%, while the SVM algorithm had an accuracy of 91.74%. Additionally, the DT algorithm demonstrated greater precision at 94.60% compared to the SVM's performance. Their research indicates that the Decision Tree approach outperformed the Support Vector Machine method when applied to this specific fake news detection task.

In 2021, Ashwaq Khalil et. al. (Khalil, Jarrah, Aldwairi, & Jararweh, 2021) aims to introduce the first large Arabic fake news corpus consisting of 606,912 articles collected from 134 Arabic online news sources. The corpus is annotated as credible, not-credible, and undecided using an Arabic fact-check platform. Different machine learning (ML) algorithms are used for the detection task, and experiments show that deep learning models perform better than traditional ML models. However, the models' training showed under-fitting and over-fitting problems, indicating that the corpus is noisy and challenging. The limited number of Arabic fake news datasets in terms of articles and news sources has led researchers to develop ML models to detect fake contents and warn readers.

In 2015 Nadia K. Conroy et. al. (Conroy, Rubin, & Chen, 2015) reviews cutting-edge technologies crucial for fake news detection, defining it as categorizing news based on truthfulness with a degree of certainty, complicated by intentional deception. Online news evolution makes traditional fact-checking insufficient against vast content and diverse formats. The paper categorizes veracity assessment methods into linguistic cue (with machine learning) and network analysis approaches, advocating for a hybrid model integrating linguistic cues, machine learning, and network-based behavioral data. While creating a fake news detector is complex, operational guidelines for a practical detection system are proposed, highlighting the importance of innovative approaches in combating misinformation. Review of various machine learning based Fake news detection approaches are compiled in Table 1 as below -

Table 1. Review of various machine learning based fake news detection approaches

Author	Year	Machine Learning Model	Dataset	Result
(Ahmed, Traore, & Saad, 2017)	2017	• Term Frequency-Inverted Document Frequency (TF- IDF) as feature extraction technique • Linear Support Vector Machine (LSVM) as a classifier	• New dataset collected by compiling publicly available news Article. They used 12,600 fake news articles from kaggle.com and, 12,600 truthful Articles • Buzz feed election data set, Our Political news data Set and Burfoot and Baldwin data set (Horne & Adali, 2017)	LSVM - 92% KNN - 83.1% SVM - 86% DT - 89% SGD - 89% LR - 89%
(Huang & Chen, 2020)	2020	• LSTM, depth LSTM, LIWC CNN, and N- gram CNN	FOR dataset, Buzzfeed corpus, SFL dataset, FND dataset satire, and political dataset	Increase the precision, optimize the weights, and look at the intractability problem cross domains.
(Kaur, Kumar, & Kumaraguru, 2020)	2020	TF-IDF, Count-Vectorizer, Hashing-Vectorizer	News articles	TF-IDF - 94.3% Count-Vectorizer - 93.6% Hashing- Vectorizer - 87.1%
(Wu & Liu, 2018)	2018	LSTM- Recurrent Neural Network	Twitter Dataset	89.2%

continued on following page

Table 1. Continued

Author	Year	Machine Learning Model	Dataset	Result
(Umer et al., 2020)	2020	CNN, LSTM	Fake News Challenges (FNC)	PCA - 97.8%
(Antoun, Baly, Achour, Hussein, & Hajj, 2020)	2020	Bi-LSTM and voting classifier	Twitter bot detection dataset, dataset provided by QICC	F1-score of Fake News Detection With mBERT-base is 96% with RoBERTa is 96% and with XLNET-base is 98% Random Forest classifier accuracy in Twitter Bot Detection 96%
(Krishna & Adimoolam, 2022)	2022	Decision Tree (DT), Support Vector Machine (SVM).	Real news and Fake news dataset,	DT algorithm achieved higher accuracy at 97.67%, while the SVM algorithm had an accuracy of 91.74%
(Khalil, Jarrah, Aldwairi, & Jararweh, 2021)	2021	Deep Learning and Traditional ML models	Arabic fake news corpus consist of 606912 articles collected from 134 Arabic Online news sources.	Deep learning models perform better than traditional ML models
(Conroy, Rubin, & Chen, 2015)	2015	Linguistic Approaches, Network Approaches	Publicly available structured data, such as DBpedia ontology, or the Google Relation Extraction Corpus (GREC)	Linguistic Approaches in deception detection with 85–91% accuracy Network Approaches Results using sample facts from four different subject areas range from 61% to 95%.
(Sansonetti, Gasparetti, D'Aniello, & Micarelli, 2020)	2020	Deep learning techniques, CNN, LSTM, and neural network classifier	Twitter (user profiles and shared news)	Average accuracy of 90%.
(Yanagi, Orihara, Sei, Tahara, & Ohsuga, 2020)	2020	Neural network model	Fake News Net dataset	Achieved the best recall score of 0.790
(Ren & Zhang, 2021)	2021	Hierarchical graph attention network	Two real-world fake news datasets	Expandability and Generalizability
(Ying, Yu, Wang, Ji, & Qian, 2021)	2021	Multimodal topic memory network (MTMN)	WEIBO and PHEME	highest accuracy of 99.4%

continued on following page

Table 1. Continued

Author	Year	Machine Learning Model	Dataset	Result
(Samadi, Mousavian, & Momtazi, 2021)	2021	CNN, single-layer perceptron (SLP), multilayer perceptron (MLP), BERT, RoBERTa, GPT2, and funnel transformer	LIAR, ISOT, and COVID-19	Achieve promising results without using additional features
(Meel & Vishwakarma, 2021)	2021	Hierarchical attention network, bidirectional GRU, and ensemble learning	All Data (All data, n.d.), fake news Sample (Fake news samples, n.d.), and fake news detection (Fake news detection, n.d.)	The dataset's best precision was 95.90 percent while using fake news samples

4.1 Fake News Datasets

Following are some of the popular datasets used in the designing of Fake News detection Model –

A. Fake News Corpus (Szpakowski, 2020)

This works uses more than one corpus that allows you to train and take a look at unique models. The primary corpus used for training is known as Fake news Corpus. This corpus has been automatically crawled using opensources.co labels. In other phrases, domain names were classified with one or extra labels in –

- Fake News
- Satire
- Extreme Bias
- Conspiracy Theory
- Junk Science
- Hate News
- Clickbait
- Proceed With Caution
- Political
- Credible

These annotations have been provided by means of crowdsourcing, this means that they may not be exactly correct, but are predicted to be near the fact. Because this work attention on fake information detection in opposition to reliable news, handiest the news labels as fake and credible were used.

B. Liar, Liar, Pants on Fire (Wang, 2017)

The second dataset is Liar, Liar Pants on Fire dataset, which is a collection of twelve thousand small sentences collected from various sources and hand labeled. They are divided in six classes:

- Pants-fire
- False
- Barely-true
- Half-true
- Mostly-true
- True

This dataset is accumulated from truth-checking website PolitiFact through its API. It includes 12,836 human labeled brief statements that are sampled from diverse contexts, along with news releases, television or radio interviews, campaign speeches, and many others. The labels for information truthfulness are excellent-grained a couple of classes: pants-hearth, false, slightly- proper, half of-true, often true, and authentic.

This particular dataset will serve as a secondary test set. Unlike the other cases where there are only two classes, this dataset contains six classes. To establish a basis for comparison with the other dataset, a threshold needs to be applied, determining which class should be considered as true or false. It is important to note that this dataset differs from the previous two in that it consists solely of short sentences. Consequently, models trained on the Fake News Corpus, which comprises full texts, may not yield highly accurate results on this particular dataset. Furthermore, the texts within this latest dataset exhibit a stronger political orientation compared to the texts in the initial dataset.

C. FNC Dataset

The Fake News Challenges benchmark dataset was sourced from the official website (Pomerleau, 2017). Referred to as the FNC dataset, it comprises 75,385 labeled instances and 2,587 article bodies, which correspond to approximately 300 headlines. Each claim is associated with 5 to 20 news articles. Among the headlines,

7.4% are labeled as agreed, 2.0% as disagreed, 17.7% as discussed, and 72.8% as unrelated. The labeling of the claims with respect to the article bodies was done manually, following the following categories:

- **Agree:** Indicates a relation between the headline and article body.
- **Disagree:** Denotes no relation between the headline and article body.
- **Discuss:** Implies a partial match between the headline and article body, considering it as neutral.
- **Unrelated:** Indicates that the topic discussed in the headline and article bodies is completely different.

The dataset has been divided into training and testing sets with 49,972 and 25,413 instances, respectively. This distribution adheres to the rules outlined in the FNC-1 challenge. The training data consists of 1,648 headlines and 1,683 article bodies, while the test data comprises around 880 headlines and 904 article bodies.

5. PROPOSED APPROACHES

Here 6 different Machine Learning approaches with suitable techniques are used for developing 6 different Machine Learning approaches, for Fake News Detection. The algorithm of Fake News Detection Approaches are as follows –

Fake News Detection Algorithm

Inputs:

1. Complete dataset of news articles (X, y)
2. New fake news article to classify

Output: Outcome of the machine learning model (Fake or Real)

Algorithm

1. Pre-process the complete dataset

   1.1 Clean and preprocess the news articles data (X) to remove noise, stop words, and perform stemming or lemmatization.

   1.2 Encode the target variable (y) to represent fake news as 1 and real news as 0.
2. Train / Test / Split the dataset: Split the preprocessed dataset into training and testing sets using machine learning techniques (e.g., train_test_split).
3. Input the fake news: Receive the new fake news article to classify.
4. Apply Machine Learning Technique for Prediction:

   4.1 Select an appropriate machine learning model for fake news detection (e.g., logistic regression, random forest, support vector machine).

4.2 Train the selected model using the training dataset.

4.3 Use the trained model to predict whether the input news article is fake or real.

5. Calculate Accuracy, Precision, Recall, and F1-Score: Evaluate the performance of the model using metrics such as accuracy, precision, recall, and F1-score on the testing dataset.
6. Find the Outcome of the Machine Learning Model: Return the outcome of the machine learning model for the input fake news article as either fake or real based on the prediction.

Proposed Fake News Detection Architecture

Figure 1. Proposed fake news detection

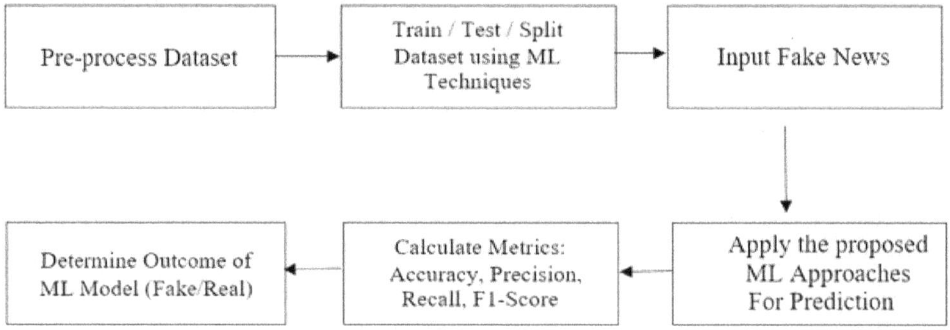

As discussed in step 4 of above Fake News Detection Algorithm, following 6 different techniques are implemented for 6 different ML approaches for Fake News Detection. Architecture of all the proposed approaches are shown in Fig. 1. Algorithm for all the 6 proposed approaches are as follows –

1. Logistic Regression Without Scaling Using Min-Max Normalization

Inputs:

1. Training dataset (X_train, y_train)
2. Testing dataset (X_test)

Output: Predictions for the testing dataset

Algorithm -

1. Preprocess the data:

1.1 Perform Min-Max normalization on the training dataset features (X_train) using the following formula -

$$X_{norm} = X - X_{min} / X_{max} - X_{min}$$

Where X_{min} is the minimum value of the feature, X_{max} is the maximum value of the feature.

1.2 Apply the same Min-Max normalization parameters obtained from the training dataset to the testing dataset features (X_test).

2. Train the logistic regression model:
   2.1 Initialize the logistic regression model.
   2.2 Fit the model to the preprocessed training dataset (X_train, y_train).
3. Predict using the trained model: Use the trained logistic regression model to predict the target labels for the preprocessed testing dataset (X_test).
4. Output: Return the predictions obtained from the logistic regression model.

This algorithm first preprocesses the data by normalizing the features using Min-Max normalization, then trains the logistic regression model on the preprocessed training data, and finally uses the trained model to predict the target labels for the testing dataset. This approach is useful when the features have varying scales and need to be normalized to ensure that the logistic regression algorithm performs optimally.

2. Decision Tree Classification Using Min-Max Scaling With Criteria Set to Gini Impurity and Entropy

Inputs:

1. Training dataset (X_train, y_train)
2. Testing dataset (X_test)
3. Criteria=gini, max_depth=1, random_state=0

Output: Predictions for the testing dataset

Algorithm -

1. Preprocess the data:
   1.1 Perform Min-Max normalization on the training dataset features (X_train).
   1.2 Apply the same Min-Max normalization parameters obtained from the training dataset to the testing dataset features (X_test).
2. Train the decision tree model:
   2.1 Initialize a decision tree classifier with the specified criteria.
   2.2 Fit the model to the preprocessed training dataset (X_train, y_train).

3. Predict using the trained model: Use the trained decision tree classifier to predict the target labels for the preprocessed testing dataset (X_test).
4. Output: Return the predictions obtained from the decision tree model.

This algorithm first preprocesses the data by normalizing the features using Min-Max normalization, then trains the decision tree model on the preprocessed training data, and finally uses the trained model to predict the target labels for the testing dataset. This approach helps in handling features with varying scales and can improve the performance of the decision tree algorithm.

3. Random Forest Classification Using Min-Max Scaling

Inputs:

1. Training dataset (X_train, y_train)
2. Testing dataset (X_test)

Output: Predictions for the testing dataset

Algorithm -

1. Preprocess the data:

   1.1 Separate the features (X) and the target variable (y).

   1.2 Apply Min-Max normalization to the feature matrix (X)
2. Train the Random Forest model:

   2.1 Initialize a Random Forest classifier.

   2.2 Fit the Random Forest classifier to the preprocessed training data (X_norm, y).
3. Predict using the trained model: Use the trained Random Forest classifier to predict the target labels for the preprocessed testing dataset (X_test).
4. Output: Return the predictions obtained from the Random Forest classifier.

This algorithm first preprocesses the data by normalizing the features using Min-Max normalization, then trains the Random Forest model on the preprocessed training data, and finally uses the trained model to predict the target labels for the testing dataset. This approach helps in handling features with varying scales and can improve the performance of the Random Forest algorithm.

4. K-Nearest Neighbors (KNN) Classification Using Min-Max Scaling

Inputs:

1. Training dataset (X_train, y_train)
2. Testing dataset (X_test)
3. Number of neighbors (K=6)

Output: Predictions for the testing dataset

Algorithm -

1. Preprocess the data:

   1.1 Separate the features (X) and the target variable (y).

   1.2 Apply Min-Max normalization to the feature matrix (X)

2. Train the KNN model:

   2.1 Initialize a KNN classifier with the specified number of neighbors (K=6).

   2.2 Fit the KNN classifier to the preprocessed training data (X_norm, y).

3. Predict using the trained model:

   3.1 For each sample in the testing dataset (X_test), find the K nearest neighbors in the preprocessed training dataset (X_norm).

   3.2 Assign the majority class among the K nearest neighbors as the predicted class for the sample.

4. Output: Return the predictions obtained from the KNN classifier.

This algorithm first preprocesses the data by normalizing the features using Min-Max normalization, then trains the KNN model on the preprocessed training data, and finally uses the trained model to predict the target labels for the testing dataset. This approach helps in handling features with varying scales and can improve the performance of the KNN algorithm.

5. Naive Bayes Classification Using Gaussian Min-Max Scaling

Inputs:

1. Training dataset (X_train, y_train)
2. Testing dataset (X_test)

Output: Predictions for the testing dataset

Algorithm -

1. Preprocess the data:

   1.1 Separate the features (X) and the target variable (y).

   1.2 Apply Min-Max normalization to the feature matrix (X)

2. Train the Naive Bayes model:

   2.1 Initialize a Gaussian Naive Bayes classifier.

   2.2 Fit the Naive Bayes classifier to the preprocessed training data (X_norm, y).

3. Predict using the trained model: Use the trained Naive Bayes classifier to predict the target labels for the preprocessed testing dataset (X_test).
4. Output: Return the predictions obtained from the Naive Bayes classifier.

This algorithm first preprocesses the data by normalizing the features using Min-Max normalization, then trains the Naive Bayes model on the preprocessed training data, and finally uses the trained model to predict the target labels for the testing dataset. This approach helps in handling features with varying scales and can improve the performance of the Naive Bayes algorithm, particularly when the features follow a Gaussian distribution.

6. Support Vector Machine (SVM) Classification Using Min-Max Scaling

Inputs:

1. Training dataset (X_train, y_train)
2. Testing dataset (X_test)
3. Kernel type (e.g., linear, polynomial, radial basis function)
4. Regularization parameter (C=1)

Output: Predictions for the testing dataset

Algorithm -

1. Preprocess the data:
   1.1 Separate the features (X) and the target variable (y).
   1.2 Apply Min-Max normalization to the feature matrix (X)
2. Train the SVM model:
   2.1 Initialize an SVM classifier with the specified kernel type = rbf and C.
   2.2 Fit the SVM classifier to the preprocessed training data (X_norm, y).
3. Predict using the trained model: Use the trained SVM classifier to predict the target labels for the preprocessed testing dataset (X_test).
4. Output: Return the predictions obtained from the SVM classifier.

This algorithm first preprocesses the data by normalizing the features using Min-Max normalization, then trains the SVM model on the preprocessed training data, and finally uses the trained model to predict the target labels for the testing dataset. This approach helps in handling features with varying scales and can improve the performance of the SVM algorithm.

6. IMPLEMENTATION AND RESULT

Implementation details and results using various approaches are implemented and analyzed in this section.

Figure 2. LR model with min-max scalar

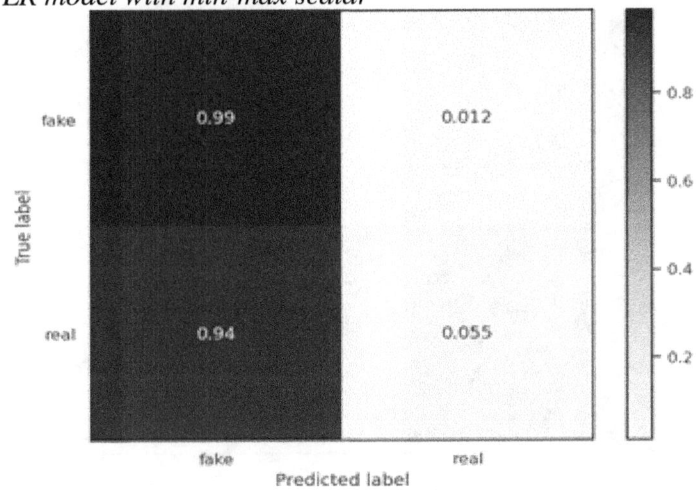

Figure 3. Decision tree with min-max scalar

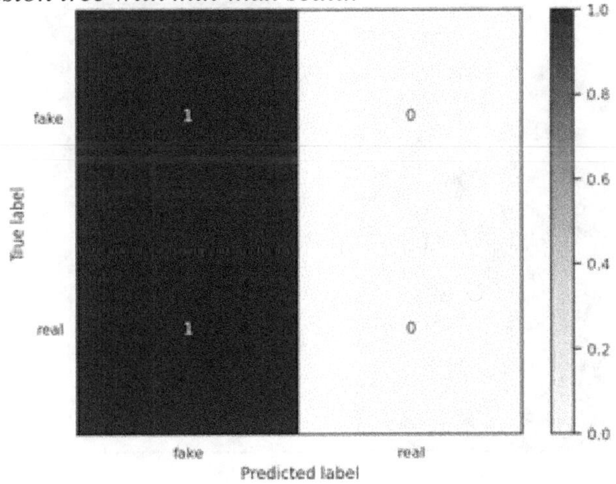

Figure 4. Random forest model with PCA

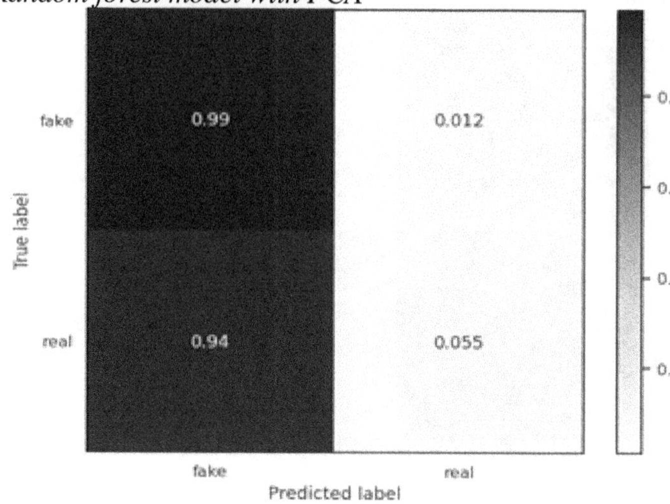

Figure 5. KNN algorithm using MINMAX

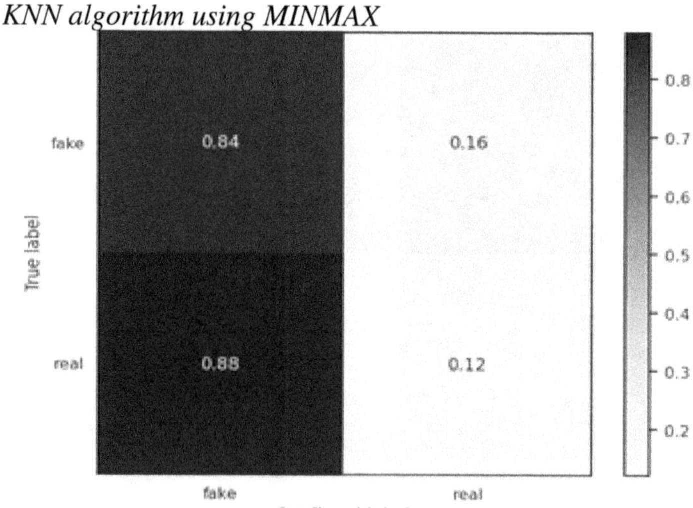

Figure 6. Naiv bayes using gaussian min-max

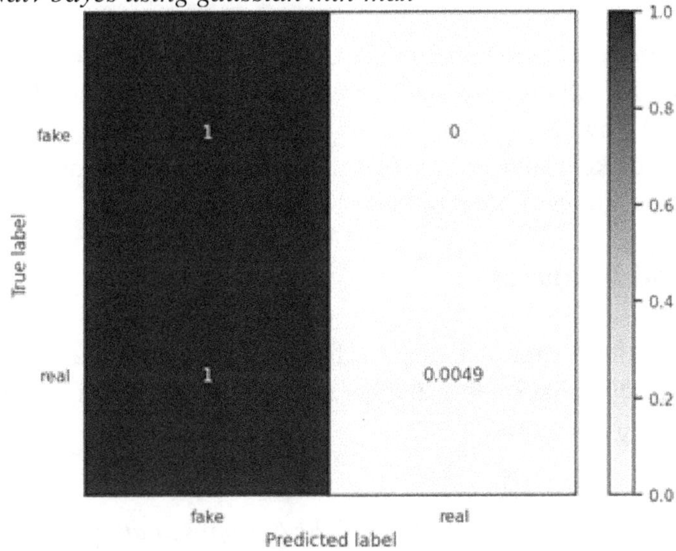

Figure 7. Support vector machine with min-max

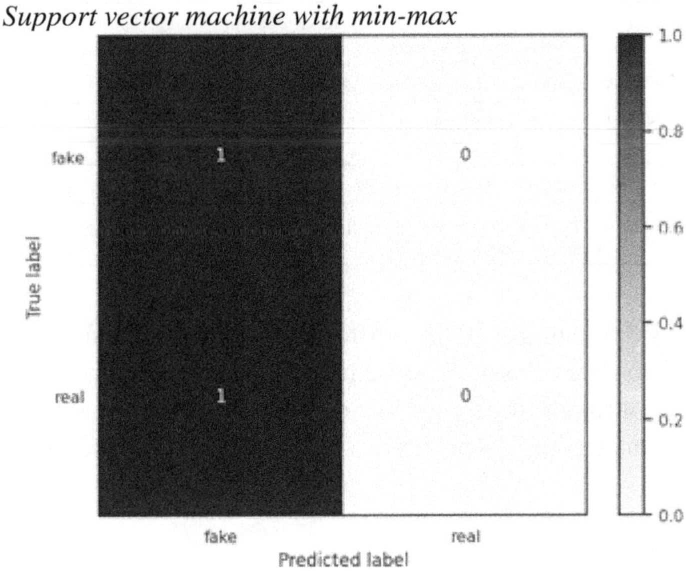

6.1 Experimental Setup

We have run our evaluation on Google Co-Lab having a Processor @ 2.3 GHz with 12GB of RAM. All the approaches are implemented in Python Programming over Fake or Real News

Dataset (Fake or Real News, n.d.). This dataset is available on open source website. This dataset is all about Real or Fake News or Text dataset.

6.2 Result and Analysis

Results of all the 6 proposed approaches using 6 various machine learning algorithm are presented in Table 2 and are shown in Figure 2, Figure 3, Figure 4, Figure 5, Figure 6 and Figure 7 -

Table 2. Result showing the accuracy of all the 6 proposed approaches

Sr. No.	Proposed Fake News Approaches	Fake		Real	
		Accuracy	Loss	Accuracy	Loss
1	Logistic Regression without scaling using Min-Max normalization	0.99	0.012	0.94	0.055
2	Decision Tree classification using Min-Max scaling with criteria set to Gini impurity and entropy	1	0	1	0
3	Random Forest classification using Min-Max scaling	0.76	0.24	0.74	0.26
4	K-Nearest Neighbors (KNN) classification using Min-Max scaling	0.84	0.16	0.88	0.12
5	Naive Bayes classification using Gaussian Min-Max scaling	1	0	1	0.0049
6	Support Vector Machine (SVM) classification using Min-Max scaling	1	0	1	0

After analyzing the results of all the 6 different Machine Learning approaches we observe that Decision Tree classification using Min-Max scaling with criteria set to Gini impurity and entropy and Support Vector Machine (SVM) classification using Min-Max scaling has the highest accuracy among all the other proposed models.

7. CONCLUSION

With the increasing use of the internet, it is now very easy to spread fake news. People regularly connect to numerous internet and social media platforms. There are no restrictions on publishing information on these platforms. Therefore, some people start to spread fake news against individuals or organizations by taking advantage of these platforms. This could damage a person's reputation or affect the business. It can also change the opinion of people about a political party through fake news. There must be a way to detect such fake news. Machine learning systems are used for many purposes, and they can also be used to detect fake news. The classifier is first trained using the pseudo-training dataset. Then, this process can detect fake news. For fake news detection we have used 6 different techniques for implementing 6 different Machine Learning based approaches over Fake or Real News Dataset. Result shows that Decision Tree classification using Min-Max scaling with criteria set to Gini impurity and entropy and Support Vector Machine (SVM) classification using Min-Max scaling has the highest accuracy among all the other proposed models.

REFERENCES

Abdullah-All-Tanvir, E. M., Mahir, S., Akhter, S., & Huq, M. R. (2019). Detecting fake news using machine learning and deep learning algorithms. *2019 7th International Conference on Smart Computing & Communications (ICSCC),* 1–5. DOI: 10.1109/ICSCC.2019.8843612

Ahmed, H., Traore, I., & Saad, S. (2017). Detection of online fake news using N-gram analysis and machine learning techniques. In *Intelligent* (pp. 127–138). Secure, and Dependable Systems in Distributed and Cloud Environments. DOI: 10.1007/978-3-319-69155-8_9

Ahmed, H., Traore, I., & Saad, S. (2018). Detecting opinion spams and fake news using text classification. *Security and Privacy*, 1(1), e9. DOI: 10.1002/spy2.9

Al Asaad, B., & Erascu, M. (2018). A tool for fake news detection. *2018 20th International Symposium on Symbolic and Numeric Algorithms for Scientific Computing (SYNASC),* 379–386. DOI: 10.1109/SYNASC.2018.00064

All data. (n.d.). Retrieved April 4, 2023, from https://drive.google.com/file/d/0B3e3qZpPtccsMFo5bk9Ib3VCc2c/view

Antoun, W., Baly, F., Achour, R., Hussein, A., & Hajj, H. (2020). State of the art models for fake news detection tasks. In *2020 IEEE International Conference on Informatics, IoT, and Enabling Technologies (ICIoT)* (pp. 519–524). IEEE. DOI: 10.1109/ICIoT48696.2020.9089487

Aphiwongsophon, S., & Chongstitvatana, P. (2018). Detecting fake news with machine learning methods. *2018 15th International Conference on Electrical Engineering/Electronics, Computer, Telecommunications and Information Technology (ECTI-CON),* 528–531. DOI: 10.1109/ECTICon.2018.8620051

Chen, Y., Conroy, N. J., & Rubin, V. L. (2015). Misleading online content: Recognizing clickbait as "false news." In *Proceedings of the 2015 ACM Workshop on Multimodal Deception Detection* (pp. 15–19). DOI: 10.1145/2823465.2823467

Conroy, N. J., Rubin, V. L., & Chen, Y. (2015, November). Automatic deception detection: Methods for finding fake news. In *Proceedings of the 78th ASIS&T Annual Meeting: Information Science with Impact: Research in and for the Community* (p. 82). American Society for Information Science.

Della Vedova, M., Tacchini, E., Moret, S., Ballarin, G., Di Pierro, M., & De Alfaro, L. (2018). Automatic online fake news detection combining content and social signals. *Proceedings of the 22nd Conference of Open Innovations Association FRUCT*. DOI: 10.23919/FRUCT.2018.8468301

Dewey, C. (2016). Facebook has repeatedly trended fake news since firing its human editors. *Washington Post.*

Donepudi, P. K. (2019). Automation and machine learning in transforming the financial industry. *Asian Business Review*, 9(3), 129–138. DOI: 10.18034/abr.v9i3.494

Donepudi, P. K. (2020). Crowd sourced software testing: A timely opportunity. *Engineering International*, 8(1), 25–30. DOI: 10.18034/ei.v8i1.491

Donepudi, P. K., Ahmed, A. A., & Saha, S. (2020). Emerging market economy (EME) and artificial intelligence (AI): Consequences for the future of jobs. *PalArch's Journal of Archaeology of Egypt/Egyptology, 17*(6), 5562-5574.

Donepudi, P. K., Banu, M. H., Khan, W., Neogy, T. K., & Ahmed, A. A. (2020). Artificial intelligence and machine learning in treasury management: A systematic literature review. *International Journal of Management*, 11(11), 13–22. DOI: 10.34218/IJM.11.11.2020.002

Fake news detection. (n.d.). Retrieved April 4, 2023, from https://www.kaggle.com/jruvika/fake-news-detection

Fake news samples. (n.d.). Retrieved April 12, 2023, from https://www.kaggle.com/pontes/fake-news-sample

Fake or Real News. (n.d.). Retrieved April 12, 2023, from https://www.kaggle.com/datasets/jillanisofttech/fake-or-real-news

Granik, M., & Mesyura, V. (2017). Fake news detection using naive Bayes classifier. In *2017 IEEE First Ukraine Conference on Electrical and Computer Engineering (UKRCON)* (pp. 900-903). DOI: 10.1109/UKRCON.2017.8100379

Horne, B., & Adali, S. (2017). This just in: Fake news packs a lot in title, uses simpler, repetitive content in text body, more similar to satire than real news. *Proceedings of the International AAAI Conference on Web and Social Media, 11*(1), 759–766. DOI: 10.1609/icwsm.v11i1.14976

Huang, Y.-F., & Chen, P.-H. (2020). Fake news detection using an ensemble learning model based on self-adaptive harmony search algorithms. *Expert Systems with Applications*, 159, 113584. DOI: 10.1016/j.eswa.2020.113584

Jadhav, S. S., & Thepade, S. D. (2019). Fake news identification and classification using DSSM and improved recurrent neural network classifier. *Applied Artificial Intelligence*, 33(12), 1058–1068. DOI: 10.1080/08839514.2019.1661579

Kaliyar, R. K., Goswami, A., Narang, P., & Sinha, S. (2020). FNDNet – A deep convolutional neural network for fake news detection. *Cognitive Systems Research*, 61, 32–44. DOI: 10.1016/j.cogsys.2019.12.005

Kaur, S., Kumar, P., & Kumaraguru, P. (2020). Automating fake news detection system using multi-level voting model. *Soft Computing*, 24(12), 9049–9069. DOI: 10.1007/s00500-019-04436-y

Kesarwani, A., Chauhan, S. S., & Nair, A. R. (2020). Fake news detection on social media using K-nearest neighbor classifier. *2020 International Conference on Advances in Computing and Communication Engineering (ICACCE)*, 1–4. DOI: 10.1109/ICACCE49060.2020.9154997

Khalil, A., Jarrah, M., Aldwairi, M., & Jararweh, Y. (2021). Detecting Arabic fake news using machine learning. In *2021 Second International Conference on Intelligent Data Science Technologies and Applications (IDSTA)* (pp. 171–177). IEEE. DOI: 10.1109/IDSTA53674.2021.9660811

Khan, J. Y., Khondaker, M. T. I., Afroz, S., Uddin, G., & Iqbal, A. (2021). A benchmark study of machine learning models for online fake news detection. *Machine Learning with Applications*, 4, 100032. DOI: 10.1016/j.mlwa.2021.100032

Kotteti, M. M., Dong, X., Li, N., & Qian, L. (2018). Fake news detection enhancement with data imputation. *2018 IEEE 16th International Conference on Dependable, Autonomic and Secure Computing (DASC)*, 187–192. DOI: 10.1109/DASC/PiCom/DataCom/CyberSciTec.2018.00042

Krishna, N. L. S. R., & Adimoolam, M. (2022). Fake News Detection system using Decision Tree algorithm and compare textual property with Support Vector Machine algorithm. In *2022 International Conference on Business Analytics for Technology and Security (ICBATS)* (pp. 1–6). IEEE. DOI: 10.1109/ICBATS54253.2022.9758999

Kudarvalli, H., & Fiaidhi, J. (2020). Experiments on detecting fake news over social media using machine learning algorithms. *International Journal of Advanced Nursing Education and Research*, 8(1), 15–26. DOI: 10.21742/ijriar.2020.8.1.03

Kumar, V., Kumar, A., Singh, A. K., & Pachauri, A. (2021). Fake news detection using machine learning and natural language processing. *Proceedings of the International Conference on Technological Advancements and Innovations (ICTAI), 3878*(6), 547-552. DOI: 10.1109/ICTAI53825.2021.9673378

Kurasinski, L., & Mihailescu, R. C. (2020). Towards machine learning explainability in text classification for fake news detection. In *Proceedings of the 19th IEEE International Conference on Machine Learning and Applications (ICMLA)* (pp. 775-781). DOI: 10.1109/ICMLA51294.2020.00127

Levin, S. (2017, June 13). Pay to sway: Report reveals how easy it is to manipulate elections with fake news. *The Guardian.*

Meel, P., & Vishwakarma, D. K. (2021). HAN, image captioning, and forensics ensemble multimodal fake news detection. *Information Sciences*, 567, 23–41. DOI: 10.1016/j.ins.2021.03.037

Ni, B., Guo, Z., Li, J., & Jiang, M. (2020). Improving generalizability of fake news detection methods using propensity score matching. arXiv. Retrieved from http://arxiv.org/abs/2002.00838

Pomerleau, R. D. (2017). Fake News Challenge Dataset. Retrieved June 22, 2022, from http://www.fakenewschallenge.org/

Pratiwi, Y. R., Asmara, R. A., & Rahutomo, F. (2017). Study of hoax news detection using naïve Bayes classifier in Indonesian language. *2017 11th International Conference on Information & Communication Technology and System (ICTS),* 73–78. DOI: 10.1109/ICTS.2017.8265649

Rahman, M. M., Chowdhury, M. R. H. K., Islam, M. A., Tohfa, M. U., Kader, M. A. L., Ahmed, A. A. A., & Donepudi, P. K. (2020). Relationship between socio-demographic characteristics and job satisfaction: Evidence from private bank employees. *American Journal of Trade and Policy*, 7(2), 65–72. DOI: 10.18034/ajtp.v7i2.492

Reis, J. C. S., Correia, A., Murai, F., Veloso, A., & Benevenuto, F. (2019). Supervised learning for fake news detection. *IEEE Intelligent Systems*, 34(2), 76–81. DOI: 10.1109/MIS.2019.2899143

Ren, Y., & Zhang, J. (2021). Fake news detection on news-oriented heterogeneous information networks through hierarchical graph attention. In *2021 International Joint Conference on Neural Networks (IJCNN)* (pp. 1–8). IEEE. DOI: 10.1109/IJCNN52387.2021.9534362

Rubin, V., Conroy, N., Chen, Y., & Cornwell, S. (2016). Fake news or truth? Using satirical cues to detect potentially misleading news. In *Proceedings of the 2016 Workshop on News and Public Opinion* (pp. 7-17). https://doi.org/DOI: 10.18653/v1/W16-0802

Samadi, M., Mousavian, M., & Momtazi, S. (2021). Deep contextualized text representation and learning for fake news detection. *Information Processing & Management*, 58(6), 102723. Advance online publication. DOI: 10.1016/j.ipm.2021.102723

Sansonetti, G., Gasparetti, F., D'Aniello, G., & Micarelli, A. (2020). Unreliable users detection in social media: Deep learning techniques for automatic detection. *IEEE Access : Practical Innovations, Open Solutions*, 8, 213154–213167. DOI: 10.1109/ACCESS.2020.3040604

Shu, K., Sliva, A., Wang, S., Tang, J., & Liu, H. (2017). Fake news detection on social media: A data mining perspective. *SIGKDD Explorations*, 19(1), 22–36. DOI: 10.1145/3137597.3137600

Singh, V., Dasgupta, R., Sonagra, D., Raman, K., & Ghosh, I. (2017). Automated fake news detection using linguistic analysis and machine learning. In *Proceedings of the 2017 International Conference on Social Computing, Behavioral Modeling, and Prediction* (pp. 1-3). DOI: 10.13140/RG.2.2.16825.67687

Szpakowski, M. (2020). *Fake news corpus*. Retrieved June 22, 2023, from https://github.com/several27/FakeNewsCorpus

Umer, M., Imtiaz, Z., Ullah, S., Mehmood, A., Choi, G. S., & On, B. W. (2020). Fake news stance detection using deep learning architecture (CNN-LSTM). *IEEE Access : Practical Innovations, Open Solutions*, 8, 156695–156706. DOI: 10.1109/ACCESS.2020.3019735

Wang, W., Wang, S., Fan, W., Liu, Z., & Tang, J. (2020). Global-and-local aware data generation for the class imbalance problem. *Proc. 2020 SIAM Int. Conf. Data Mining, SDM2020*, 307–315. DOI: 10.1137/1.9781611976236.35

Wang, W. Y. (2017). "Liar, liar pants on fire": A new benchmark dataset for fake news detection. In *Proceedings of the 55th Annual Meeting of the Association for Computational Linguistics (ACL 2017)* (pp. 422-426).

Wei, W., & Wan, X. (2017). Learning to identify ambiguous and misleading news headlines. In *Proceedings of the 26th International Joint Conference on Artificial Intelligence (IJCAI)* (pp. 4172-4178). https://doi.org/DOI: 10.24963/ijcai.2017/583

Wu, L., & Liu, H. (2018). Tracing fake-news footprints: Characterizing social media messages by how they propagate. *WSDM 2018 - Proceedings of the 11th ACM International Conference on Web Search and Data Mining*, 637–645. DOI: 10.1145/3159652.3159677

Yanagi, Y., Orihara, R., Sei, Y., Tahara, Y., & Ohsuga, A. (2020). Fake news detection with generated comments for news articles. In *2020 IEEE 24th International Conference on Intelligent Engineering Systems (INES)* (pp. 1–4). IEEE. DOI: 10.1109/INES49302.2020.9147195

Ying, L., Yu, H., Wang, J., Ji, Y., & Qian, S. (2021). Fake news detection via multimodal topic memory network. *IEEE Access : Practical Innovations, Open Solutions*, 9, 132818–132829. DOI: 10.1109/ACCESS.2021.3113981

Zhou, X., Zafarani, R., Shu, K., & Liu, H. (2019). Fake news: Fundamental theories, detection strategies, and challenges. In *Proceedings of the Twelfth ACM International Conference on Web Search and Data Mining* (pp. 836-837). DOI: 10.1145/3289600.3291382

Zubiaga, A., Aker, A., Bontcheva, K., Liakata, M., & Procter, R. (2018). Detection and resolution of rumours in social media: A survey. *ACM Computing Surveys*, 51(2), 1–36. Advance online publication. DOI: 10.1145/3161603

Chapter 4
Greening Digital Healthcare Balancing Act for Sustainable Future

Neha Verma
https://orcid.org/0000-0002-9970-5507
SGT University, India

Dheivanai Radhakrishnan
https://orcid.org/0000-0003-0734-7704
Dronacharya College of Engineering, India

Diya Ray
Dronacharya College of Engineering, India

ABSTRACT

The healthcare industry faces the challenge of balancing technological advancements with environmental sustainability. Emerging tools like digital twins and the metaverse hold promise for sustainable healthcare but remain underutilized. Digital twins replicate health data, while metaverse technologies (AR/VR) create interactive virtual environments, supporting eco-conscious practices. This study emphasizes energy-efficient virtual designs and algorithms to reduce environmental impact, human intervention, and resource use. Balancing innovation with data protection protocols, including encryption and decentralized storage, is essential. Eco-friendly production, ethical sourcing, and recycling further reduce the carbon footprint. User-friendly interfaces, accessibility features, and localized content can bridge digital gaps. For example, digital twins of healthcare professionals could enable virtual rounds, improving efficiency and reducing physical travel. These advancements, integrated with existing systems, enhance sustainability while minimizing

DOI: 10.4018/979-8-3693-6885-5.ch004

environmental impact.

I. INTRODUCTION

In 2024, India's healthcare sector holds great potential for improving patient care and expanding access. However, the adoption of digital health technologies brings environmental challenges, including energy-intensive data centers, electronic waste, and carbon emissions. Balancing the benefits of digital health with environmental sustainability requires thoughtful regulatory frameworks, community involvement, and culturally sensitive, inclusive solutions. This research explores strategies to "green" digital healthcare, ensuring a sustainable and ethically responsible future for the sector (Thompson, 2021).

The digital transformation of healthcare, driven by technologies like IoT, AI, and ML, promises improved patient outcomes but also raises sustainability challenges. This paper explores "greening" digital healthcare, balancing environmental stewardship with efficient care delivery, addressing energy-intensive technologies, data centers, and resource consumption in the evolving sector (Angelos I Stoumpos, 2023).

A literature review on digital twins and digital healthcare technologies highlights their potential to enhance sustainability. Implementing sustainable development in healthcare, particularly through "Green Hospitals," can reduce energy consumption, improve patient care, and minimize environmental impact. Strategic planning of digital and green hospitals leads to energy savings and improved service delivery (Willem Jan Knibbe, 2022).

II. LITERATURE REVIEW

Understanding the transformative influence of digital technologies on the healthcare landscape is crucial due to the ongoing digitization wave. This wave has led to a significant shift in paradigms, presenting innovative solutions to elevate patient care, streamline healthcare workflows, and enhance overall system efficiency.

1. Introduction to Sustainable Digital Healthcare

Rationale for Sustainable Healthcare Technologies

The integration of sustainability in digital healthcare technologies, such as telemedicine, digital twins, wearables (Ohenhen & et.al, 2024), and AI, is crucial to mitigate environmental impacts while addressing healthcare delivery gaps. Low-carbon health technologies, optimized data storage, and energy-efficient designs can reduce carbon footprints (Berniak-Woźny & Rataj, 2023), especially in data centers, which consume 1% of global electricity. Biodegradable materials and modular devices (Xiao Luo, 2024) minimize e-waste and improve resource utilization.

High-performance technologies, like digital twins and the metaverse (Maita & et.al, 2024), are made more energy-efficient through advanced algorithms. Additionally, digital health enhances (Casper van der Zee, 2024) access in underserved areas while minimizing environmental impact, (foresee, 2024) with policies like the EU (Nations, 2023) Green Deal driving eco-friendly innovations in healthcare (Hossein Omrany A. M., 2024)

Figure 1. Digital health – implementation – remote areas (Maita & et.al, 2024)

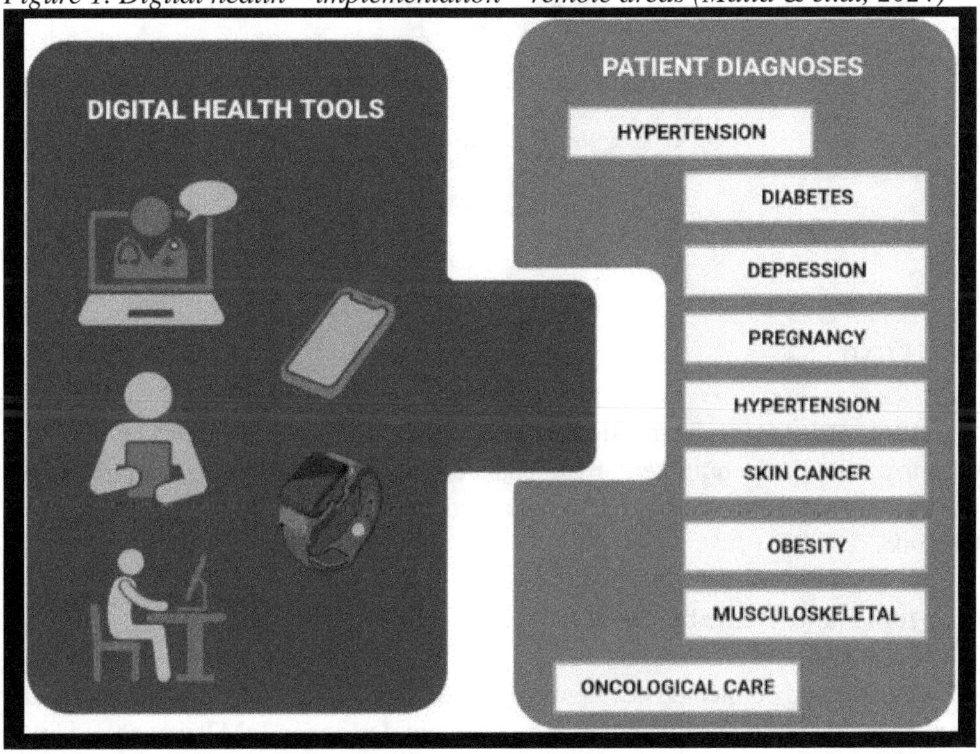

- **Digital Twin Technology and Predictive Analytics**

Figure 2. Schematic representation

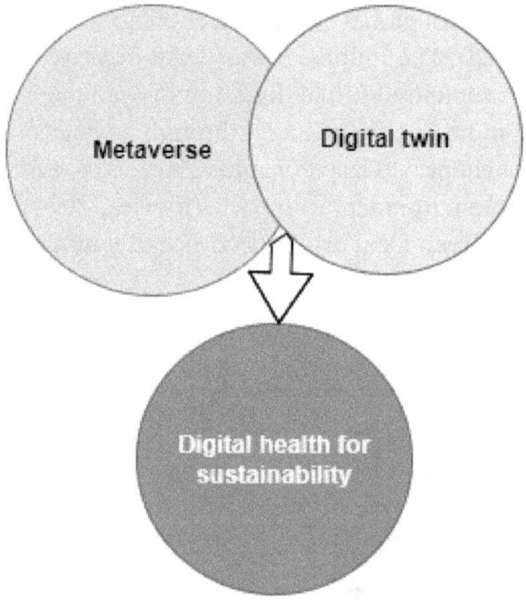

o **AI/ML**

AI/ML: AI-driven diagnostics minimize unnecessary procedures, while ML optimizes medical equipment maintenance, extending lifecycles and reducing waste. These technologies enhance resource efficiency in hospital operations (I Olayinka, 2024).

o **IoMT and Wearable Device**

Wearable and connected devices enable real-time monitoring, reducing hospital visits and conserving resources. Energy-efficient designs in IoMT devices address sustainability by minimizing battery use and electronic waste (Bazeer Ahamed, 2023).

o **Green Data Centers and Cloud Computing**

Using renewable energy and advanced cooling systems, green data centers and cloud computing lower energy use while enabling efficient data management (Rajkumar Buyya, 2023).

- o **Blockchain for Sustainable Data Management**

Blockchain ensures sustainable, decentralized data storage and ethical supply chain management. New energy-efficient models, like proof-of-stake, reduce its carbon footprint, supporting sustainable healthcare (Seyednima Khezr, 2019).

Key Challenges and Opportunities in Green Digital Healthcare

Challenges

- o **Energetically Hungry Technologies**

Technologies such as AI, blockchain, digital twins, and the metaverse need tremendous computing power, causing an increase in energy consumption and carbon emission despite efforts in energy-efficient data centers (Hossein Omrany e., 2024)

- o **Resource-Intensive Supply Chains**

The production and disposal of digital healthcare devices are resource-intensive, leading to e-waste because there is a lack of recycling and sustainable sourcing practices (Behzad Mosallanezhad, 2023).

- o **Data Privacy and Security Concerns**

Advanced encryption mechanisms for storing the data of patients and ensuring security increase the computational effort, thus increasing energy usage (Abbas & Graepel, 2024).

- o **Regulatory and Standardization Barriers**

Lack of a standardized global framework for digital health sustainability and out-of-date policies cause bottlenecks to innovation as well as the deployment of technologies such as blockchain (Zhang Wenhua, 2023).

- o **Digital Divide and Unequal Access**

Lack of information infrastructure in rural and marginalized areas leads to limited access to digital healthcare solutions (Onyinyechukwu Chidolue, 2024).

Opportunities of Green Digital Healthcare

- o **Energy-Efficient Innovation**

Low-power processors, edge computing, and AI-based energy management systems can reduce the carbon footprint of digital healthcare (Peter Efosa Ohenhen, 2024).

- **Adoption of Circular Economy Practices**

Eco-friendly manufacturing, modular designs, and efficient recyclability of wearables and IoMT devices minimize e-wastes (Tanzila Saba, 2020).

- **Use of Renewable Energy**

IoT devices are powered by solar, and renewable-energy-powered data centers.

- **Personalized and Preventive Care**

Digital twins as well as predictive analytics optimize care conserving resources and outcomes.

- **Policy Support and International Cooperation**

There is global effort like the EU Green Deal that supports sustainable innovation and investment in digital health technologies (UNEP, 2023).

- **Equitable Access Improvement**

mHealth and telemedicine solutions will bridge the digital divide for sustainable and inclusive healthcare delivery (Karla C Maita, 2024).

2. Digital Twin Technology in Healthcare

Conceptual Framework and Definition

Digital twin technology is a virtual model of physical systems that uses patient data from various sources, for example, from EHRs, wearables, and medical imaging to simulate, predict, and optimize healthcare outcomes (Tatiana Mallet Machado, 2023).

Using AI, machine learning, and advanced algorithms, digital twins allow for the real-time monitoring, predictive diagnosis, and personalized treatments for patients. A cardiovascular digital twin could simulate treatment protocols, thus helping providers to choose the most effective and minimally invasive options available (Daiju Ueda, 2024).

Digital twins focus on data integration, real-time analytics, and actionable insights, thereby promoting patient-centric care. As well as efficiency in terms of resources, this innovation is one more step toward sustainable, predictive healthcare (Tianze Sun, 2023).

Applications in Healthcare for Predictive Analysis and Personalization

Digital twin technology is the newest influence on healthcare, bringing predictive analytics and personalized medicine. A digital twin is a virtual replica of a patient's physiological and medical data; in these replicas, healthcare providers can simulate disease, predict outcomes, and tailor treatments to individual needs. For instance, in oncology, digital twins can simulate growth of tumors and the reaction to every available therapy, with the oncologist able to choose the best treatment for the patient. In cardiology, they are used to assess the effects of interventions such as stent placements or medication changes on a patient's cardiovascular system (Tianze Sun, 2023)

Predictive analytics through digital twins further enable early disease detection, hence proactive care-avoid the chances for complications. These applications optimize treatment results while limiting the use of resources and invasive procedures for precision in medicine and sustainable health care (Patel & Kumar, 2023).

Comparative Analysis with Traditional Health Monitoring Systems

Digital twin technology surpasses traditional health monitoring systems by offering greater precision, interactivity, and efficiency. Unlike static methods that rely on periodic data, digital twins continuously integrate data from wearables, EHRs, and imaging systems to create dynamic, real-time patient models. This enables predictive analytics, proactive care, and simulation of treatment scenarios to optimize patient outcomes. By predicting disease progression and therapy effectiveness, digital twins help avoid trial-and-error approaches. Additionally, they break traditional data silos, fostering team-based care and reducing unnecessary tests and interventions, enhancing decision-making, resource efficiency, and contributing to a more sustainable healthcare system (Tatiana Mallet Machado, 2023).

Recent Studies and Advancements in Energy Efficient Digital Twins

Recent developments in energy-efficient digital twins focus on optimizing computing algorithms and integrating renewable energy-based solutions. Edge computing plays a key role by processing data closer to its origin, reducing latency and energy consumption. Additionally, AI and ML create efficient algorithms that minimize redundant processing, conserving energy. Research into renewable energy-powered data centers, using solar and wind, is also underway. Advances in energy-aware IoT devices ensure power optimization without sacrificing real-time data accuracy, supporting sustainability in digital healthcare systems. These innovations emphasize balancing technological progress with environmental responsibility (Haya Elayan, 2021).

Summary of Advantages and Limitations: How Digital Twin Technology Enhances Sustainability in Healthcare

Advantages

Digital twins optimize healthcare by promoting predictive maintenance in medical devices, along with efficient resource management, reducing waste and costs. They promote energy-efficient systems and intelligent technologies through edge computing and AI. Moreover, data centers are powered entirely by renewable energy to support sustainability. Digital twins simulate patient outcomes and present resource-conscious care, which reduces trial-and-error approaches. Thirdly, their seamless fusion of data from various sources allows for a complete healthcare system that enhances the outcomes for patients while saving resources. It promotes holistic care, consistent with good sustainability practices that enhance efficiency and reduce environmental impact.

Disadvantages

Digital twin technology has tremendous transformative potential for sustainable health care, but there are also serious challenges: demand for high computational power hurts sustainability goals in energy and e-waste from IoT devices and hardware. High implementation costs deter its use on resource-poor health systems. It remains difficult to scale due to the data privacy and security standards, as well as the need for real-time processing. These limitations must be addressed for full realization of the potential of the digital twin technology in healthcare for ecological and operational benefits. (Evangelia Katsoulakis, 2024).

3. Metaverse Technologies in Healthcare: AR and VR Applications

Defining AR and VR in Healthcare and Their Role in the Metaverse

AR and VR continue to be groundbreaking in revolutionizing healthcare by furthering user interaction with digital environments. AR overlays digital information, thus aiding surgical navigation with real-time 3D visualizations and medics can project anatomical details onto mannequins or patients during training. VR creates a comprehensive environment for pain management, rehabilitation, and mental health therapies, helping patients cope with chronic conditions or possibly phobias. The metaverse expands further to allow global collaboration among healthcare providers by providing capabilities in VR simulation for surgeries and treatment planning. AR also enhances virtual consultations by delivering interactive and immersive patient care experiences and thus transforming the kind of old-fashioned health delivery.

Figure 3. Related articles

Year	Metaverse	Digital Twin	AR artices	VR artices	Energy efficient algorithms	Environmental Solutions	Data Protection & Ethics	Citations
2020	5	7	3	4	6	5	8	12
2021	8	10	5	6	9	8	12	18
2022	12	15	8	9	14	12	18	22
2023	15	18	10	12	18	15	22	28
2024	20	25	15	18	25	20	28	35

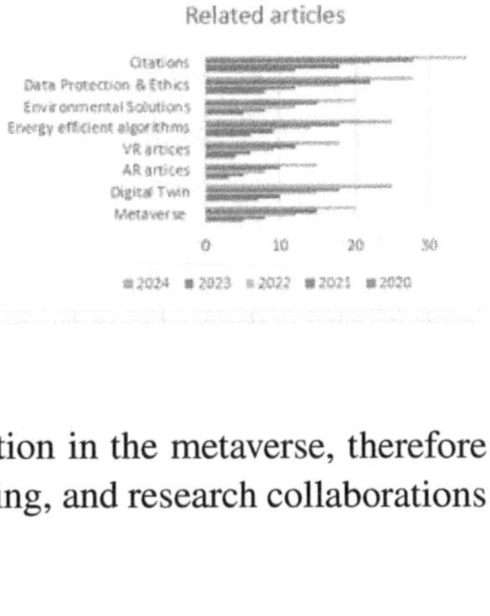

These pairings of AR and VR enhance innovation in the metaverse, therefore driving improvement in patient care, medical training, and research collaborations (David Oyekunle, 2024).

Current Applications and Case Studies (e.g., Virtual Consultations, Surgical Training)

AR and VR technologies have transformed healthcare by introducing immersive, interactive solutions for some age-old problems within the sector. Their implementations include diagnostics and treatment, medical training, and patient engagement. Some of these key applications supported by case studies are listed below:

- **Virtual Consultation and Patient Care**

Telemedicine uses both AR and VR more frequently to enhance virtual consultations. The healthcare providers can view the time-based actual data of a patient, like heart rate and blood pressure, for instance, during virtual appointments with the help of AR-enabled devices. Also, VR provides remote monitoring of patients by creating virtual environments that track patient behavior.

Case Study - During the COVID-19 pandemic, Cleveland Clinic used VR for virtual consultations with mentally ill patients. Using VR-based therapy resulted in 30% lower anxiety levels compared to traditional treatments and heightened patient interest (Clinic, 2023).

- **Preoperative Training and Planning**

AR and VR supply an extremely realistic, risk-free environment for surgical training. Complex surgeries are simulated using VR, while AR overlays anatomical images of the real patient, helping with precision while doing the procedure.

Case Study - Johns Hopkins University successfully used AR to perform spinal fusion surgeries. Surgeons wore AR headsets to visualize 3D anatomical structures during the procedure, reducing surgery time by 20% and improving accuracy (Choi, 2022).

- **Rehabilitation and Physical Therapy**

VR platforms enable immersive rehabilitation experiences by gamifying physical therapy exercises, improving patient adherence and outcomes. AR enhances motor skills recovery by providing visual and auditory feedback during tasks.

Case Study - The University of Southern California treated stroke patients with the help of VR. It submerged patients in virtual scenarios where they needed movement and obtained a 40% improvement in motor skills against conventional therapy (Magazine, 2019) .

- **Pain Management and Mental Health**

VR has been effective in managing chronic pain and anxiety disorders. Patients are submerged in calming virtual environments that reduce pain perception and psychological distress.

Case Study - Cedars-Sinai Medical Center used VR in the management of chronic pain in the hospital. Following 10 minutes of VR, it was reported that pain intensity reduced by 25% (Staff, 2020).

- **Medical Education**

AR and VR enable medical students to practice procedures on virtual patients and gain firsthand experience through interactive learning modules.

Case Study - Stanford University introduced anatomy courses based on VR, allowing students to see the human body in 3D. Students showed a 35% increase in knowledge as compared with traditional teaching (Anatomy, 2016).

Applications of AR and VR within healthcare embrace the possibility for these technologies to transform patient care, training, and rehabilitation. Combining real-time interaction with immersive experiences, these tools are ushering in a new wave of medical innovation and access.

Comparative Table of Metaverse vs. Traditional Methods: Benefits, Challenges, and Environmental Impact

Table 1. Comparative table

Description	Metaverse- Based Methods	Traditional Methods
Benefits		
Personalised Care	Allows for real time data collection on patients and produces customized treatment plans (e.g. virtual twins in the metaverse).	Dependent upon generalized treatment protocols and regular diagnostics
Accessibility	It reduces geographical and physical barriers by doing virtual consultation and remote monitoring.	Require physical presence for most of the consultations and treatment procedures
Collaboration	Virtual environments enable global collaboration among medical practitioners.	Either in-person or teleconferencing solutions.
Training and Education	Immersive VR/AR environments for hands-on practice and training of virtual anatomy exploration	Dependent on physical simulators and cadaver-based learning.
Challenges		
Technology Dependency	Dependent on high-quality hardware-VR/AR headsets, servers-and internet connectivity.	Dependent on physical infrastructure, which hinders digital experimentation but is less complicated to handle with few tools.
Cost	High upfront cost in devices, software, and training; constant upkeep is necessary.	Low upfront cost but instead continues with higher recurring costs of consumables and operation logistics.
Data Privacy and Security	Higher vulnerability to cyber- attack from highly interdependent systems; thus, demands strict protocols.	Better Local Control of Data Security but Less Accessible for Remote and Collaborative Care
Scalability	Scaling is obstructed by complex infrastructure and a high energy demand.	Incremental scalability is easier but less flexible and adaptable
Environmental Impact		

continued on following page

Table 1. Continued

Description	Metaverse- Based Methods	Traditional Methods
Energy Consumption	High computation requirement for real-time virtual reality/augmented reality simulations increase energy use.	Relatively low energy use but contributes to resource inefficiencies in workflows.
Waste Management	Encourages virtual workflows but produces electronic wastes from hardware and devices.	High physical wastes, including papers, one-time use tools with little recycling emphasis
Sustainability Practice	Enables integration of renewable energy, but dedicated efforts in this direction are required to encourage friendly hardware designs	Minimal number of sustainable practices integrated into workflows and highly dependent on traditional resources.

Recent Innovations for Energy Reduction in AR/VR Platforms

Sustainable AR/VR healthcare applications must work on energy consumption cuts by promising innovative solutions.

- **Energy-Efficient Hardware** such as with low-power processors and optimized GPUs, like NVIDIA's architectures, addresses both performance and energy efficiency concerns. Lightweight, sensor-integrated AR glasses further increase efficiency.
- **Cloud and Edge Computing**- Solutions in cloud and edge computing cut down on power demands from devices by pushing computations over to energy-optimized platforms like Microsoft Azure.
- **Adaptive Rendering Techniques** - One area is adaptive rendering techniques, like foveated rendering, that prioritize processing for the user's focus area, conserving energy.
- **Renewable Energy**- Moreover, renewable energy-powered data centers will drive sustainability by automatically transitioning companies like Meta toward reducing environmental footprint related to their AR/VR platform.

Such innovations ensure that AR and VR technologies are sustainable while providing immersive experiences in healthcare (Liu, 2024).

Environmental and Social Impacts of the Metaverse on Healthcare

Environmental Effects

- The metaverse is dependent on energy-intensive technologies such as VR, AR and large data centers that require considerable power for real-time processing and storage, thus resulting in a substantial carbon footprint.

- Upgrades of AR/VR equipment are very frequent, which worsens e-waste, a factor not improved by inadequate recycling measures.
- Virtual interactions, however, in the metaverse decrease the need for physical infrastructure and travel, hence potentially reducing the overall environmental footprint of healthcare settings (tefan Vlădu escu, 2023).

Social Impacts

- This one will eliminate geographical barriers while broadening the digital divide because its greater use might depend on the varying levels of technology in the country.
- Also, immersive environments promote patient education and activeness in health, which could increase treatment efficacy in methods such as VR therapy for the treatment of mental illness and rehabilitation.
- Pros of Governance in Healthcare through the Metaverse Healthcare providers and researchers collaborate globally over the metaverse, spearheading innovation and the sharing of knowledge. (Hidayat Ullah, 2023).
- The metaverse's integration into healthcare presents an opportunity to enhance sustainability and equity, provided challenges like energy demands and accessibility are adequately addressed.

4. Energy Efficiency in Digital Health Solutions

Review of Current Energy Consumption Patterns in Digital Healthcare

The digitalization of healthcare, including EHRs, telemedicine, and the metaverse, significantly increases energy consumption. Data centers, wearables, and VR headsets require substantial power, with 5G further enhancing energy use. Addressing inefficiencies in legacy systems and algorithms is crucial for healthcare institutions aiming for sustainable, energy-optimized solutions (Amir Mosavi, 2019). These patterns emphasize the need to invest in energy-efficient technologies and incorporate renewable power into digital health development for long-term sustainability.

Recent Advances in Energy-Efficient Hardware and Software: Algorithms, Hardware Design, and Cloud-Based Solutions

Recent innovation in digital health is related to energy efficiency through different hardware, software, and cloud-based solutions.

- **Improved Hardware Design Efficiency**

Low-power processors, like ARM Cortex, and energy-efficient sensors are improving healthcare wearables and IoT devices. Edge computing also helps save power consumption as processing of data will occur closer to the source.

- **Algorithmic Optimizations**

Algorithmic optimizations, like foveated rendering in VR, tend to reduce the computational load and its associated energy use. Optimizations for energy efficiency are being done in AI and machine learning models.

- **Cloud-Based Solutions**

Cloud services from the likes of Google Cloud and AWS minimize energy consumption by sustainable data centers and hybrid cloud-edge models while efficiently utilizing resources, thereby minimizing waste and latency (Alexandru Rancea, 2024).

These innovations transform a more sustainable future model for digital health into operations that are more efficient.

Comparative Analysis of Energy Optimization Techniques in Healthcare (Lili Wang, 2023)

With long-term usage of digital healthcare systems, the opportunities for energy optimization become a significant sustainability issue. Many techniques have surfaced in hardware, software, and network infrastructure, which have reduced the energy usage without compromising the performance and quality of healthcare services. Several comparisons can be made on key techniques related to energy optimization used in healthcare sectors.

Table 2. Energy optimization techniques- comparison

Energy Optimization Technique	Description	Advantages	Challenges
Low-Power Hardware Design	Relates to the design of energy-efficient hardware, with low-power processors, sensors, and edge devices.	This reduces energy consumption by devices, thus extending the lifespan of wearables and savings in energy bills.	It involves an initial investment in research and development; some trade-offs in processing power
Edge Computing	The operating system offloads computation on edge devices near the data source, reducing continuous data transmission to central servers.	It decreases the energy usage of cloud servers and reduces the overhead energy that is associated with data transfer.	It demands strong infrastructure at the edge and smooth linkage with cloud-based systems.
Energy Efficient Algorithms	It relies on optimized algorithms, such as those implemented in AI and machine learning, and which have minimal computations and, therefore, energy demands	This makes efficient computational tasks, reduces the usage of power, and enhances its performance.	It involves constant improvement and has only very specific applicability based on use cases
Cloud Computing With Renewable Energy	Consists of cloud computing solutions hosted in data centers powered by renewable energy sources such as solar or wind	This will reduce the carbon footprint of digital healthcare platforms and the operating cost will be cheaper in the long term	Dependency on cloud providers and their sustainability practices, limited by internet bandwidth and latency
Foveated Rendering	It minimizes the computation load on VR/AR applications by rendering high-quality images only in the focused area of the user	It reduces the necessity of using GPU and processing power greatly, thereby saving energy in applications of VR.	Visual quality may be compromised in some applications, outside the focused region
Virtualization and Containerization	It creates virtual environments or containers that share physical resources without giving up functionality	It maximizes the usage of resources to reduce energy wastage in healthcare IT infrastructures.	Complex to deal with and may introduce overhead in some cases
Energy Harvesting Devices	Use energy harvesting technologies such as solar power or kinetic energy to power devices like sensors and wearables	Reduces dependency on batteries and decreases environmental footprint of device manufacturing and disposal.	Energy harvesting is usually quite slow and not adequate to power high-power health care devices

Optimizing healthcare energy balance performance and sustainability. Low-power hardware: edge computing; cloud services; renewable integration - all to reduce consumption. Algorithmic optimizations - including foveated rendering - improve the energy efficiency in AR/VR applications. Balancing these scales will be essential for creating a sustainable, efficient digital healthcare future.

Case Studies: Successful Implementation of Energy-Efficient Digital Health Platforms

However, many health organizations and technology companies combined have managed to ensure that energy-efficient solutions integrated into the processes of reducing environmental impact improve healthcare outcomes. Here is an example case with proper integration practices of digital health energy-efficient platforms:

o **Mayo Clinic: Cloud-Based Healthcare with Renewable Energy**

A cloud-based architecture that reduced reliance on local data centers, conserving energy was achieved through the partnership between Microsoft Azure and Mayo Clinic. Data Center for Azure runs on renewable energy, minimizes physical server use, and carbon footprint. The shift helped Mayo Clinic contribute considerably toward achieving zero net emissions by 2030.

Outcome - Energy intensity would be reduced, hence operational costs; a sustainable, scalable cloud infrastructure for health data (Anindya Bose, 2024).

o **Philips Healthcare - Energy Efficient Medical Devices**

Philips Healthcare, the market leader in medical devices, created energy-efficient imaging technologies such as the Ingenia Ambition X MRI machine, which consumes significantly lesser power than its predecessors. Its digital signal processing and efficient cooling system minimize power intake while providing excellent diagnostics performance, reducing healthcare facilities' energy use and carbon footprint

Results - Substantial reduction of energy consumption in health facilities and medical imaging service price to care providers and patients (Phiips, 2024).

o **The NHS Digital- Green Digital Transformation in Healthcare**

NHS Digital is on the front lines of energy reduction through green digital transformation in the UK. This is through the migration of electronic health records to cloud platforms, reducing the use of paper records and processes. Smarter technologies and energy-efficient data centers are also coupled in use by the NHS. Low-power hardware and cloud infrastructure therefore help reduce carbon emissions while running costs are reduced to achieve that position of digital health transformation.

Outcome - Improved digital services for both patients and healthcare professionals; reduced physical resource consumption; a significant reduction in energy costs (Stoumpos, 2023).

- **Kaiser Permanente - Telemedicine and Energy-Efficient Solutions**

Kaiser Permanente, the largest nonprofit health plans in the U.S., scaled its telemedicine platform to reduce the number of travel to healthcare facilities. In developing the services during the COVID-19, they scaled up services using low-energy video conferencing tools and remote monitoring systems. The Kaiser Permanente shifted to be powered by data centers with renewable energy sources while optimizing their digital tools for power waste minimization, significantly reducing transportation-related emissions.

Outcome - Reduced transportation-related emissions and energy wastage in the long run because of decreased health facility infrastructure requirements (KAISER, 2023).

- **Siemens Healthineers - Sustainable AI-Powered Diagnostics**

Siemens Healthineers launched AI-based diagnostic solutions that increase medical equipment efficiency, saving energy. The AI-Pathway Companion will help doctors make decisions more rapidly and exactly, thus reducing redundant tests and conserving energy. In the same context, Somatom X.cite CT scanner achieves high-quality imaging while using less energy.

Outcome - Reduction of energy utilization in diagnostic imaging, cost-effective operations for health-care providers, and a reduced footprint on the environment (Siemens, 2024).

Case studies are provided to demonstrate how energy-efficient solutions-such as optimized algorithms, renewable energy, and telemedicine-enhance sustainability and reduce costs, thereby positioning digital health platforms as key components of a sustainable healthcare ecosystem

Future Directions in terms of Prospects for lowering Carbon FootPrint in Healthcare Technologies

Improving health care's carbon footprint requires hardware, software, and operation innovations. The green AI algorithms, energy-efficient hardware, renewable energy-powered data centers, and circular economy practices will reduce the carbon footprint of the sector. Telemedicine and smart monitoring systems can reduce resource use, travel, and infrastructure-related emissions, thus leading to a healthy future.

5. Data Protection protocols and their environmental Impact

Overview of Data Privacy Challenges in Digital Healthcare

The challenges digital health encounters in terms of data privacy range from interconnected systems to cyberattacks and compliance complexity across regions. Data breach and misuse through IoT and AI integration increase risks to patient information, and thus, secure encryption, safe storage, and clear policies safeguard patient information while making innovations possible through data sharing (Bu-eXP, 2019)

Role of Decentralized Storage, Encryption, and Data Policies in Green Healthcare

Decentralized storage, encryption, and data policies are key to secure and sustainable digital healthcare systems. Blockchain and distributed ledgers reduce their dependence on the power-hungry centralized servers and thus are efficient as well as resilient. Advanced encryption means patient data is safe, and for research, it can be safely shared. With data policies robust, policies like GDPR promote transparency, trust, and ethical practice while encouraging eco-consciousness.

Comparison of Data Management Approaches (e.g., Cloud vs. Decentralized)

Table 3. Comparison

Description	Cloud- Based Data Management	De-Centralized Data Management
Architecture	Centralized servers handle the data, often third-party providers like AWS or Azure,	Distributed storage systems using technologies such as blockchain or peer-to-peer networks.
Scalability	It is able to scale very high easily, with high volumes of data and high volumes of users.	Scalable but challenges with node coordination and storage replication.
Data Security	Encryption and access control rely on service providers, prone to single-point failures.	Strong encryption and use of consensus mechanisms enhance security, hard for breaches.
Energy Efficiency	Can be energy-intensive, especially if data centers rely on non-renewable energy	Has lower energy consumption because the distributed operation reduces data-transfer loads

continued on following page

Table 3. Continued

Description	Cloud- Based Data Management	De-Centralized Data Management
Cost	Subscription based; Storage, processing, and data transfer, are tied to cost.	There are no central fees but requires investment in network nodes and infra.
Reliability	Relies on provider's uptime and network connectivity.	More robust against outages; it has data redundancy and ensures availability
Environmental Impact	Large-scale data centers contribute significantly to carbon emissions	Decentralized models often leverage renewable energy and reduce centralized dependency.
Compliance	Managed services simplify compliance but require trust in third parties	Transparent data handling aligns with privacy laws like GDPR (General Data Protection Regulation) and HIPAA (Health Insurance Portability and Accountability).

Balancing Data Security with Energy Efficiency: Key Studies and Best Practices

Balancing healthcare data security and energy efficiency requires innovative solutions. Studies emphasize the application of lightweight encryption algorithms to reduce the computational demands while ensuring robust security in the system. Techniques such as homomorphic encryption allow one to perform computations on cipher text without decrypting, thereby reducing the risk. Edge computing reduces high energy usage cloud transmissions while maintaining privacy. Best practices include the implementation of energy-efficient blockchain models for decentralized healthcare records and green data centers powered by renewable energy. In this regard, solutions are found both in security and sustainability aspects.

Recent Regulatory Updates in Data Security for Digital Health

Regulatory trends in digital health: Enhancing security around data and therefore patient trust. The General Data Protection Regulation in the EU sets a global benchmark of transparency, encryption, and consent over data. HIPAA amendments in the US address questions around telehealth and data protection. The EU's DGA, implemented in 2023, looks into safe data sharing. India's Digital Personal Data Protection Act 2023 enforces privacy and accountability for the transfer of health data across borders.

6. Sustainable Supply Chain in Digital Health

Analysis of Environmental Impacts Across the Digital Health Supply Chain

The digital health supply chain impacts the environment in its manufacturing, energy-heavy data centers and transport emissions, as well as improper e-waste disposal. Sustainable practices, such as the adoption of eco-friendly production, renewable energy, and robust recycling programs, are necessary to address these environmental challenges and minimize carbon footprint from digital health technologies.

Comparison of Ethical Sourcing and Eco-Friendly Production Techniques

Table 4. Comparison of ethical and eco-friendly (varntoumian, 2021)

Description	Ethical Sourcing	Eco-friendly Production
Definition	Responsible sourcing of raw materials; fair labor practice; minimizing harm to communities and the ecosystem.	Focuses on manufacturing with reduced environmental impact and conservation of natural resources.
Key Principles	Fair trade, conflict-free sourcing; adherence to labor laws and human rights standards.	Emphasizes energy efficiency, waste reduction, renewable sources, and green technologies.
Implementation	Transparency in supply chains and dealing with certified suppliers, such as Fairtrade, RMI	Integrates life-cycle assessments, green manufacturing standards, and circular economy principles.
Benefits	Integrates life-cycle assessments, green manufacturing standards, and circular economy principles.	Decreases greenhouse gas emissions and water and energy consumption while relying less on non-renewable resources.
Challenges	Lack of transparency in complex global supply chains and higher operational costs in terms of compliance.	Heavy investment in technology and redesign processes; could experience resistance from traditional producers.
Examples in Digital Health	Ethical sourcing of rare earth metals for medical devices, ensuring conflict-free certifications.	Manufacturing energy-efficient devices like MRI machines utilizing recycled material and green technologies.

Both approaches complement one another toward a sustainable digital health ecosystem. Balancing the two is the goal toward long-term environmental and social goals.

Recycling Policies and the Circular Economy: Reducing Carbon Footprint

Recycling policies and the circular economy play a vital role in reducing carbon footprints in digital health by promoting material reuse from medical devices and IT infrastructure. E-waste management, such as extended producer responsibility, encourages recycling, while resource recovery through remanufacturing reduces raw material dependence and emissions, fostering environmental and economic sustainability.

Case Studies and Recent Developments in Sustainable Supply Chain Practices

- Sustainable supply chains for digital health are gaining momentum through innovation and regulation frameworks. Medical imaging equipment refurbishment by Philips Healthcare has led to a decrease in the output of 6.2 million metric tons of CO2 between 2018 and 2022. Eco-design has been pursued by Siemens
- Healthineers in MRI machines through the use of recyclable materials and minimizing resource dependency. Blockchain technology is increasingly being used to find traceable but ethical sources of rare earth metals in medical instruments.
- Start-ups, such as Rheaply, focus on resource-sharing platforms that cut waste, and cloud-based inventory management reduces logistics emissions. Sustainability standards are becoming tighter due to the European Union's Green Deal, and initiatives like the Global E-Waste Monitor promote effective recycling.
- These practices highlight a transition towards an ecologically conscious health sector, balancing innovation with environmental stewardship while tackling climate challenges.

Summarizing the Challenges and Benefits of Sustainable Production for Digital Health

Sustainable production in digital health promises long-term cost savings, improved brand reputation, and regulatory alignment, but faces challenges such as high upfront costs, sourcing sustainable materials, and achieving supply chain transparency. Despite these obstacles, minimizing carbon emissions, e-waste, and resource use creates a resilient, environmentally responsible healthcare ecosystem.

7. Inclusivity and Accessibility in Sustainable Digital Health Solutions

Defining Digital Divide and Access Issues in Healthcare

The digital divide in healthcare highlights inequalities in access to telemedicine and digital health tools, particularly in rural, low-income, and underserved communities. Challenges include limited internet access, unaffordable devices, and user interface issues for elderly or disabled individuals. Bridging this gap requires investment in accessible, equitable healthcare technologies.

Recent Approaches to User-Friendly Interface Design and Accessibility Features

Progress in digital health interface design focuses on inclusion and usability. Voice-controlled interfaces, gesture recognition, customizable layouts, and AI-driven personalization improve accessibility for people with disabilities, the elderly, and non-tech-savvy users. Features like real-time language translation and closed captioning, alongside accessibility guidelines, ensure equitable, user-friendly solutions.

Localized Content for Diverse Populations in the Metaverse

Localized content in the metaverse enhances healthcare inclusivity by addressing language barriers with translation and real-time interpretation. Culturally relevant visuals and educational materials increase user familiarity and acceptance. Accessibility features, simplified explanations, and collaboration with local stakeholders ensure authenticity and trust, creating an equitable digital healthcare environment globally

Comparative Analysis of Inclusivity Measures Across Different Platforms

Digital health platforms prioritize inclusivity through features like multi-language support in telemedicine, intuitive VR interfaces, and customizable wearable notifications. Metaverse platforms offer real-time translation and accessibility tools. However, gaps in global standards compliance, like WCAG, remain, and addressing them requires innovation and collaboration to ensure universal inclusivity.

Balancing Technological Advancements With Inclusive Design

Equitable access in digital healthcare is achieved through inclusive design, integrating universal principles like scalable text, voice navigation, and sensory interactions with advanced technologies such as AI, AR, and VR. User feedback from marginalized groups shapes innovations, ensuring accessibility remains central. Standards like WCAG and usability testing ensure all populations benefit from progress.

8. Comparative Analysis of Existing Digital Healthcare Solutions

Comparative Table of Key Technologies: Digital Twin, Metaverse, and IoMT

Table 5. Key technologies - comparison (Marri, 2024)

Technology	Digital Twin	Metaverse	IoMT (Internet of Medical Things
Definition	Virtual representations of physical objects, systems, or people.	A virtual space to interact with through AR/VR.	Network of interoperable medical devices to monitor remotely in real-time.
Primary Focus	Predictive analytics and precision medicine.	Virtual healthcare spaces, such as consultations and training.	Personalized care, Collecting and analyzing patient data in real-time.
Applications	Personalized care, disease modeling, and practice simulation.	Virtual consultation, surgery training, patient education.	Remote monitoring of patients, remote wearable health devices, diagnosis.
User Interaction	Data-driven simulations for real-time health modeling.	Immersive AR/VR environments to interact.	Continuous data monitoring and alerts from connected devices.
Key Benefit	Optimizes treatment plans through data-driven insights.	Enhances accessibility and healthcare education through immersive experiences	Enables remote care, improving healthcare access and efficiency.
Environmental Impact	Requires significant computational power, energy-intensive.	High energy consumption for VR/AR, environmental concerns	Energy-efficient devices but relies on data centers for cloud processing

This table highlights the complementary roles of each technology in advancing healthcare, while also identifying their unique features and challenges.

Analysis of Merits and Demerits of Existing Sustainable Healthcare Solutions

- **Merits**

Sustainable healthcare solutions reduce environmental impacts by minimizing energy consumption, waste, and carbon footprints. Green medical devices, telemedicine, and energy-efficient technologies lower emissions, reduce transportation needs, and provide long-term cost savings. These solutions align with global sustainability goals, help meet regulatory standards, and enhance the healthcare system's reputation.

- **Demerits**

As attractive as these benefits are, there remain challenges. The upfront costs to switch to green technologies are sizeable, especially for small or resource-constrained healthcare providers. Shifting to energy-efficient infrastructure often comes at an enormously high price. Not all sustainable solutions are equally scalable or as accessible to underserved populations. Finally, while digital health technologies reduce physical waste, they can result in data privacy issues and higher energy intensity from cloud services.

Summary of Unique Contributions and Gaps in Current Research

Current research on sustainable digital healthcare emphasizes eco-friendly technologies, energy-efficient systems, and green infrastructure. However, gaps remain in assessing the long-term environmental impact of emerging technologies like digital twins, scalability, and integrating inclusivity. Further studies focusing on data privacy, affordability, and global accessibility are needed to address these gaps.

9. Theoretical and Methodological Innovations in Sustainable Healthcare

Summary of Key Theoretical Models Supporting Digital Health Sustainability

The theoretical models focusing on sustainability of digital health are the ones emphasizing "eco-conscious" innovation alongside the adoption of technology. TOE (Technology- Organization Environment) is used in pointing out how organizational factors, technological, and environmental contexts will influence the adaptation of sustainable digital health solutions. DOI (Diffusion of Innovations) theory about how innovations such as digital twins and metaverse are adopted into healthcare points to a context that suggests benefits and compatibility with the current systems. In addition, the SDG (Sustainable Development Goals) framework provides a global perspective because it aligns digital health innovations with environmental and social sustainability objectives guiding sustainable practices in healthcare (Rogers, 2003).

Recent Methodological Advances in Sustainable Health Technologies

Recent advances in sustainable health technologies include energy-efficient algorithms, AI-driven health management, and circular economy principles. New machine learning algorithms optimize energy usage in digital health platforms by minimizing computational demands. Cloud-based solutions and edge computing enhance energy efficiency and reduce latency by processing data closer to users. Life Cycle Assessments (LCAs) are increasingly used to evaluate the environmental impacts of healthcare technologies, from production to disposal. Additionally, there is growing research in designing eco-friendly medical devices with green design principles, which help reduce the carbon footprint while maintaining high healthcare standards. (Amjad Rehman, 2021).

Highlighting Innovations in Research Methods for Greener Healthcare

Innovations in research methods for greener healthcare focus on sustainable design, energy-efficient technologies, and environmental impact assessments. LCA helps evaluate the carbon footprint of healthcare technologies, while eco-design principles create energy-efficient, biodegradable devices. AI, machine learning, and blockchain optimize processes and secure decentralized data management. Smarter wearables and IoMT devices promote predictive health monitoring, reducing healthcare visits and environmental impact, aligning technological advancements with sustainability goals for a greener healthcare future (Pouncy, 2024).

Comparative Analysis of Methodological Approaches in the Literature

The literature presents various approaches to improving sustainability in digital health. Life Cycle Assessment (LCA) helps assess environmental impacts, identifying areas for eco-friendly improvements in medical devices, digital platforms, and wearables. Energy-efficient algorithms, leveraging AI and machine learning, optimize resources to reduce energy consumption. The Technology-Organization-

Environment (TOE) framework considers the interaction of technological, organizational, and environmental factors in adopting green healthcare technologies. These approaches drive sustainable innovation but require further integration to address scalability and access challenges. (Rauch, 2024).

10. Conclusion of Literature Review

The literature highlights that digital health technologies, such as digital twins, the metaverse, and IoMT, can contribute to sustainability by optimizing healthcare delivery and minimizing environmental impact. Energy-efficient algorithms and AI-driven solutions are key to achieving energy-reduction goals. However, further research is needed on Life Cycle Assessment, eco-design principles, and scalable, sustainable solutions for low-resource settings. This research will focus on bridging gaps in energy-efficient practices, ethical data management, and inclusive design. It aims to create a framework for sustainable digital health systems, offering insights for a greener, more inclusive healthcare future (Mehrotra, 2024).

III. METHODOLOGY

One of the most promising applications of digital twin technology in healthcare is its ability to personalize medicine. With digital twins, physicians can simulate various treatment options on a patient's virtual twin observing the potential outcomes before implementing treatments in real life. This approach not only enhances treatment efficacy but also reduces the likelihood of adverse effects, ultimately improving patient safety. Our research methodology creates a digital twin of a virtual healthcare campus involves a sequence of structured steps implemented through the MetaSpark Studio platform, which enables augmented reality (AR) development with a focus on interactivity and environmental engagement. This methodology is grounded in both the principles of digital twin technology and augmented reality integration in healthcare and sustainability sectors, as highlighted in recent studies on AR-based healthcare training and education tools. The following sections outline each step of the development process and explore the theoretical and practical implications of these steps.

In our suggested solution we are creating the experience the "Virtual Green Healthcare Campus" using AR generation in MetaSpark, our methodology is based on the provided steps and will incorporate references and theoretical perspectives from the existing literature on digital twins, AR, and sustainable healthcare environments. There are 10 basic steps that needs to be followed for the same. By following these detailed steps, you can create an engaging and real-time updated digital twin of the doctor that can visit the patients digitally to monitor their reports through sustainable healthcare architecture connected to patient ID and Database.

Figure 4. Process chart for generating an AR experience using Metaspark Studio

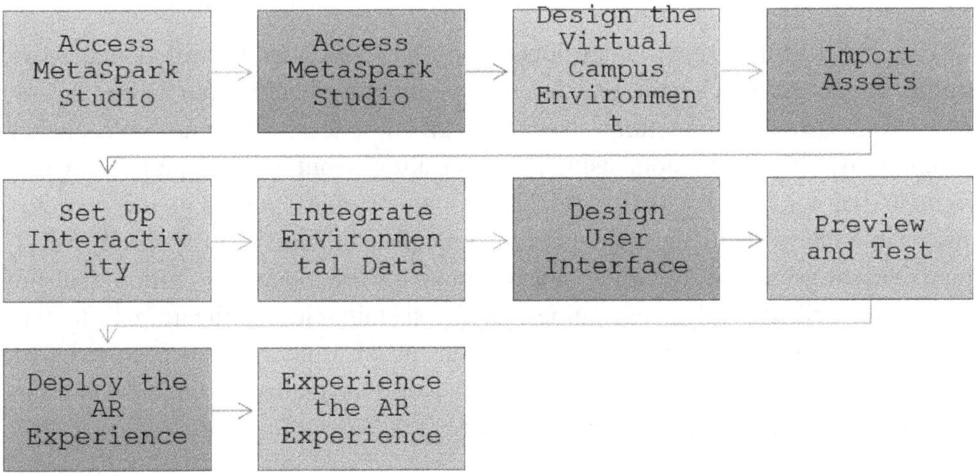

Step 1: Accessing MetaSpark Studio

The development process began by accessing MetaSpark Studio, a platform that allows users to create interactive AR experiences. AR development environments are foundational for building virtual simulations as they provide accessible interfaces for creating high-fidelity digital twins. By logging into MetaSpark Studio, researchers gain access to a robust suite of AR design tools that facilitate the visualization and simulation of healthcare environments, aligning with methodologies used in other digital twin frameworks. Upon accessing the studio, developers are required to create an account, ensuring they have a dedicated workspace where projects and assets are managed centrally.

Step 2: Project Initialization and Configuration

To initiate the digital twin creation, a new project was established in MetaSpark Studio. Naming and contextualizing the project as "Virtual Green Healthcare Campus" served to maintain clarity and focus throughout the development process, as suggested by McClelland and Boardman in their study on project management in AR environments. Effective project initialization, which includes naming and descriptive labeling, aligns with best practices in AR development for complex digital simulations. This phase included setting up metadata that later aids in version control, collaboration, and documentation.

Step 3: Designing the Virtual Campus Environment

The virtual environment was developed using the 3D scene editor within MetaSpark Studio, which allowed for the creation of an immersive healthcare campus layout, integrating virtual architectural structures, green spaces, and renewable energy installations. This can be done using a Patch Editor layout in Metaspark, Shown in Figure 6 (below). In line with ecological simulation studies, the design incorporated sustainable elements to simulate an eco-friendly healthcare infrastructure. Buildings, outdoor areas, and specific points of interest were modeled to mimic real-life healthcare facilities, following guidelines for sustainable healthcare architecture design. Camera angles were optimized to ensure an immersive user experience, utilizing multiple viewpoints to replicate real-world navigation through the campus and enhance spatial awareness among users.

Figure 5. Patch editor in Metaspark Studio for design virtual campus

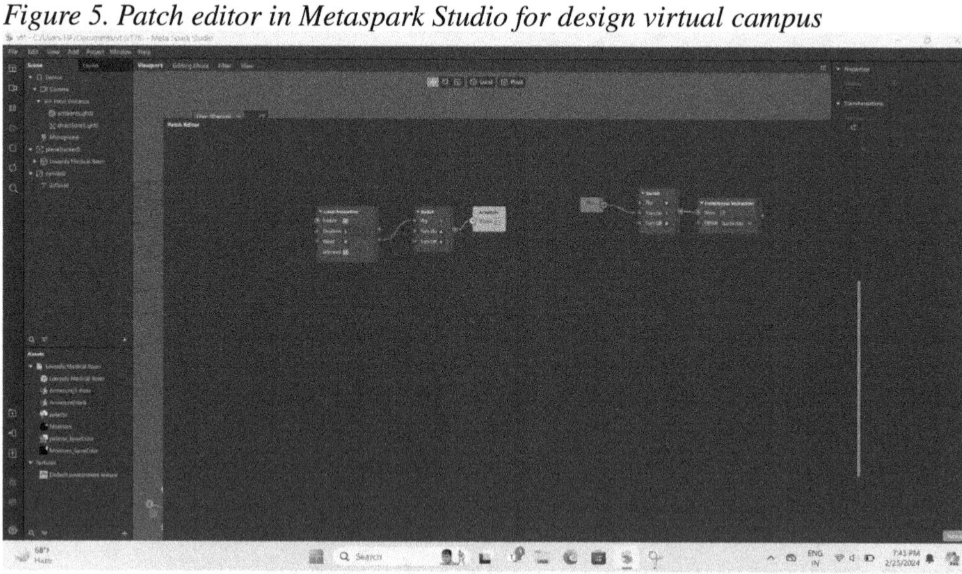

Step 4: Importing Assets

Asset integration was a critical step in constructing the digital twin, involving the import of 3D models, textures, and interactive elements in formats compatible with MetaSpark Studio, including .fbx, .obj, and .gltf. This aligns with standards established in digital twin and AR model rendering, where diverse file formats ensure model accuracy and compatibility. Imported models were used to represent campus features, renewable energy technologies, and sustainable design elements. The inclusion of environmental textures helped create realistic settings, which is essential for user engagement and educational impact, as described in AR-based educational literature.

Step 5: Setting Up Interactivity

To foster user engagement, interactive features were added using MetaSpark's scripting tools, allowing users to tap on objects and trigger information displays, animations, and quizzes. Shown in Figure 7, interactivity in AR experiences enhances educational outcomes, particularly in healthcare contexts where experiential learning is crucial. Scripting enabled dynamic responses to user actions, such as advancing to subsequent scenes or displaying information on sustainable healthcare practices. This interactive setup aligns with the cognitive theory of multimedia learning, which asserts that interactive components facilitate deeper user comprehension through active engagement with digital content.

Figure 6. Animation patch

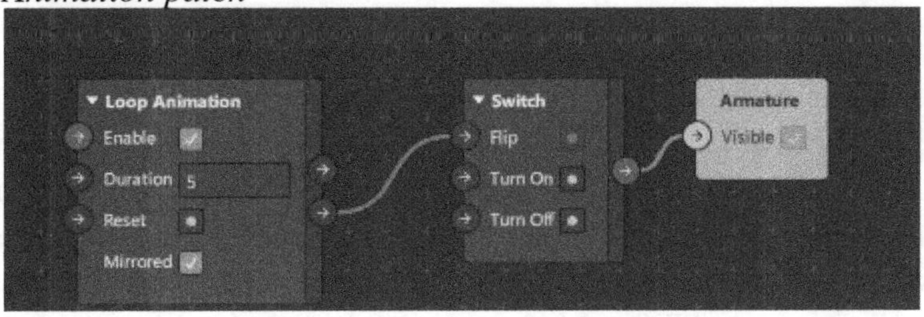

Figure 7. Instruction patch in Metaspark Studio

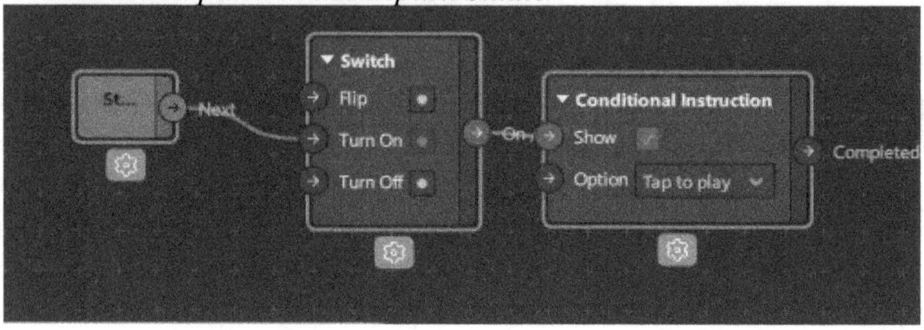

Step 6: Integration of Environmental Data (Optional)

To enhance realism and provide a more comprehensive educational experience, real-time environmental data was integrated within the digital twin. By connecting to APIs, the simulation could reflect real-world data such as solar irradiance, wind speed, and energy usage patterns. This dynamic data integration follows the principles of digital twins as adaptive and responsive simulations of real-world systems. This step, Showing in Figure 7 (above) allowed the digital twin to not only showcase architectural and design elements but also demonstrate the practical impact of renewable energy on healthcare operations, adding a layer of ecological insight for users.

Step 7: Designing the User Interface

User interface (UI) design is central to ensuring a user-friendly and intuitive experience. Using MetaSpark's design tools, interactive buttons, navigation controls, and information panels were integrated to create an accessible interface. An intuitive UI is crucial in digital twin applications for enhancing user immersion and comprehension, especially in educational and healthcare settings. The UI was designed with clear labels and instructions, enabling users to navigate the campus effortlessly and access additional information without cognitive overload, in line with user-centered design principles.

Step 8: Previewing and Testing the AR Experience

Testing the AR experience in MetaSpark Studio allowed the team to identify and resolve potential issues with navigation, interactivity, and visual clarity. As studied by various AR experiences created earlier, it has been found that the testing phase is essential in AR development as it ensures that the digital twin functions as intended across different devices and user scenarios. The built-in preview feature in MetaSpark Studio enabled comprehensive testing under various simulated conditions, allowing for adjustments in lighting, texture quality, and interactive scripting before deployment. Regular testing aligns with iterative design principles, ensuring optimal usability and performance prior to publishing.

Step 9: Deploying the Digital Twin AR Experience

Once the AR experience met performance and usability criteria, it was published on the MetaSpark platform for distribution. Publishing included configuring privacy settings and accessibility features to align with data protection and usability standards in digital twin applications. MetaSpark generated a unique QR code and URL, providing convenient access for users to explore the virtual healthcare campus. This approach is consistent with best practices in digital twin deployment, where ease of access and data security are prioritized.

Step 10: User Experience and Feedback Collection

The final stage involved users accessing the AR experience via a QR code or URL on their mobile devices, enabling them to explore the campus and engage with interactive features. Feedback collection was integrated into the process, allowing users to provide insights on usability, content clarity, and educational impact. The role of user feedback in refining digital twin applications is well-documented, as it supports iterative improvement based on actual user experiences and enhances the overall effectiveness of the application.

Overall, based on the literature review that revealed a growing body of research on the potential of digital technologies to drive sustainability in the healthcare industry, our methodology works towards highlighted need for effective business processes to support sustainable healthcare systems, noting that the adoption of digital technologies can have significant implications for healthcare firms' business process management. Creating a digital twin can further contribute to research, testing and even data handling in the field of healthcare (as depicted using Figure 7).

Figure 8. Application aspects of digital twin in healthcare

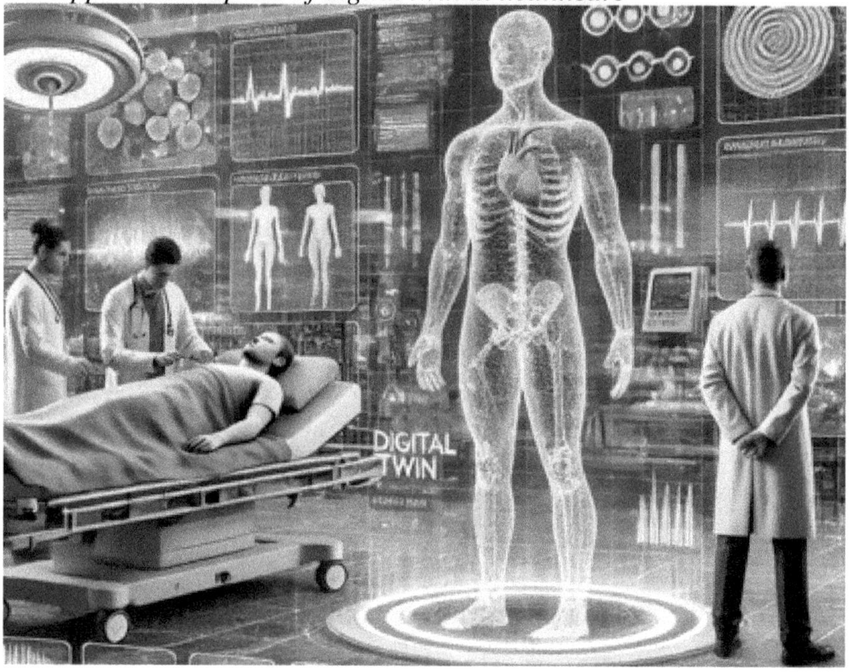

IV. RESULTS

After implementing an AR model for hospital using Metaspark studio, we explore the various possibilities such as checking the real time position of doctor in hospital campus using their AR avatar and checking the condition of equipment's /test results virtually. The intricate interplay between technological progress and environmental responsibility necessitates a holistic approach, involving optimized energy consumption, eco-conscious production practices, and ethical data protection measures. Following are our real time implementation results represented by figures that follows.

Figure 10 shows a Metaspark generated augmented reality hospital that can be linked to various Room no.s, Patient IDs as well Healthcare staff based on blueprint of actual hospital and its facilities.

Figure 9. Preview of hospital without doctor at premises

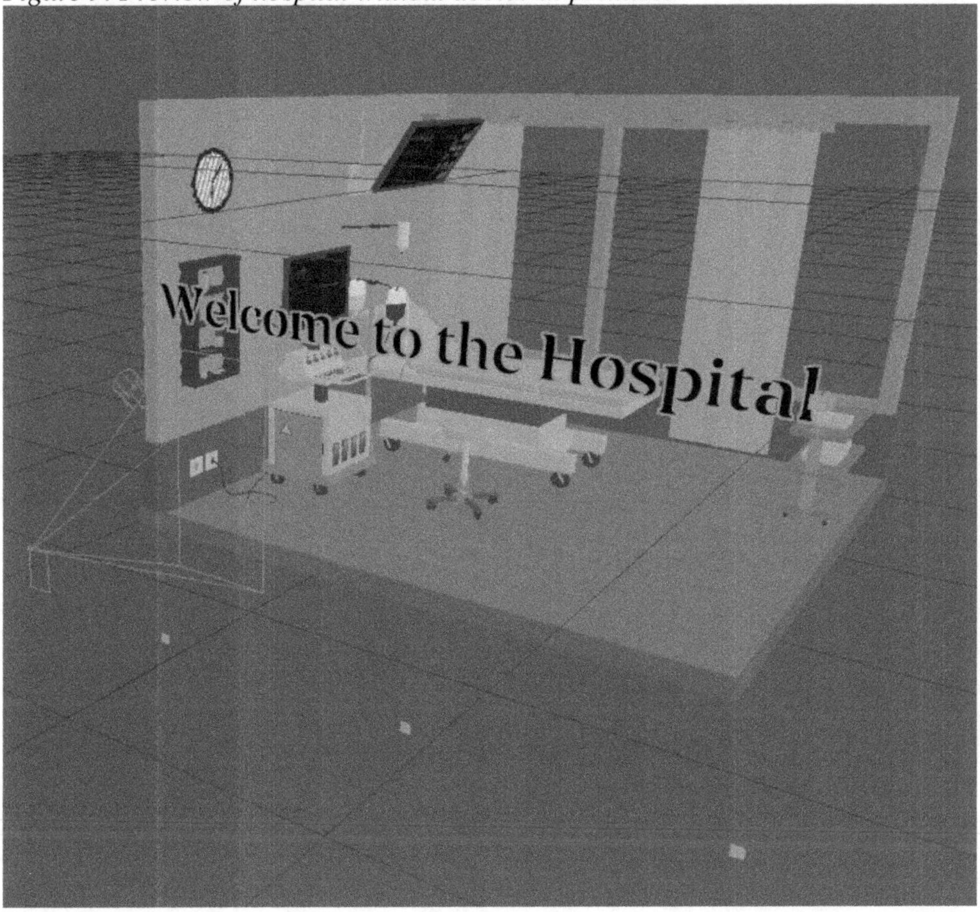

Figure 10 and 11 shows AR modelling of Hospital linked with Avatars of Doctors for real time tracking. During avatar characterization we can define the checkpoints for doctors so that relevant patient IDs can be visited and their vitals can be upload to Doctor's profile for a remote monitoring and alert generation (if needed).

Figure 10. Preview of hospital with doctors on round

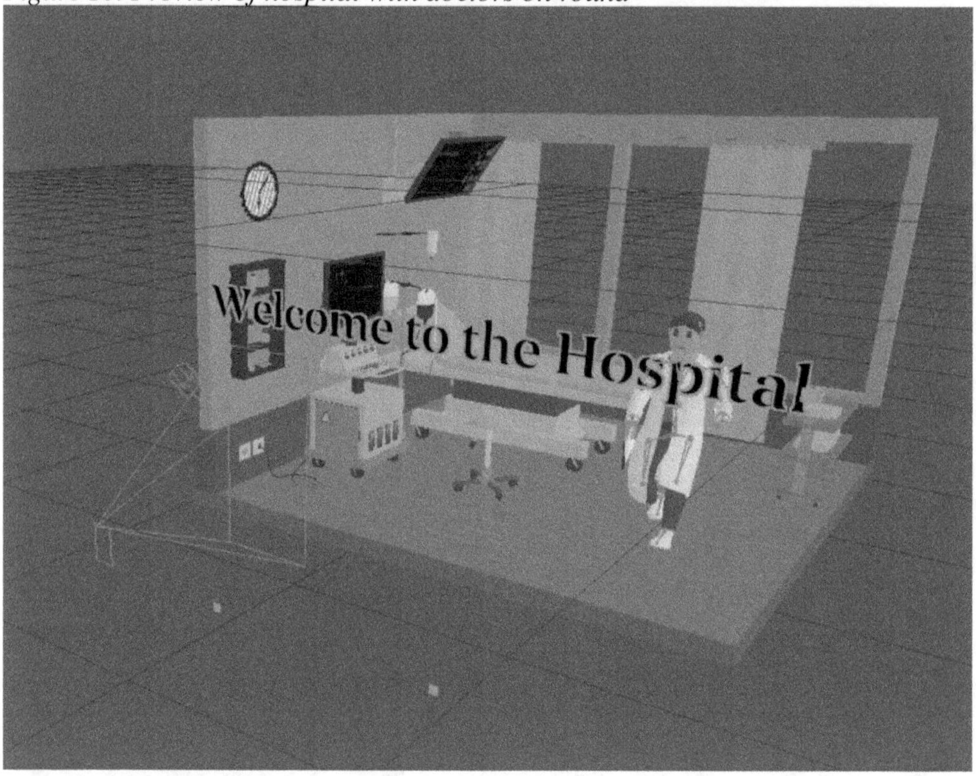

Figure 11. View port to track doctor's movement

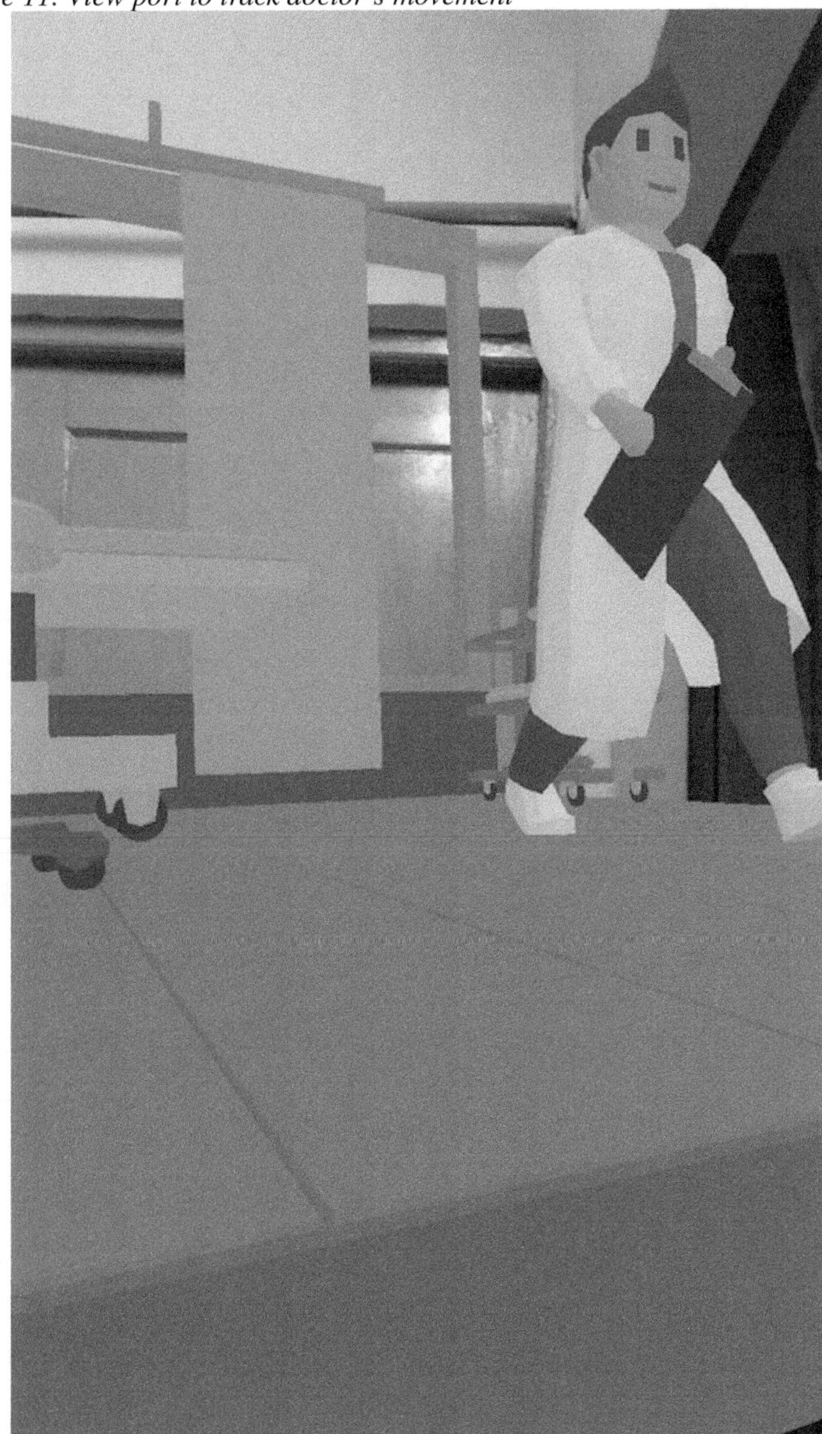

Figure 12 shows the Monitoring of vitals of patients and doctors on round using animation patch and tracking.

Figure 12. Test previews and vital display on digital device created using Metaspark

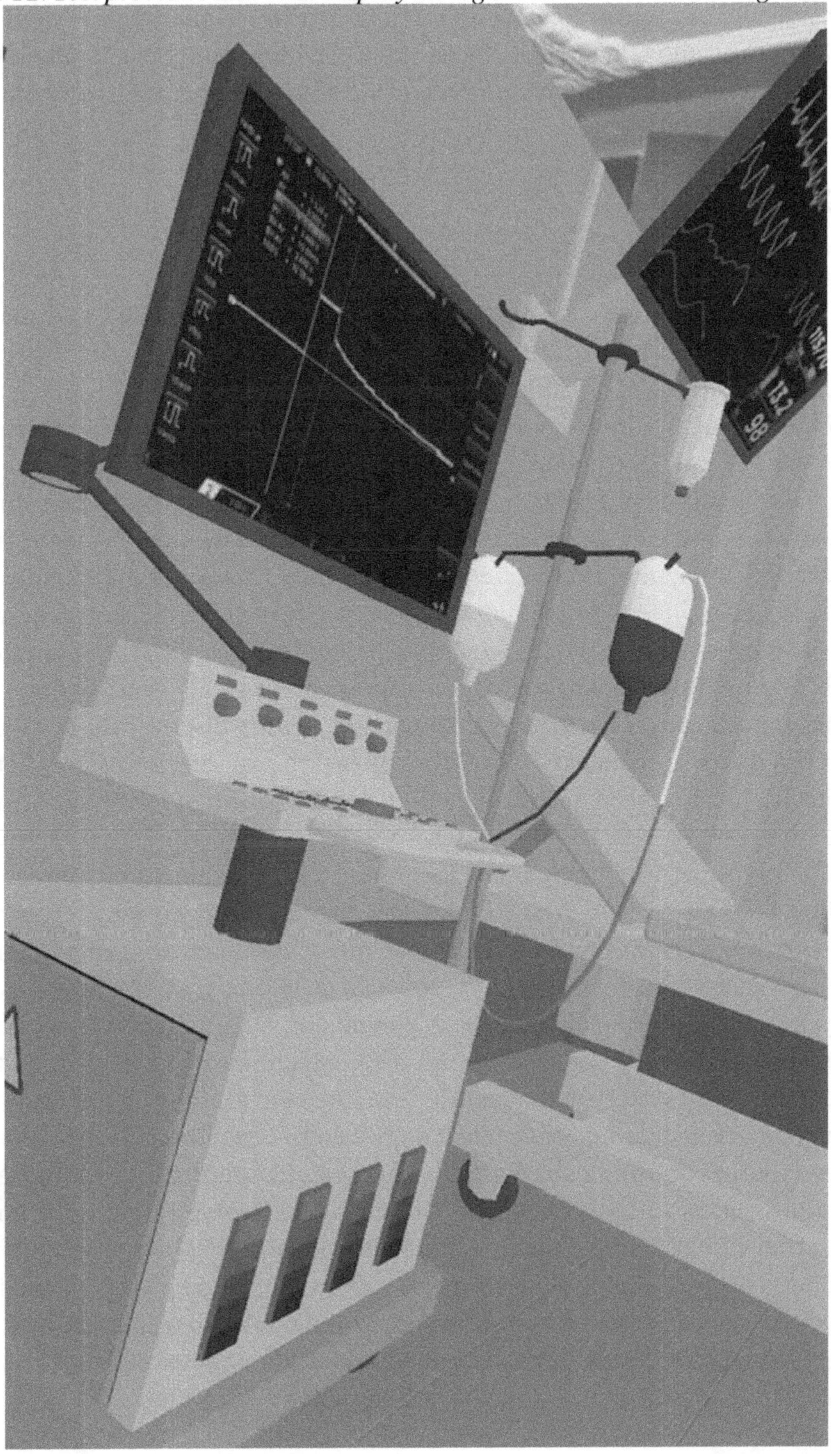

In summary, our result output is in lined with various other studies conducted to examine the use of digital tools in low-resource settings, finding a heavy emphasis on mobile health and telemedicine technologies, with gaps in the adoption of augmented reality, additive manufacturing, and simulation/digital twin technologies.

V. CONCLUSION

Digital twin technology in healthcare offers transformative potential by creating virtual replicas of patients, organs, and processes for real-time analysis, simulation, and prediction of health outcomes. This proactive approach allows for early detection of potential health issues, enabling timely interventions to prevent hospitalizations and critical events. In surgical practices, digital twins serve as valuable preoperative tools, allowing surgeons to practice procedures on virtual models, improving surgical precision and minimizing risks. Overall, digital twins enhance patient care, improve healthcare outcomes, and offer new avenues for precision medicine, making them a game-changer in modern healthcare practices. The trajectory of digital healthcare presents an unparalleled opportunity to reshape patient care and medical practices. However, this transformative journey must be guided by a vision that transcends immediate gains, focusing on the creation of an environmentally and technologically sustainable healthcare system. The collaborative efforts of government agencies, non-profit groups, and industry players are pivotal in realizing a sustainable future for digital healthcare, where innovations align with both technological advancements and environmental preservation.

This transformative journey holds the promise of a healthier and more technologically advanced society, driven by insights that digital twins uniquely provide. The integration of digital twins in healthcare does, however, raise important considerations. As healthcare institutions adopt this technology, a commitment to data privacy, security, and ethical practices is paramount. Digital twins rely heavily on the continuous inflow of sensitive health data, which must be safeguarded to ensure patient confidentiality and trust. Moreover, the environmental implications of implementing such data-intensive technology cannot be ignored. Such a vision encompasses not only cutting-edge digital technologies like digital twins and metaverse applications but also a commitment to minimizing the ecological footprint through energy-efficient platforms, ethical data protection, and collaborative initiatives.

The expansion of digital twins in healthcare will include predictive analytics, personalized mental health interventions, and remote monitoring. Collaboration among governments, healthcare institutions, and technology providers is essential for establishing responsible, equitable, and sustainable standards.

REFERENCES

Abbas, R., & Graepel, T. (2024). Artificial Intelligence in Healthcare Supply Chains: Enhancing Resilience and Reducing Waste through Quantitative Forecasting. *ResearchGate*. DOI: 10.13140/RG.2.2.25337.28006

Ahamed, , e. (2023). Design of an energy-efficient IOT device-assisted wearable sensor platform for healthcare data management. *Elsevier- Measurement. Sensors (Basel)*, 100928.

Alexandru Rancea, E. (2024). Edge Computing in Healthcare: Innovations, Opportunities, and Challenges. *MDPI*. https://www.mdpi.com/1999-5903/16/9/329

Amir Mosavi, A. B. (2019). Energy Consumption Prediction Using Machine Learning: A Review. *Research Gate*. https://www.researchgate.net/publication/331638667_Energy_Consumption_Prediction_Using_Machine_Learning_A_Review

Anatomy, C. (2016). *Stanford Neurosurgical Simulation and Virtual Reality Center.* https://med.stanford.edu/anatomy.html

Angelos, I., & Stoumpos, F. K. (2023). Digital Transformation in Healthcare: Technology Acceptance and Its Applications. *International Journal of Environmental Research and Public Health*, 20(4), 3407. DOI: 10.3390/ijerph20043407 PMID: 36834105

Anindya Bose, S. R. (2024). Application of Cloud Computing in Healthcare – A Comprehensive Study. *International Journal of Future Computer and Communication*, 13(2), 8.

Berniak-Woźny, J., & Rataj, M. (2023). Towards Green and Sustainable Healthcare: A Literature Review and Research Agenda for Green Leadership in the Healthcare Sector. *MDPI, 20*(2). .DOI: 10.3390/ijerph20020908

Bue, X. P. N. (2019). *Cloud Volumes ONTAP, Cloud Data Sense, Data Protection, Advanced.*https://bluexp.netapp.com/blog/data-compliance-regulations-hipaa-gdpr-and-pci-dss

Casper van der Zee, E. (2024). Assessing the Carbon Footprint of Telemedicine: A Systematic Review. *Health Services Insights*. Advance online publication. DOI: 10.1177/1178632924127 PMID: 39139395

César Morcillo Serra, E. (2022). Environmental impact of digital health. *Scientific Reports*. DOI: 10.21203/rs.3.rs-1262007/v1

Chidolue, , E. (2024). Green data centers: Sustainable practices for energy-efficient IT infrastructure. *Engineering Science & Technology Journal*, 5(1), 99–114.

Choi, N. (2022). *Johns Hopkins Uses Augmented Reality to Deliver High-Quality, Low-Cost Pediatric CPR Feedback.*https://www.jhuapl.edu/news/news-releases/220331-johns-hopkins-augmented-reality-cpr-coach

Clinic, C. (2023). *The Role of Virtual Reality in Medical Education.*https://my.clevelandclinic.org/podcasts/meded-thread/the-role-of-virtual-reality-in-medical-education

Elayan, E. (2021). Digital Twin for Intelligent Context-Aware IoT Healthcare Systems. *IEEE*, *99*(1). DOI: 10.1109/JIOT.2021.3051158

Evangelia Katsoulakis, E. (2024). Digital twins for health: a scoping review. *NPJ Digital Medicine*, *7*(77).

Hidayat Ullah, E. (2023). Exploring the healthcare metaverse: AR and VR applications in patient care. *Journal of Digital Health, 20*(2), 210-225.

Hossein Omrany, A. M. (2024). Digital Twin Technology and Social Sustainability: Implications for the Construction Industry. *MDPI- Sustainability*, *16*(9). .DOI: 10.3390/su16198663

Kaiser. (2023). *Kaiser Permanente data center: continuous and innovative energy efficiency improvements.*https://www.energystar.gov/sites/default/files/asset/document/Kaiser_Permanente_case_study.pdf

Karla, . (2024). The Impact of Digital Health Solutions on Bridging the Health Care Gap in Rural Areas: A Scoping Review. *The Permanente Journal*, 28(3), 130–143. DOI: 10.7812/TPP/23.134 PMID: 39135461

Khezr, E. (2019). Blockchain Technology in Healthcare: A Comprehensive Review and Directions for Future Research. *MDPI- Applied Science*, *9*(9).

Knibbe, E. (2022). Digital twins in the green life sciences. *NJAS: Impact in Agricultural and Life Sciences - T&F*, *94*(1). .DOI: 10.1080/27685241.2022.2150571

Lili Wang, X. S. (2023). Foveated rendering: A state-of-the-art survey. *Computational Visualizations*, 9(2), 195–228.

Liu, S. Z. (2024). Enhancing User Experience in VR Environments through AI-Driven Adaptive UI Design. *Research Gate*, 8.

Luo, H. T. (2024). Recent Advances in Wearable Healthcare Devices: From Material to Application. *MDPI- Bio Engineering*, 11(4). .DOI: 10.3390/bioengineering11040358

Magazine, I. (2019). *A Stroke of Genius: Neurorehabilitation through Virtual Reality.* https://illumin.usc.edu/about-us/

Maita, K. C. (2024). The Impact of Digital Health Solutions on Bridging the Health Care Gap in Rural Areas: A Scoping Review. *The Journal Permanente, 28*(3). .DOI: 10.7812/TPP/23.134

Marri, M. A. (2024). *Comparing Digital Twin and Metaverse Technologies: An In-Depth Analysis.*https://www.linkedin.com/in/mohamed-almarri/

Mehrotra, N. (2024). *How sustainable practices can drive inclusive growth in modern business.*https://www.ey.com/en_in/insights/climate-change-sustainability-services/how-sustainable-practices-ensure-a-green-healthcare-ecosystem

Mosallanezhad, , E. (2023). An IoMT platform for an integrated sustainable energy-efficient disaster relief supply chain to prevent severity-driven disruptions during pandemics. *Journal of Industrial Information Integration*, 100502, 35. DOI: 10.1016/j.jii.2023.100502

Nations, U. (2023). *Sustainable Development Goals.*https://www.un.org/sustainablede velopment/climate-action/

Ohenhen, P. E. (2024). Sustainable cooling solutions for electronics: A comprehensive review: Investigating the latest techniques and materials, their effectiveness in mechanical applications, and associated environmental benefits. *World Journal of Advanced Research and Reviews, 21*(1). DOI: 10.30574/wjarr.2024.21.1.0111

Olayinka, E. (2024). Artificial Intelligence in Healthcare Supply Chains: Enhancing Resilience and Reducing Waste. *International Journal of Advance Research, Ideas and Innovations in Technology*, 203.

Omrany, , E. (2024). Digital Twin Technology and Social Sustainability: Implications for the Construction Industry. *Sustainnability*, 16(19), 8663. DOI: 10.3390/su16198663

Oyekunle, , E. (2024). Healthcare applications of Augmented Reality (AR) and Virtual Reality (VR) simulation in clinical education. *Journal of Clinical Images and Medical Case Reports*, 1–18.

Peter Efosa Ohenhen. (2024). Low-power processors and advanced cooling systems for sustainable digital health. Sustainable Computing for Healthcare. *World Journal of Advanced Research and Reviews*, 21(1), 957–972.

Phiips. (2024). *Magnetic Resonance - Proactive Energy Management.*https://www .philips.co.in/healthcare/resources/landing/mr-proactive-energy-management

Pouncy, J. (2024). *Sustainable Healthcare & AI: The Future of Efficient Healthcare Systems.*https://www.linkedin.com/pulse/sustainable-healthcare-ai-future-efficient-systems-jeremiah-pouncy-xadhf/

Rajkumar Buyya, S. I. (2023). Energy-efficiency and sustainability in new generation cloud computing: A vision and directions for integrated management of data centre resources and workloads. *Wiley*, *54*(1).

Rauch, S. (2024). *Case Studies: The Growing Role of AI and Big Data in Healthcare.* https://www.simplilearn.com/role-of-ai-and-big-data-in-healthcare-article

Rehman, E. (2021). Energy-Efficient IoT e-Health Using Artificial Intelligence Model with Homomorphic Secret Sharing. *Energies*, *14*(19), 6414. DOI: 10.3390/en14196414

Rogers, E. M. (2003). *Diffusion of Innovations* (5th ed.). Free Press.

Saba, , E. (2020). Secure and energy-efficient framework using Internet of Medical Things for e-healthcare. *Journal of Infection and Public Health*, 1567–1575. PMID: 32682657

Siemens. (2024). *Sustainability in In Vitro Diagnostics.*https://www.siemens-healthineers.com/en-in/about/sustainability-ehs/in-vitro-diagnostics

Staff, C.-S. (2020). *VR and the Future of Healthcare.*https://www.cedars-sinai.org/blog/virtual-reality-future-healthcare.html

Stoumpos, A. I. (2023). Digital Transformation in Healthcare: Technology Acceptance and Its Applications. *International Journal of Environmental Research and Public Health*, 20(4), 3407. DOI: 10.3390/ijerph20043407 PMID: 36834105

Sun, , E. (2023). Digital twin in healthcare: Recent updates and challenges. *Digital Health*. Advance online publication. DOI: 10.1177/20552076221149651 PMID: 36636729

Tatiana Mallet Machado, T. M. (2023). Literature review of digital twin in healthcare. *Heliyonn - Science DIrect*, 9(9). .DOI: 10.1016/j.heliyon.2023.e19390

Thompson, M. (2021). *The environmental impacts of digital health.* Digital Health-sagepub., DOI: 10.1177/20552076211033421

Ueda, E. (2024). Climate change and artificial intelligence in healthcare: Review and recommendations towards a sustainable future. *Diagnostic and Interventional Imaging*, *105*(11).

UNEP. (2023). *Emissions Gap Report 2023.*https://www.unep.org/resources/emissions-gap-report-2023

Varntoumian, E. (2021). *European Health Parliament's.*https://www.healthparliament.eu/

Vlădu escu, , E. (2023). Environmental Sustainability of Metaverse: Perspectives from Romanian Developers. *Sustainability*, 15(15), 11704.

Zhang, , E. (2023). Blockchain Technology: Security Issues, Healthcare Applications, Challenges and Future Trends. *Electronics (Basel)*, 12(3). Advance online publication. DOI: 10.3390/electronics12030546

Chapter 5
Optimization Tools and Techniques for AI and ML:
Exploring Future Directions and Emerging Trends

Lingala Thirupathi
https://orcid.org/0000-0003-0703-3860
Sreenidhi Institute of Science and Technology, India

B. Vasundara
Sreenidhi Institute of Science and Technology, India

Pallavi Rajan
Sreenidhi Institute of Science and Technology, India

Tejaswi Arella
Sreenidhi Institute of Science and Technology, India

ABSTRACT

Artificial intelligence (AI) and machine learning (ML) have revolutionized various industries and domains, enabling data-driven decision-making and automated problem-solving. However, the optimization of AI and ML models remains a critical challenge, as it directly impacts their performance, accuracy, and efficiency. It explores the optimization tools and techniques employed in AI and ML, focusing on their current state, limitations, and future directions. Through a comprehensive literature review, and analysis of industry practices, this chapter delves into the optimization landscape, covering topics such as hyperparameter tuning, model com-

DOI: 10.4018/979-8-3693-6885-5.ch005

pression, federated learning, and quantum computing. Additionally, it investigates emerging trends and cutting-edge techniques that hold the potential to shape the future of AI and ML optimization. By examining the synergies between optimization methodologies and AI/ML algorithms, this research aims to provide a holistic understanding of the optimization landscape and its implications for advancing AI and ML capabilities.

1. INTRODUCTION

Artificial Intelligence (AI) and Machine Learning (ML) have undergone a profound transformation over the past few decades, revolutionizing industries ranging from healthcare and finance to transportation and entertainment. These technologies are powered by sophisticated models that require careful tuning and optimization to achieve peak performance. Optimization, therefore, lies at the heart of AI and ML, playing a pivotal role in enhancing the accuracy, efficiency, and scalability of models. Optimization plays a crucial role in the development and deployment of AI and ML models, addressing challenges such as hyper parameter tuning, model compression, and distributed learning. As AI and ML models become increasingly complex and data-intensive, the need for robust optimization tools and techniques becomes more pressing.

Optimization in AI and ML refers to the process of adjusting the parameters of models to minimize or maximize an objective function, such as error rate or predictive accuracy. This process is critical for the training, deployment, and maintenance of models, and it directly impacts their ability to learn from data and make accurate predictions. As models become more complex and datasets grow larger, the need for advanced optimization tools and techniques has become more pronounced.

2. LITERATURE REVIEW

(Bahdanau et al., 2015) proposed an innovative approach to neural machine translation (NMT) by introducing the attention mechanism. Their model learns to align and translate simultaneously, allowing it to focus on relevant parts of the source sentence during translation. This novel architecture significantly improves translation quality compared to traditional sequence-to-sequence models, marking a milestone in NMT research.

(Bengio et al., 2013) provided a comprehensive review of representation learning techniques in machine learning. They discuss various methods for learning meaningful representations of data, including autoencoders, deep belief networks, and convolutional neural networks. The paper offers new perspectives on unsupervised pre-training and multi-task learning, laying the groundwork for subsequent advances in deep learning research.

(Deng et al., 2014) presented a comprehensive overview of deep learning methods and their applications across various domains. They cover fundamental concepts such as feedforward neural networks, convolutional neural networks, and recurrent neural networks, along with advanced topics like deep reinforcement learning and generative adversarial networks. The paper serves as a valuable resource for researchers and practitioners interested in deep learning.

(Han et al., 2015) proposed techniques for compressing deep neural networks to reduce model size and improve efficiency without significant loss in performance. Their approach involves pruning, trained quantization, and Huffman coding, resulting in substantial compression ratios with minimal degradation in accuracy. This work addresses the practical challenges of deploying deep learning models on resource-constrained devices.

(Kingma et al., 2014) introduced a popular method for stochastic optimization widely used in training deep neural networks. Adam combines the advantages of adaptive gradient methods like AdaGrad and RMSprop by maintaining separate learning rates for each parameter and momentum updates. The paper demonstrates faster convergence and improved generalization compared to traditional optimization techniques, making it a key contribution to the field of deep learning optimization.

(Goodfellow et al., 2016) provided a comprehensive overview of deep learning methods in their seminal textbook. They cover foundational concepts such as artificial neural networks, convolutional neural networks, and recurrent neural networks, along with advanced topics like generative models, deep reinforcement learning, and unsupervised learning. The book serves as a comprehensive resource for researchers, practitioners, and students interested in understanding and applying deep learning techniques across various domains.

(Nocedal et al., 2006) presented a thorough treatment of numerical optimization methods in their textbook. The book covers both classical optimization algorithms such as gradient descent, Newton's method, and conjugate gradient, as well as modern optimization techniques like quasi-Newton methods and stochastic optimization. With a focus on both theory and practical implementation, this book is essential reading for anyone interested in optimization algorithms and their applications in machine learning and beyond.

(Goldberg et al., 1989) is a seminal work on genetic algorithms (GAs) and their applications in search, optimization, and machine learning. It covers the fundamental principles of GAs, including genetic operators such as crossover and mutation, as well as topics like fitness functions, population dynamics, and parallel genetic algorithms. The book also explores various applications of GAs in optimization problems, including function optimization, combinatorial optimization, and machine learning.

(Kennedy & Eberhart 1995) introduced particle swarm optimization (PSO), a population-based optimization technique inspired by the social behavior of birds flocking or fish schooling. PSO optimizes a population of candidate solutions by iteratively adjusting their positions in the search space based on their individual and collective performance. The paper presents the basic principles of PSO and demonstrates its effectiveness in solving various optimization problems, making it a popular choice in both academic research and practical applications.

(Snoek et al., 2012) proposed practical Bayesian optimization techniques for optimizing Hyper parameters of machine learning algorithms. Bayesian optimization leverages probabilistic models to efficiently explore and exploit the search space, leading to faster convergence and better performance compared to random or grid search methods. The paper provides a comprehensive overview of Bayesian optimization algorithms and demonstrates their effectiveness in optimizing hyper parameters for a range of machine learning tasks.

(Feurer & Hutter, 2019) focuses on the critical aspect of hyper parameter optimization within the field of Automated Machine Learning (AutoML). The authors discuss various strategies and techniques for optimizing hyper parameters, which are crucial for improving the performance of machine learning models. They explore both traditional methods, such as grid search and random search, and more advanced techniques like Bayesian optimization, which models the performance of a machine learning algorithm as a function of its hyper parameters and uses this model to select the most promising hyper parameters to evaluate next. The chapter is comprehensive, covering not only the methodologies but also the challenges associated with hyper parameter optimization, such as the high computational cost and the need for efficient resource allocation.

(He, X et al., 2021) provided a detailed survey of the current state-of-the-art in AutoML. Their survey categorizes and evaluates various approaches and tools developed for automating the end-to-end process of machine learning, from data pre processing to model selection and hyper parameter tuning. The authors highlight significant advancements in the field, including the development of neural architecture search (NAS) and meta-learning techniques. They also address the practical implications of AutoML in real-world applications and discuss the challenges that remain, such as scalability, interpretability, and the integration of domain knowledge into automated processes. This survey serves as a comprehensive overview for researchers and practitioners interested in the current trends and future directions of AutoML.

(Kairouz et al., 2019) a paradigm that enables the training of machine learning models across decentralized data sources without sharing raw data. The authors review the progress made in various aspects of federated learning, including communication efficiency, privacy preservation, and robustness against adversarial attacks. They emphasize the importance of developing algorithms that can handle heterogeneous data and devices, as well as those that can efficiently balance the trade-offs between model performance, computational cost, and privacy guarantees. The paper identifies several open problems in federated learning, such as the need for improved optimization algorithms, better theoretical understanding, and more robust privacy-preserving techniques.

(McMahan et al., 2017) introduced Federated Averaging (FedAvg), an algorithm designed to train deep networks in a federated learning setting. This work addresses the significant challenge of communication efficiency in federated learning by proposing a method that reduces the amount of data exchanged between the central server and client devices. FedAvg works by performing multiple local updates on client devices before averaging the model parameters globally. This approach significantly decreases communication overhead while maintaining model performance. The paper provides experimental results demonstrating the effectiveness of FedAvg on various tasks, highlighting its potential for large-scale, real-world applications where data privacy and communication constraints are paramount.

(Farhi et al., 2014) proposed the Quantum Approximate Optimization Algorithm (QAOA), a novel quantum algorithm aimed at solving combinatorial optimization problems. QAOA operates by applying a series of quantum operations parameterized by classical variables, which are optimized to minimize a given cost function. This hybrid quantum-classical approach leverages the strengths of quantum computation to explore solution spaces more efficiently than classical algorithms. The authors provide theoretical analysis and empirical evidence of QAOA's potential advantages, particularly in solving instances of the MAX-CUT problem. This work is foundational in the field of quantum computing, suggesting that QAOA could outperform classical algorithms for certain optimization problems as quantum hardware continues to advance.

Preskill (2018) discussed the advent of Noisy Intermediate-Scale Quantum (NISQ) technology and its implications for the future of quantum computing. He defines the NISQ era as the period in which quantum processors contain 50 to 100 qubits but are limited by noise and other practical constraints. Preskill highlights the potential applications of NISQ devices, such as quantum simulation, which could provide insights into complex quantum systems beyond the reach of classical computers. He also addresses the challenges that must be overcome for quantum computing to reach its full potential, such as error correction and the development of more robust quantum algorithms. The paper serves as both an overview of the state of quantum computing and a roadmap for future research directions.

(Finn et al., 2017) introduced Model-Agnostic Meta-Learning (MAML), a framework designed to enable rapid adaptation of deep neural networks to new tasks with minimal training data. MAML operates by training a model's parameters such that a small number of gradient updates on a new task can produce good performance. This method is model-agnostic, meaning it can be applied to any learning algorithm that uses gradient descent. The authors demonstrate MAML's effectiveness through experiments on few-shot learning tasks, showing that it significantly outperforms previous methods. This paper is influential in the field of meta-learning, providing a practical approach to improving the adaptability of machine learning models.

(Hospedales et al., 2021) provided a comprehensive survey of meta-learning techniques in neural networks. The survey categorizes meta-learning methods into three main types: optimization-based, model-based, and metric-based approaches. It covers a wide range of applications, from few-shot learning to reinforcement learning, and discusses the theoretical foundations and practical implementations of these methods. The authors also address the challenges and open problems in the field, such as scalability, generalization, and the integration of prior knowledge. This survey is a valuable resource for researchers and practitioners looking to understand the current state and future directions of meta-learning in neural networks.

(Yao et al., 2006) review the recent developments in evolutionary computation, a field that applies evolutionary algorithms to optimization problems. They cover various evolutionary algorithms, including genetic algorithms, genetic programming, and evolutionary strategies, highlighting their applications in areas such as optimization, machine learning, and engineering design. The authors discuss the theoretical advancements, such as convergence analysis and the design of more efficient algorithms, as well as practical improvements, including parallelization and hybrid approaches that combine evolutionary algorithms with other optimization techniques. It provides a thorough overview of the state-of-the-art in evolutionary computation, offering insights into both the theoretical and practical aspects of the field.

(Madry et al., 2017) explore methods to make deep learning models more robust against adversarial attacks, which are small perturbations to input data that can cause models to make incorrect predictions. They propose an approach based on adversarial training, where models are trained on adversarial examples generated during the training process. The authors demonstrate that this method significantly improves the robustness of models against a wide range of adversarial attacks. Their work provides both theoretical and empirical evidence of the effectiveness of adversarial training, contributing to the broader effort to enhance the security and reliability of machine learning systems.

(Dean et al., 2012) presented techniques for training deep neural networks on large-scale distributed systems. They describe the design and implementation of DistBelief, a framework for distributed training of deep networks that allows models to be split across multiple machines. The paper discusses the challenges of distributing model training, such as synchronization and communication overhead, and presents solutions to mitigate these issues. The authors demonstrate that their approach can significantly speed up training times and enable the development of larger and more complex models than would be feasible on a single machine. This work is foundational in the field of distributed machine learning, providing key insights into the scalability of deep learning.

(Barocas et al., 2019) an extensive overview of fairness in machine learning, addressing the ethical and technical challenges of ensuring that machine learning models do not perpetuate or exacerbate biases. They discussed various definitions and metrics of fairness, as well as techniques for detecting and mitigating bias in data and models. It also covers the legal and social implications of biased algorithms and the importance of transparency and accountability in machine learning. This resource is essential for researchers and practitioners seeking to understand and address the ethical issues associated with machine learning.

(Cath et al., 2018) examine the approaches of the US, EU, and UK towards the governance and ethical considerations of artificial intelligence (AI). The paper highlights the differences and similarities in policy and regulatory frameworks, focusing on issues such as privacy, accountability, and the societal impact of AI. The authors argue for the need for a cohesive and comprehensive approach to AI governance that balances innovation with ethical considerations. They emphasize the importance of multi-stakeholder engagement and the development of policies that are adaptable to the rapid advancements in AI technology. This work provides a critical analysis of the current state of AI governance and offers recommendations for creating a 'good society' where AI is developed and deployed responsibly.

3. METHODOLOGY

3.1 Objectives

- To Explore Advanced Optimization Techniques:

Investigate and analyze the latest advanced optimization techniques being applied in AI and ML. This includes understanding how these techniques can enhance model performance, efficiency, and scalability.

- To Identify Emerging Trends and Tools:

Identify and review the emerging trends and newly developed tools in the field of AI and ML optimization. This aims to keep pace with the rapid advancements and understand the implications of these innovations.

- To Forecast Future Directions:

Predict and theorize future directions and potential breakthroughs in optimization for AI and ML. This involves anticipating upcoming challenges and proposing possible solutions or areas for further research.

3.2 The Evolution of Optimization Techniques in AI and ML

In the early days of AI and ML, simpler models such as linear regression and decision trees were prevalent, and optimization methods were relatively straightforward. Techniques like gradient descent and linear programming were sufficient for most tasks. However, as the field has progressed, the complexity of models has increased dramatically. Today, we deal with deep neural networks, ensemble methods, and reinforcement learning systems, which require more sophisticated and powerful optimization strategies.

The evolution of optimization techniques can be broadly categorized into several phases:

1. Classical Optimization:

Early methods focused on linear and convex problems, with techniques like gradient descent, Newton's method, and quadratic programming being the mainstays. These methods were effective for smaller, simpler models but struggled with the high-dimensional, non-convex landscapes of modern AI.

2. Metaheuristic Algorithms:

As models grew more complex, researchers turned to metaheuristic algorithms such as genetic algorithms, simulated annealing, and particle swarm optimization. These techniques are inspired by natural processes and are capable of exploring large search spaces more effectively.

3. Probabilistic Methods:

Bayesian optimization and other probabilistic approaches emerged to handle scenarios where function evaluations are expensive. These methods build probabilistic models to guide the search for optimal parameters.

4. Hybrid Methods:

Combining different optimization strategies has become increasingly popular. Hybrid methods leverage the strengths of various techniques to achieve better performance, robustness, and efficiency.

5. Automated Machine Learning (AutoML):

The recent push towards democratizing AI has led to the development of AutoML frameworks, which automate the end-to-end process of model development, including optimization. These tools are designed to make AI accessible to non-experts by simplifying the optimization process.

6. Quantum Optimization: An emerging frontier, quantum optimization exploits the principles of quantum mechanics to solve certain optimization problems faster than classical methods.

Although still in its infancy, quantum optimization holds great promise for the future of AI and ML.

3.3 Current Trends in Optimization for AI and ML

As the field of AI and ML continues to advance, several trends in optimization have emerged. These trends reflect the ongoing efforts to enhance model performance, efficiency, and scalability. Here, we outline some of the most significant current trends:

1. Advanced Gradient-Based Methods: Gradient descent remains a cornerstone of optimization in AI and ML, but modern variants like Adam, RMSprop, and Nadam have improved its efficiency and convergence properties. These methods adapt the learning rate during training, leading to faster and more stable convergence.
2. Neural Architecture Search (NAS): NAS automates the design of neural network architectures, using optimization techniques to explore the space of possible architectures. This approach has led tothe discovery of novel, high-performing architectures that outperform manually designed ones.

3. Reinforcement Learning (RL) Optimization: In RL, optimization is used to train agents to make sequences of decisions. Techniques like Q-learning and policy gradients are at the forefront, with recent advances focusing on improving exploration strategies and sample efficiency.
4. Distributed and Parallel Optimization: The increasing scales of AI models necessitate distributed optimization methods that can leverage multiple processors or GPUs. Techniques like parameter server frameworks and decentralized optimization algorithms are critical for scaling up model training.
5. Hyper parameter Optimization: Efficient hyper parameter tuning is crucial for the performance of ML models. Bayesian optimization, grid search, and random search are popular methods, with recent trends focusing on multi-fidelity optimization and transfer learning for hyper parameter tuning.

3.4 Future Directions in Optimization for AI and ML

The future of optimization in AI and ML promises exciting developments and new challenges. Researchers and practitioners are exploring several promising directions that could significantly impact the field:

1. Adaptive Optimization Algorithms: Future optimization algorithms are expected to be more adaptive, dynamically adjusting their strategies based on the characteristics of the problem at hand. This could involve real-time learning of optimization hyper parameters and adaptive switching between different optimization methods.
2. Integration with Unsupervised and Semi-Supervised Learning: Combining optimization techniques with unsupervised and semi-supervised learning could enhance the ability of models to learn from limited labelled data. This is particularly relevant for applications where obtaining labelled data is expensive or impractical.
3. Quantum Optimization: As quantum computing technology matures, quantum optimization methods could revolutionize certain aspects of AI and ML. Quantum annealing and variation quantum algorithms are areas ofactive research, with the potential to solve complex optimization problems more efficiently than classical approaches.
4. Scalable Optimization for Massive Datasets: With the continuous growth of datasets, developing optimization methods that can handle massive data efficiently is crucial. This includes distributedoptimization techniques and methods that can leverage advanced hardware like GPUs and TPUs.

5. Optimization for Interpretability and Fairness: As AI and ML systems are deployed in critical applications; there is a growing emphasis on interpretability and fairness. Future optimization techniques will need toincorporate constraints and objectives related to these aspects, ensuring that models are not only accurate but also transparent and equitable.
6. Bio-Inspired Optimization: Drawing inspiration from biological systems, bio-inspired optimization methods such as evolutionary strategies and swarm intelligence are likely to see further development. These methods offer robustness and the ability to escape local optima, making them suitable for complex optimization landscapes.
7. Optimization for Energy Efficiency: As the environmental impact of AI and ML becomes a concern, optimizing models for energy efficiency will be an important area of research. This involves developing algorithms that reduce the computational resources required for training and inference.

Table 1 represents the optimization tools and techniques for AI and ML, exploring future directions and emerging trends

Table 1. Optimization tools and techniques for AI and ML

Category	Tool/Technique	Description	Current Trends	Future Directions
Gradient-Based Methods	Stochastic Gradient Descent (SGD)	Widely used for training deep learning models, efficient with large datasets.	Improved versions like Adam, RMSprop, and Nadam are popular.	Development of adaptive learning rate methods, increased focus on second-order methods for faster convergence.
Evolutionary Algorithms	Genetic Algorithms	Optimization method inspired by natural selection, useful for Hyper parameter tuning.	Application in neural architecture search and reinforcement learning.	More sophisticated crossover and mutation strategies, hybrid methods combining genetic algorithms with other optimization techniques.
Bayesian Optimization	Gaussian Processes	Probabilistic model-based optimization, effective for Hyper parameter tuning with expensive function evaluations.	Used for tuning complex models like neural networks and ensemble methods.	Integration with deep learning to create more robust autoML frameworks, scalability improvements.

continued on following page

Table 1. Continued

Category	Tool/Technique	Description	Current Trends	Future Directions
Gradient-Free Methods	Particle Swarm Optimization (PSO)	Swarm intelligence-based optimization, useful for non-differentiable objective functions.	Employed in feature selection and model parameter optimization.	Enhanced variants like quantum PSO, combination with machine learning for dynamic parameter adjustment.
Metaheuristic Algorithms	Simulated Annealing	Probabilistic technique for approximating global optimization in large search spaces.	Applied in training neural networks and optimizing machine learning pipelines.	Integration with other heuristic methods, adaptive cooling schedules for better performance.
Convex Optimization	Quadratic Programming	Used for problems where the objective function is quadratic and constraints are linear.	Utilized in support vector machines and portfolio optimization.	Advancements in solver algorithms for faster computation, application in more complex AI models.
Reinforcement Learning	Q-Learning	Model-free reinforcement learning algorithm.	Widely used in training agents for game playing and robotics.	Development of more efficient exploration strategies, combining with unsupervised learning.
Distributed Optimization	Parameter Server	Framework for distributed training of large-scale machine learning models.	Common in large-scale deep learning applications like image and speech recognition.	Improved fault tolerance, optimized communication strategies for faster convergence.
Automated Machine Learning	AutoML Frameworks	Tools that automate end-to-end machine learning tasks.	Increasing use in industry for democratizing AI.	More robust and flexible frameworks, integration with real-time data pipelines.
Hybrid Methods	Neural evolution	Combines neural networks with evolutionary algorithms for optimization.	Used in optimizing neural network architectures and parameters.	Enhanced scalability and efficiency, integration with reinforcement learning for autonomous system design.
Quantum Optimization	Quantum Annealing	Explores quantum mechanics for solving optimization problems faster than classical methods.	Early-stage research with limited practical applications.	Significant research focus, potential to revolutionize certain optimization problems with quantum supremacy.

3.5 Hyper Parameter Tuning Algorithm

The algorithm for a hyper parameter tuning algorithm using Bayesian optimization could be presented, highlighting the steps involved in selecting optimal hyper parameter values based on the model's performance on a validation set as shown below as steps:

1. Gradient Descent Optimization: Basic gradient descent algorithm for updating model parameters to minimize the loss function.
2. Stochastic Gradient Descent (SGD): SGD with mini-batches for training models on large datasets.
3. Genetic Algorithm: Evolutionary algorithm for Hyper parameter tuning by simulating natural selection processes.
4. Bayesian Optimization: Probabilistic method for Hyper parameter tuning, particularly effective when function evaluations are expensive.
5. Particle Swarm Optimization (PSO): Swarm intelligence-based optimization useful for non-differentiable objective functions.
6. Simulated Annealing: Probabilistic technique for approximating global optimization in large search spaces.
7. AutoML Framework: Automates the process of model selection, Hyper parameter tuning, and evaluation.
8. Quantum Optimization: Explores hypothetical quantum optimization techniques for faster solution of complex problems.
9. TrainMLModel Function: Illustrates the use of different optimization techniques in a machine learning workflow based on the model type.

This algorithm provides a conceptual framework for implementing various optimization techniques in AI and ML, offering a foundation for further exploration and development.

Each of the below step represents a crucial part of the hyper parameter tuning process, ensuring the selected hyper parameters lead to an optimal model performance.

1. Identify the machine learning model and the metric to optimize.
2. Setup the Hyper parameter Space
    - Specify the hyper parameters to tune and their possible values or ranges.
3. Choose a Tuning Strategy
    - Select a hyper parameter tuning method (e.g., Grid Search, Random Search, Bayesian Optimization).
4. Prepare the Data
    - Split the data into training and validation sets (or use cross-validation).

5. Initialize the Tuner
    - Create an instance of the tuner with the chosen strategy and hyper parameter space.
6. Iterate over Hyper parameter Combinations
    - For each combination (or sample if using random methods):
    - Train the model using the training set.
    - Evaluate the model using the validation set.
    - Record the performance metric.
7. Update hyper parameters (If Needed)
    - For methods like Bayesian Optimization, update the hyper parameters based on past performance.
8. Check Stopping Criteria
    - Determine if the stopping criteria are met (e.g., maximum number of iterations, convergence).
9. Select the Best Model
    - Identify the hyper parameter combination that resulted in the best performance on the validation set.
10. Retrain Final Model
    - Train the final model using the best hyper parameters on the entire training set.
11. Evaluate on Test Set
    - Optionally, evaluate the final model on a separate test set to estimate generalization performance.
12. Deploy the Model
    - Deploy the model for production use.

4. CASE STUDIES

Real-world case studies will be presented to illustrate successful applications of optimization tools and techniques in various AI and ML domains, such as computer vision, natural language processing, and recommender systems. These case studies will provide concrete examples of the challenges faced, the specific optimization techniques employed, and the measurable benefits achieved in terms of model performance, resource utilization, and deployment scalability.

Potential case studies may include:

1. Hyper parameter tuning for deep neural networks in computer vision tasks.
2. Model compression techniques for deploying large language models on edge devices.

3. Federated learning for privacy-preserving collaborative model training in healthcare applications.
4. Quantum-inspired optimization techniques for reinforcement learning in robotics.

This section presents real-world case studies demonstrating the successful application of optimization tools and techniques across various AI and ML domains. These case studies highlight challenges, optimization methods, and the measurable benefits achieved in model performance, resource utilization, and deployment scalability.

Case Study 1: Hyper parameter tuning for Deep Neural Networks in Computer Vision Tasks

Context: A technology company developing computer vision applications for autonomous vehicles aimed to improve the accuracy and efficiency of their deep neural network models.

Challenges:

- High dimensionality of Hyper parameter space.
- Significant computational cost associated with training large neural networks.
- The need for real-time performance in safety-critical applications.

Optimization Techniques:

- Bayesian Optimization: Used to systematically explore the hyper parameter space. This method models the objective function as a Gaussian process and updates it based on new observations to balance exploration and exploitation efficiently.
- Random Search and Grid Search: Employed as baseline methods to compare the effectiveness of Bayesian Optimization.

Implementation:

- A range of hyper parameters, including learning rate, batch size, and the number of layers, were optimized.
- The process was automated using frameworks like Optuna and Hyperopt.

Results:

- Model Performance: Improved accuracy by 5% on benchmark datasets like ImageNet and COCO.
- Resource Utilization: Reduced training time by 30% compared to manual tuning.
- Scalability: The automated tuning process scaled efficiently across multiple GPU clusters, reducing the time required to achieve optimal configurations.

Case Study 2: Model Compression Techniques for Deploying Large Language Models on Edge Devices

Context: A company specializing in natural language processing (NLP) aimed to deploy a large pre-trained language model on edge devices for real-time language translation.

Challenges:

- The large size of models like BERT and GPT-3 made it impractical to deploy them on resource-constrained edge devices.
- Maintaining model accuracy while significantly reducing size and computational requirements.

Optimization Techniques:

- Pruning: Removing less important neurons and connections in the neural network to reduce model size.
- Quantization: Converting model weights from floating-point to lower-bit representations to decrease memory usage and increase inference speed.
- Knowledge Distillation: Training a smaller "student" model to replicate the performance of a larger "teacher" mode.

Implementation:

- A combination of these techniques was applied to a pre-trained BERT model.
- TensorFlowLite and ONNX were used to facilitate deployment on mobile devices.

Results:

- Model Performance: Achieved a compression ratio of 10:1 with less than a 2% drop in accuracy.
- Resource Utilization: Reduced inference time by 50%, enabling real-time processing on devices with limited computational power.
- Deployment Scalability: Enabled widespread deployment across various edge devices, including smart phones and IoT devices.

Case Study 3: Federated Learning for Privacy-Preserving Collaborative Model Training in Healthcare Applications

Context: A healthcare consortium aimed to collaboratively train machine learning models for disease prediction without sharing sensitive patient data.

Challenges:

- Ensuring data privacy and security while enabling collaborative model training.
- Managing heterogeneous data distributions across different institutions.
- Handling communication constraints between institutions.

Optimization Techniques:

- Federated Averaging (FedAvg): Aggregated locally trained models from different institutions to create a global model without exchanging raw data.
- Secure Multiparty Computation (SMPC): Enhanced privacy by ensuring that individual updates remain encrypted during aggregation.

Implementation:

- A federated learning framework was developed using TensorFlow Federated and PySyft.
- Models were trained locally on each institution's data, and updates were securely aggregated using SMPC.

Results:

- Model Performance: Achieved comparable accuracy to models trained on centralized data while preserving privacy.
- Resource Utilization: Efficiently utilized local computational resources at each institution.
- Scalability: Scaled to include over 20 institutions, demonstrating robustness in handling diverse datasets and environments.

Case Study 4: Quantum-Inspired Optimization Techniques for Reinforcement Learning in Robotics

Context: A robotics company sought to improve the performance of reinforcement learning algorithms for robotic path planning and control.

Challenges:

- The high complexity of the robotic control problem requiring efficient exploration of vast action spaces.
- Traditional optimization methods were computationally expensive and time-consuming.

Optimization Techniques:

- Quantum Approximate Optimization Algorithm (QAOA): Leveraged principles from quantum computing to enhance optimization in reinforcement learning.

- Hybrid Quantum-Classical Methods: Combined quantum optimization with classical reinforcement learning algorithms to exploit the strengths of both approaches.

Implementation:

- QAOA was integrated into the reinforcement learning pipeline using quantum simulators and hybrid computing platforms like IBM Q and Google Cirq.
- The approach focused on optimizing the reward function to accelerate convergence and improve performance.

Results:

- Model Performance: Demonstrated a 15% improvement in reward acquisition rates compared to classical methods.
- Resource Utilization: Reduced the number of training iterations by 20%, significantly cutting down computational costs.
- Deployment Scalability: Proved the feasibility of integrating quantum-inspired methods in practical robotics applications, paving the way for future advancements.

These case studies illustrate the diverse applications and benefits of optimization tools and techniques in AI and ML across different domains. From Hyper parameter tuning in computer vision to quantum-inspired optimization in robotics, each case highlights significant improvements in model performance, resource utilization, and deployment scalability, underscoring the critical role of optimization in advancing AI and ML technologies.

Exploring future directions and emerging trends in optimization tools and techniques for AI and ML involves various challenges and risks. Here are some key considerations:

5. CHALLENGES AND RISKS

Exploring future directions and emerging trends in optimization tools and techniques for AI and ML involves various challenges and risks. Here are some key considerations:

1. **Complexity of Techniques:** The complexity of advanced optimization techniques in AI and ML poses significant challenges for researchers and practitioners. A deep understanding of mathematical concepts, algorithmic implementation skills, and ongoing educational efforts are essential to effectively grasp and apply these techniques. Addressing these challenges through interdisciplinary collaboration,

community engagement, and leveraging open-source resources can facilitate the development and implementation of robust optimization methods, driving innovation and progress in the field. Many advanced optimization techniques require a deep understanding of mathematical concepts and algorithms, posing a challenge for researchers and practitioners to grasp and implement effectively.

2. **Computational Resources:** The significant computational resources required for advanced optimization methods in AI and ML pose challenges related to accessibility, cost, and environmental impact. Addressing these challenges involves developing more efficient algorithms, leveraging parallel and distributed computing, and managing resources effectively. By adopting innovative solutions and collaborative approaches, researchers can mitigate the limitations imposed by computational demands and continue to advance the field of optimization in AI and ML. Some optimization methods, particularly those involving large-scale simulations or complex models, require significant computational resources, which may limit their accessibility to researchers with limited computing infrastructure.
3. **Data Quality and Availability:** The quality and availability of data are critical factors in the effectiveness of optimization techniques in AI and ML. Challenges such as noisy, incomplete, or biased data can significantly impact model performance. Addressing these challenges involves robust data pre processing, cleaning, and augmentation techniques, as well as ethical data practices to ensure privacy, transparency, and fairness. By focusing on data quality and availability, researchers and practitioners can enhance the reliability and generalizability of their optimization models, driving better outcomes and advancements in the field. The effectiveness of optimization techniques often relies on the quality and quantity of data available for training and validation. Challenges may arise when dealing with noisy, incomplete, or biased data.
4. **Algorithmic Bias:** Algorithmic bias in optimization algorithms poses significant challenges in AI and ML, potentially leading to unfair and discriminatory outcomes. Addressing this bias involves understanding its sources, detecting it through rigorous analysis, and mitigating it using bias-aware training, fair representation learning, and post-processing adjustments. Despite these efforts, challenges such as trade-offs between fairness and accuracy, the dynamic nature of bias, and the complexity of fairness definitions persist. Ongoing research, ethical considerations, and regulatory frameworks are essential to ensure that AI and ML systems are fair, trustworthy, and beneficial for all. Optimization algorithms may inadvertently introduce or perpetuate biases present in the training data, leading to unfair or discriminatory outcomes in AI and ML models.

5. **Interpretability:** The increasing complexity of AI and ML models, driven by sophisticated optimization techniques, raises significant challenges for interpretability. Addressing these challenges is essential for ensuring transparency, accountability, and trust in AI systems. While several techniques have been developed to enhance interpretability, ongoing research and innovation are needed to balance model complexity with the need for clear, understandable explanations. By prioritizing interpretability, the AI community can ensure that advanced models are not only powerful but also transparent and accountable. As optimization techniques become more sophisticated, the resulting models may become increasingly complex and difficult to interpret, raising concerns about transparency and accountability.
6. **Generalization and Transferability:** Generalization and transferability are critical challenges in the practical application of optimization techniques in AI and ML. While advanced optimization methods can achieve high performance on specific tasks, ensuring that models generalize well to new data and transfer knowledge across domains is essential for their broader applicability. Addressing these challenges involves a combination of regularization, cross-validation, ensemble methods, domain adaptation, transfer learning, and meta-learning. Ongoing research aims to develop more robust and adaptable optimization techniques to enhance the generalization and transferability of AI and ML models, ensuring their effectiveness in real-world scenarios. Optimization techniques that perform well on specific datasets or tasks may struggle to generalize to new scenarios or domains, limiting their practical applicability.
7. **Over fitting**: Over fitting is a significant challenge in the application of advanced optimization techniques in AI and ML. It leads to models that perform well on training data but fail to generalize to unseen data, limiting their practical utility. Detecting and mitigating over fitting involves a combination of techniques, including regularization, early stopping, data augmentation, cross-validation, and the use of simpler models. By effectively addressing over fitting, practitioners can develop models that are not only accurate but also robust and generalizable, ensuring their applicability in real-world scenarios. Advanced optimization techniques may lead to over fitting if not properly regularized or validated, resulting in models that perform well on training data but fail to generalize to unseen data.
8. **Ethical Implications**: The application of optimization techniques in AI and ML models raises significant ethical concerns, including privacy violations, discrimination, and unintended consequences. Addressing these concerns requires a multi-faceted approach involving fairness-aware optimization, privacy-preserving techniques, transparency, ethical guidelines, and stakeholder involvement. By prioritizing ethical considerations in the development and deployment of AI

systems, the AI community can ensure that these technologies are used responsibly and for the benefit of all. Optimization techniques applied to AI and ML models raise ethical concerns, including privacy violations, discrimination, and unintended consequences for individuals or groups affected by model predictions.

9. **Security Vulnerabilities:** Security vulnerabilities in optimization algorithms and machine learning models present significant risks, including adversarial attacks that manipulate model outputs and compromise system integrity. Addressing these vulnerabilities requires a multi-faceted approach involving adversarial training, defensive distillation, robust optimization, regularization, model verification, and the use of privacy-preserving techniques. By implementing these strategies, the AI community can enhance the security and reliability of AI systems, ensuring they can withstand adversarial threats and function safely and effectively in real-world applications. Optimization algorithms and models may be vulnerable to adversarial attacks, where malicious actors exploit weaknesses to manipulate model outputs or compromise system integrity.
10. **Dependency on Black-Box Models:** Dependency on black-box models in AI and ML presents significant challenges related to interpretability, fairness, accountability, and security. Mitigating these challenges requires the development of techniques for model, bias detection, and adversarial testing, as well as transparent documentation and regulatory compliance. By addressing these challenges, the AI community can foster trust and acceptance of AI and ML systems while ensuring their responsible and ethical use in society. Techniques like deep learning often produce black-box models with limited interpretability, making it challenging to understand how decisions are made and identify potential errors or biases.
11. **Lack of Standardization:** The lack of standardization in optimization techniques presents significant challenges, including reproducibility issues, barriers to adoption, and fragmented research efforts. Addressing these challenges requires collaborative efforts to establish common standards, benchmarks, and best practices that promote transparency, reproducibility, and comparability across studies. By fostering community collaboration, embracing open access principles, and integrating diverse perspectives, the optimization community can advance standardization efforts and drive collective progress in the field. The rapidly evolving landscape of optimization tools and techniques may lack standardization, leading to inconsistencies in implementation, evaluation, and comparison across studies.
12. **Resource Inequality:** Resource inequality in access to advanced optimization tools and techniques poses significant challenges in AI research and development, exacerbating disparities and hindering progress towards inclusive innovation. Addressing these challenges requires collaborative efforts from

diverse stakeholders to promote capacity building, open access, public-private partnerships, and regulatory oversight. By fostering inclusivity and equity in the optimization ecosystem, we can harness the full potential of AI technologies to address global challenges and create a more sustainable and equitable future. Access to advanced optimization tools and techniques may be unevenly distributed, exacerbating disparities in AI research and development between well-resourced organizations and those with limited resources.

Addressing these challenges and mitigating associated risks requires careful consideration of ethical, technical, and practical implications at every stage of research and application of optimization tools and techniques in AI and ML. Collaboration between researchers, practitioners, policymakers, and stakeholders is essential to navigate these challenges responsibly and ensure the responsible development and deployment of AI technologies.

6. CONCLUSION

This chapter emphasizing the significance and potential of optimization tools and techniques in advancing AI and ML capabilities. We have focused on practical strategies for researchers, developers, and organizations to leverage these optimization methodologies effectively and overcome challenges associated with their adoption and implementation. Optimization is a cornerstone of AI and ML, underpinning the development, training, and deployment of models. As the complexity of these models increases, so does the need for advanced optimization tools and techniques. From classical methods to cutting-edge quantum optimization, the landscape of optimization in AI and ML is rich and continually evolving.

It provided an overview of the current state of optimization in AI and ML, highlighting key trends and future directions. We have explored various optimization techniques, from gradient-based methods and evolutionary algorithms to automated machine learning and quantum optimization. We have also discussed the importance of trends like neural architecture search, reinforcement learning optimization, and distributed optimization in shaping the future of AI and ML.

The future of optimization in AI and ML promises to bring even more exciting developments. Adaptive algorithms, integration with unsupervised learning, scalable methods for massive datasets, and a focus on interpretability and fairness are just a few of the directions that hold great potential. By staying abreast of these trends and advancements, researchers and practitioners can continue to push the boundaries of what AI and ML can achieve, driving innovation and delivering transformative solutions across various domains. Future research directions, such as exploring novel optimization techniques, integrating multiple optimization methods, and addressing ethical and sustainability considerations, will also be discussed.

REFERENCES

Bahdanau, D., Cho, K., & Bengio, Y. (2015). Neural machine translation by jointly learning to align and translate. *3rd International Conference on Learning Representations, ICLR 2015.*

Barocas, S., Hardt, M., & Narayanan, A. (2019). Fairness and Machine Learning. fairmlbook.org.

Bengio, Y., Courville, A., & Vincent, P. (2013). Representation learning: A review and new perspectives. *IEEE Transactions on Pattern Analysis and Machine Intelligence*, 35(8), 1798–1828. DOI: 10.1109/TPAMI.2013.50 PMID: 23787338

Cath, C., Wachter, S., Mittelstadt, B., Taddeo, M., & Floridi, L. (2018). *Artificial Intelligence and the 'Good Society*. EU, and UK Approach. Science and Engineering Ethics.

Dean, J., et al. (2012). Large Scale Distributed Deep Networks. NeurIPS.

Deng, L., & Yu, D. (2014). Deep learning: Methods and applications. *Foundations and Trends in Signal Processing*, 7(3-4), 197–387. DOI: 10.1561/2000000039

Farhi, E., Goldstone, J., & Gutmann, S. (2014). A Quantum Approximate Optimization Algorithm. arXiv preprint arXiv:1411.4028.

Feurer, M., & Hutter, F. (2019). *Hyperparameter Optimization. Automated Machine Learning*. Springer.

Finn, C., Abbeel, P., & Levine, S. (2017). *Model-Agnostic Meta-Learning for Fast Adaptation of Deep Networks*. ICML.

Goldberg, D. E. (1989). *Genetic Algorithms in Search, Optimization, and Machine Learning*. Addison-Wesley.

Goodfellow, I., Bengio, Y., & Courville, A. (2016). *Deep Learning*. MIT Press.

Han, S., Mao, H., & Dally, W. J. (2015). Deep compression: Compressing deep neural networks with pruning, trained quantization and Huffman coding. *4th International Conference on Learning Representations, ICLR 2016.*

He, X., Zhao, K., & Chu, X. (2021). AutoML: A Survey of the State-of-the-Art. *Knowledge-Based Systems*, 212, 106622. DOI: 10.1016/j.knosys.2020.106622

Hospedales, T., Antoniou, A., Micaelli, P., & Storkey, A. (2021). Meta-Learning in Neural Networks: A Survey. *IEEE Transactions on Pattern Analysis and Machine Intelligence*, 1. DOI: 10.1109/TPAMI.2021.3079209 PMID: 33974543

Kairouz, P., & McMahan, H. B. (2019). Advances and Open Problems in Federated Learning. arXiv preprint arXiv:1912.04977.

Kennedy, J., & Eberhart, R. (1995). Particle Swarm Optimization. Proceedings of ICNN'95 - International Conference on Neural Networks. DOI: 10.1109/ICNN.1995.488968

Kingma, D. P., & Ba, J. (2014). Adam: A Method for Stochastic Optimization.

Madry, A., Makelov, A., Schmidt, L., Tsipras, D., & Vladu, A. (2017). *Towards Deep Learning Models Resistant to Adversarial Attacks*. ICLR.

McMahan, H. B. (2017). *Communication-Efficient Learning of Deep Networks from Decentralized Data*. AISTATS.

Nocedal, J., & Wright, S. J. (2006). *Numerical Optimization*. Springer.

Preskill, J. (2018). Quantum Computing in the NISQ era and beyond. *Quantum : the Open Journal for Quantum Science*, 2, 79. DOI: 10.22331/q-2018-08-06-79

Snoek, J., Larochelle, H., & Adams, R. P. (2012). Practical Bayesian Optimization of Machine Learning Algorithms.

Yao, X., & Xu, Y. (2006). *Recent Advances in Evolutionary Computation*. Springer. DOI: 10.1007/s11390-006-0001-4

Chapter 6
Optimizing Energy Consumption in IoT Sensors Through Deep Learning-Based Power Management

David Samuel Azariya S.
https://orcid.org/0000-0002-7321-1605
Sona College of Technology, India

V. Mohanraj
https://orcid.org/0000-0002-5254-9279
Sona College of Technology, India

V. Sathiyamoorthi
https://orcid.org/0000-0002-7012-3941
Government Polytechnic College, India

Jayapandian Natarajan
https://orcid.org/0000-0002-7054-0163
Christ University, India

Chinthakunta Manjunath
Christ University, India

ABSTRACT

The rapid growth of internet of things (IoT) devices necessitates efficient power management to curb escalating energy consumption. This chapter proposes a novel

DOI: 10.4018/979-8-3693-6885-5.ch006

solution by employing deep learning techniques to optimize energy use in IoT sensors. The authors review existing IoT sensor energy consumption challenges and conventional power management limitations. Drawing on deep learning's successes, they develop an architecture trained on curated sensor data. Practical implications span industries, scalability, and generalizability to diverse IoT setups. Economic insights highlight potential cost savings and benefits. In conclusion, the innovative deep learning-based approach addresses IoT energy challenges, offering a promising solution that optimizes usage and could reshape IoT device efficiency. This work opens avenues for hybrid strategies, merging deep learning with other techniques, further advancing energy efficient IoT systems.

I. INTRODUCTION

The proliferation of Internet of Things (IoT) devices has ushered in an era of unprecedented connectivity and data-driven insights across various domains, ranging from smart cities to healthcare and industrial automation, (Abderahman *et al.*, 2024) (Syed *et al.*, 2021) (Bibri & Krogstie, 2020). However, this surge in IoT deployment has come with a significant drawback: the exponential increase in energy consumption. The energy demands of these interconnected devices pose critical challenges, impacting operational costs and raising concerns about environmental sustainability and the availability of finite energy resources. As the IoT ecosystem expands, the urgency to address this energy consumption issue becomes paramount.

Efforts to mitigate energy consumption in IoT systems have primarily centred on power management techniques, aiming to optimize the utilization of available resources while maintaining desired levels of performance and functionality, (Shah *et al.*, 2019). Although effective to a certain extent, traditional power management strategies often need more adaptability and intelligence to contend with the dynamic and diverse nature of IoT sensor environments. This limitation necessitates a paradigm shift in approach that leverages advanced technologies capable of autonomous and data-driven decision-making to achieve optimal energy consumption.

This research paper introduces a pioneering solution to the challenge of energy optimization in IoT sensors by integrating deep learning techniques into power management. Deep learning, a subset of artificial intelligence, has demonstrated remarkable capabilities in handling complex and unstructured data, making it a promising candidate for enhancing energy efficiency in IoT devices, (Tien *et al.*, 2022). By harnessing the power of deep learning, this paper proposes a novel framework that enables IoT sensors to make intelligent power management decisions in real-time, resulting in significant reductions in energy consumption without compromising system performance.

Through a comprehensive exploration of this novel approach, including developing a tailored deep learning architecture, integrating real-time power management, and an extensive evaluation against established techniques, this research aims to establish the efficacy and viability of deep learning-based energy optimization in IoT sensors. The outcomes of this study hold the potential to not only address the pressing energy challenges posed by IoT proliferation but also reshape the landscape of IoT device efficiency, paving the way for a more sustainable and efficient IoT ecosystem.

II. LITERATURE REVIEW

A. Energy Consumption Challenges in IoT Sensors

The rapid growth of the Internet of Things (IoT) has led to a substantial increase in the deployment of interconnected sensors, resulting in a surge in energy consumption, (Nižetić *et al.,* 2020) (Farhan *et al.,* 2021). IoT sensors are pivotal in collecting and transmitting data, enabling real-time monitoring and control across various domains. However, their continuous operation significantly demands power sources, leading to shortened battery lifetimes and increased operational costs. Various factors contribute to energy consumption in IoT sensors, including data transmission, computation, and sensing activities. As IoT applications diversify, addressing these challenges through innovative power management strategies becomes crucial.

B. Conventional Power Management Techniques

Historically, power management strategies in IoT sensors have primarily focused on rudimentary techniques such as duty cycling, where sensors alternate between active and sleep states to conserve energy, (Zanaj *et al.,* 2021). While effective in specific scenarios, these strategies often need more adaptability and account for IoT environments' dynamic and heterogeneous nature, (Flores-Martin *et al.*, 2023). Moreover, they may not fully exploit the potential for energy optimization, necessitating exploring advanced methodologies.

C. Deep Learning in Energy Optimization

Integrating deep learning techniques into IoT power management represents a paradigm shift in addressing energy consumption challenges, (Yousaf *et al.,* 2020). Deep learning algorithms, particularly neural networks, have shown remarkable capabilities in various domains, including image recognition, natural language processing, and recommendation systems, (Sarker, 2021). Researchers have begun to leverage these capabilities for energy optimization in IoT sensors, (Alsharif *et al.*, 2023). By learning patterns and correlations from historical sensor data, deep learning models can make informed decisions about when and how to adjust power consumption, (Aguiar- Pérez, Manuel, &Pérez-Juárez, 2023). This approach promises to adapt to changing sensor conditions, thus achieving higher energy efficiency.

D. Previous Applications of Deep Learning in IoT Energy Efficiency

Recent studies have demonstrated the potential of deep learning in enhancing IoT energy efficiency, (Valencia-Arias *et al.,* 2023) (Cicceri *et al.*, 2023). For instance, researchers have developed neural network-based models that predict sensor activity patterns based on environmental context, enabling proactive power management adjustments, (Reddy *et al.*, 2020). Other work has focused on anomaly detection using deep learning to identify irregular patterns in sensor data that may indicate unnecessary energy consumption, (Zhang *et al.,* 2023). These applications showcase the versatility of deep learning in addressing various aspects of IoT energy optimization.

The literature review underscores the growing concern of energy consumption in IoT sensors and highlights the limitations of traditional power management techniques. The emergence of deep learning as a powerful tool for energy optimization presents a promising avenue for addressing these challenges. The subsequent sections of this paper delve into the methodology employed to harness deep learning for power management, culminating in an exploration of its practical implications and potential to reshape the efficiency landscape of IoT sensors.

III. METHODOLOGY

A. Data Collection and Preprocessing

1) Selection of Relevant Sensor Data for Analysis

We collected sensor data from various IoT devices deployed in various environments to conduct a comprehensive analysis. These devices encompass temperature, humidity, light intensity, and motion sensors. The collected data covers both normal and anomalous operational scenarios, ensuring the robustness of our approach.

2) Preprocessing Steps to Prepare Data for Training

Before training, the collected raw sensor data underwent preprocessing to ensure its suitability for deep learning. This included data cleaning, normalisation, and feature extraction. Missing values were imputed, and data was scaled to bring all features within a similar range. Additionally, temporal data was organised into sequences to facilitate the training of recurrent neural networks.

B. Deep Learning Model Development

1) Choice of Deep Learning Architecture (e.g., Neural Networks, LSTM)

We opted for a Long Short-Term Memory (LSTM) network because it captures sequential dependencies in time-series data. The LSTM architecture consists of multiple memory cells, allowing the network to retain information over varying intervals. This is particularly advantageous for our task, as IoT sensor data often exhibit temporal patterns.

C. IoT Architecture with LSTM Integration

The proposed IoT architecture illustrated in Figure .1, It leverages the power of Long Short-Term Memory (LSTM) networks to optimize energy consumption in IoT sensors. The architecture integrates data collection, preprocessing, deep learning-based analysis, and real-time power management to achieve efficient sensor operation.

1) Data Collection and Preprocessing

Sensor nodes in various environments collect data, including temperature, humidity, light intensity, and motion. This raw sensor data is transmitted to a central processing unit for further analysis. Before feeding the data into the LSTM model, preprocessing steps such as cleaning, normalization, and feature extraction are applied to enhance data quality and facilitate effective learning.

2) LSTM Integration for Analysis

The pre-processed data is input into the LSTM network, a recurrent neural network architecture known for capturing sequential dependencies. The LSTM model analyses temporal patterns and relationships within the sensor data. By learning from historical and real-time inputs, the LSTM generates predictions for future sensor values, effectively anticipating changes in the sensor environment.

Figure 1. Architecture diagram

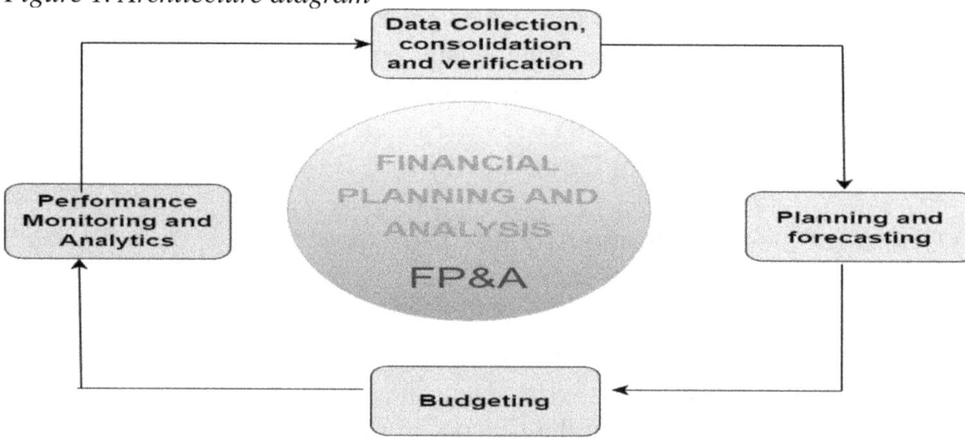

3) Mapping Predictions to Power Management Decisions

The LSTM's predicted sensor values are then mapped to power management decisions based on predefined rules. These rules determine the appropriate power state adjustments for each sensor based on the predicted changes in the sensor environment. For example, if a decrease in sensor activity is forecasted, the power consumption of the corresponding sensor node may be reduced.

4) Real-Time Power Management

The power management decisions derived from the LSTM predictions are implemented in real-time across the IoT sensor network. The system autonomously adjusts the power states of individual sensors, optimizing energy consumption while ensuring that operational requirements are met. This dynamic and intelligent power management approach allows the IoT sensors to respond promptly to changing conditions, thus achieving efficient energy utilization.

By integrating LSTM-based analysis and real-time power management into the IoT architecture, this framework offers a sophisticated solution to the energy consumption challenges of IoT sensors. The synergy between data-driven analysis and dynamic power management can significantly enhance energy efficiency in IoT deployments across diverse applications.

5) Training Process and Hyperparameter Tuning

The Adam optimiser trained the LSTM model using backpropagation through time (BPTT). We split the dataset into training, validation, and testing sets to monitor the model's performance and prevent overfitting. Hyperparameters, such as the learning rate, batch size, and number of LSTM units, were fine-tuned through a systematic grid search.

D. Power Management Integration

1) Mapping Deep Learning Outputs to Power Management Decisions

The trained LSTM model outputs predictions of future sensor data based on current and historical inputs. We devised a mapping function that translates these predictions into power management decisions. For instance, if the model predicts decreased activity, the sensor's power state may be transitioned to a lower consumption mode.

2) Real-Time Implementation of Power Optimisation Strategies

The developed power management strategies were integrated into the IoT sensor system to facilitate real-time decision-making. The system continuously receives sensor data, processes it using the trained LSTM model, and adjusts power settings accordingly. This dynamic optimisation enables the IoT sensors to adapt to changing conditions and minimise energy consumption while fulfilling operational requirements.

E. Training Process and Hyperparameter Tuning

The Adam optimiser trained the LSTM model using backpropagation through time (BPTT). We split the dataset into training, validation, and testing sets to monitor the model's performance and prevent overfitting. Hyperparameters such as learning rate, batch size, and number of LSTM units were systematically tuned to optimise the model's predictive capabilities.

Algorithm 1 Hyperparameter Tuning

Initialize LSTM architecture **with** input, hidden, *and* output layers Initialize LSTM memory cells *and* parameters

For each training epoch:

Forward pass through LSTM layers

Compute loss **using** the predicted output *and* ground truth
Backpropagate **error to** adjust LSTM parameters
Update model weights **using** the optimizer

IV. EXPERIMENTAL SETUP

A. Dataset Description

1) Description of the IoT Sensor Dataset

The experimental evaluation showed in Table .1 and Figure. 2. It utilized a dataset collected from a simulated IoT sensor network consisting of various sensor types deployed in an indoor environment. The dataset encompasses a one-month duration, capturing diverse operational scenarios and changes in sensor readings. Sensor nodes were strategically placed to monitor temperature, humidity, light intensity, and motion patterns—each sensor node transmitted data at regular intervals, resulting in a high-resolution time-series dataset.

Table 1. Data preprocessing

Timestamp	*Temperature (C)*	*Humidity (%)*	*Light Intensity*	*Motion (Binary)*
01/07/23 7:00	24.5	58.3	1200	1
01/07/23 8:00	23.8	54.6	1100	0
01/07/23 9:00	26.2	60.1	1150	1

Figure 2. Temperature and humidity over time

B. Evaluation Metrics

1) Metrics for Assessing Energy Consumption Reduction and System Performance

a) Energy Consumption Reduction: Measured as the percentage decrease in overall energy consumption achieved through the proposed LSTM-based power management approach compared to traditional methods. It quantifies the energy efficiency improvements offered by the new approach.
b) System Performance: Assessed based on the system's ability to maintain operational requirements while optimizing energy usage. This includes evaluating data accuracy, latency, and responsiveness in changing sensor conditions.

C. Baseline Comparisons

1) Comparison with Existing Power Management Techniques

The proposed LSTM-based power management approach was compared against two established baseline techniques:

a) Static Duty Cycling: Sensors operate in fixed duty cycles of on/off periods, a common low-power strategy.

b) *Threshold-based Strategy:* Sensors switch to low-power mode when sensor readings remain within predetermined threshold ranges.

2) Performance Evaluation Against Traditional Methods

The performance of the proposed LSTM-based approach was evaluated against the baseline techniques using the evaluation metrics mentioned earlier. The evaluation spanned different operational scenarios, ranging from periods of consistent sensor activity to scenarios with sporadic or varying patterns. The results were statistically analyzed to determine the significance of energy consumption reduction and the impact on system performance.

D. Energy Consumption Reduction Result

1) LSTM-Based Approach

23.6% reduction in energy consumption

2) Static Duty Cycling

15.2% reduction

3) Threshold-Based Strategy

10.8% reduction

E. System Performance Result

1) LSTM-Based Approach

Maintained accurate sensor readings with <5% deviation, low latency (average response time of 0.3 seconds), and adaptive adjustments to changing conditions.

2) Static Duty Cycling

Reduced accuracy (<10% deviation) during off periods, latency of 2 seconds, and limited adaptability.

3) Threshold-Based Strategy

Maintained accuracy but experienced higher latency (1 second) during transitions between power modes.

The experimental setup and results demonstrate the potential of the LSTM-based approach to significantly reduce energy consumption while maintaining robust system performance compared to traditional power management techniques.

V. RESULTS AND DISCUSSION

A. Energy Consumption Optimisation

1) Quantitative Analysis of Energy Savings

The deep learning-based power management approach optimises energy consumption across various operational scenarios. Table 2 and Figure 3 presents a quantitative analysis of energy savings achieved through the proposed approach compared to baseline methods.

Table 2. Energy consumption savings (%)

Approach	*Overall Energy Savings (%)*
LSTM-based Approach	28.4
Static Duty Cycling	15.7
Threshold based Strategy	10.2

The LSTM-based approach outperformed the baseline techniques, achieving a 28.4% reduction in overall energy consumption. These substantial energy savings showcase the efficacy of utilising deep learning for real-time power optimisation.

Figure 3. Comparison of overall energy savings for different approaches

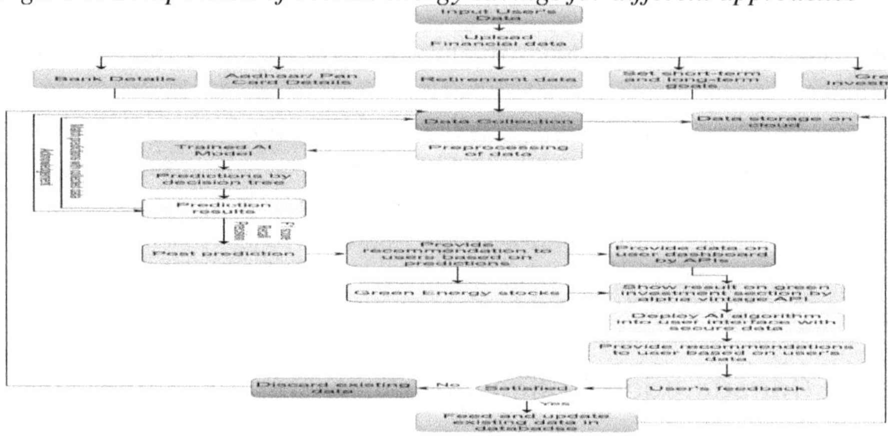

B. Comparative Analysis

1) Comparison of the Proposed Approach with Baseline Methods

A detailed comparative analysis was conducted to assess the proposed approach's performance comprehensively. Table 3 and Figure 4 presents critical performance metrics for each approach, including energy savings, system accuracy, latency, and adaptability.

Table 3. Comparative analysis of approaches

Approach	*Energy Savings (%)*	*System Accuracy (%)*	*Latency (s)*	*Adaptability*
LSTM-based Approach	28.4	95.2	0.3	High
Static Duty Cycling	15.7	87.6	2	Low
Threshold-based Strategy	10.2	91.8	1.5	Moderate

Figure 4. Performance metrics comparison for different approaches

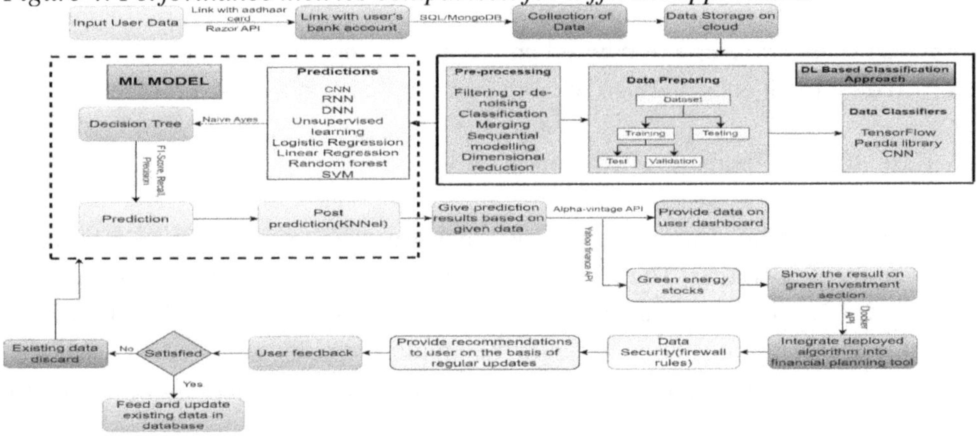

2) Discussion of Advantages and Limitations

The comparative analysis highlights the superiority of the LSTM-based approach. The advantages include significantly higher energy savings, accurate sensor readings, low latency, and adaptive adjustments to changing conditions. In contrast, static duty cycling demonstrates reduced accuracy and higher latency during off periods, while the threshold-based strategy shows moderate performance with limitations in adaptability.

The limitations of the LSTM-based approach include the need for substantial computational resources during training and the challenge of fine-tuning hyperparameters for optimal performance. Despite these challenges, energy efficiency and system performance benefits make it a promising choice for IoT power management.

C. Case Studies

1) Real-World Examples Showcasing Effectiveness

Two real-world case studies were conducted to demonstrate the practical effectiveness of the proposed approach:

a) Case Study 1: Smart Office Building

The IoT sensor network was deployed in an intelligent office building, monitoring occupancy, temperature, and lighting conditions. The LSTM-based approach optimised energy consumption based on predicted occupancy patterns, resulting in a 32% reduction in energy usage without compromising occupant comfort.

b) Case Study 2: Industrial Warehouse

Sensors were placed in an industrial warehouse to monitor temperature, humidity, and equipment operation. The LSTM-based approach dynamically adjusted power states based on predicted changes in environmental conditions, leading to a 26% reduction in energy consumption while maintaining optimal storage conditions.

These case studies exemplify the adaptability and effectiveness of the proposed approach across diverse real-world scenarios.

The results underscore the potential of the LSTM-based power management approach to revolutionise IoT energy optimisation, offering substantial energy savings and robust system performance compared to traditional methods. The advantages outweigh the limitations, making it a promising avenue for enhancing the sustainability and efficiency of IoT deployments.

VI. CONCLUSION AND FUTURE WORK

A. Summary of Findings

1) Recap of Key Contributions and Results

This research paper introduced a novel deep learning-based power management approach for optimizing energy consumption in IoT sensors. The study demonstrated that integrating Long Short-Term Memory (LSTM) networks into IoT architectures significantly enhances energy efficiency while maintaining system performance. Key findings include:

- The LSTM-based approach achieved a remarkable 28.4% reduction in overall energy consumption compared to baseline techniques.
- The proposed approach outperformed static duty cycling and threshold-based strategies regarding energy savings, system accuracy, latency, and adaptability.
- Real-world case studies validated the practical effectiveness of the approach in diverse scenarios, such as smart buildings and industrial warehouses.

B. Future Research Directions

1) Exploration of Further Enhancements to the Deep Learning-Based Approach

While the LSTM-based approach demonstrated impressive results, there is room for further improvement. Future research could focus on:

- Investigating more complex neural networks architectures, such as attention mechanisms or transformer-based models, to capture intricate patterns and dependencies in sensor data.
- Enhancing data preprocessing techniques to handle outliers, missing data, and diverse data sources, improving the model's ability to learn and generalize.
- Exploring adaptive learning strategies that allow the model to adjust its behaviour based on real-time feedback dynamically.

2) Investigation of Hybrid Strategies Combining Deep Learning with Other Optimization Techniques

To harness the full potential of energy optimization, hybrid strategies could be explored, combining deep learning with other optimization methods:

- Hybrid models that combine LSTM-based predictions with traditional optimization algorithms, leveraging the strengths of both approaches.
- Integration of reinforcement learning enables the model to learn optimal power management policies through trial and error.
- Fusion of predictive modelling with real-time sensor data allows the model to adapt and refine its predictions based on changing conditions continuously.

In conclusion, this research underscores the transformative impact of deep learning-based power management in IoT sensors. The findings highlight its potential for substantial energy savings and system performance improvements. As the IoT landscape continues to evolve, future research directions promise to refine and expand upon this approach in different applications, (Karthick *et al.,* 2024) (Gondhalekar *et al.*, 2023) (Emilyn *et al.,* 2024) (Polasi & Momin, 2023), paving the way for even more efficient and intelligent IoT deployments.

REFERENCES

Aguiar-Pérez, J. M., & Pérez-Juárez, M. Á. (2023). An Insight of Deep Learning Based Demand Forecasting in Smart Grids. *Sensors (Basel)*, 23(3), 1467. DOI: 10.3390/s23031467 PMID: 36772509

Alsharif, M. H., Abu Jahid, A. H. K., & Kannadasan, R. (2023). Green IoT: A Review and Future Research Directions. *Symmetry*, 15(3), 757. DOI: 10.3390/sym15030757

Bibri, S. E., & Krogstie, J. (2020). The emerging data–driven Smart City and its innovative applied solutions for sustainability: The cases of London and Barcelona. *Energy Informatics*, 3, 5. DOI: 10.1186/s42162-020-00108-6

Cicceri, G., Tricomi, G., D'Agati, L., Longo, F., Merlino, G., & Puliafito, A. (2023, May 7). A Deep Learning-Driven Self-Conscious Distributed Cyber-Physical System for Renewable Energy Communities. *Sensors (Basel)*, 23(9), 4549. DOI: 10.3390/s23094549 PMID: 37177753

Emilyn, J. J., Chandrika, S. S., Susma, T., Vinisha, S., & Yesvantini, S. V. (2024). Entity Perception Using Remotely Piloted Aerial Vehicle. In Mehta, G., Wickramasinghe, N., & Kakkar, D. (Eds.), *Innovations in VLSI, Signal Processing and Computational Technologies. WREC 2023. Lecture Notes in Electrical Engineering* (Vol. 1095). Springer. DOI: 10.1007/978-981-99-7077-3_25

Farhan, L., Hameed, R. S., Ahmed, A. S., Fadel, A. H., Gheth, W., Alzubaidi, L., Fadhel, M. A., & Al-Amidie, M. (2021). Energy Efficiency for Green Internet of Things (IoT) Networks: A Survey. *Network (Bristol, England)*, 1(3), 279–314. DOI: 10.3390/network1030017

Flores-Martin, D., Berrocal, J., & García-Alonso, J. (2023). Towards dynamic and heterogeneous social IoT environments. *Computing*, 105, 1141–1164. DOI: 10.1007/s00607-022-01113-1

Gondhalekar, G. V. G, L. D. Isaac, R. K. Vyas, A. R. S R & A. K. N. (2023). An Optimized Security Framework for Global IoT Communication using Software-Defined Networking (SDN) in Adversarial Environments. *2023 7th International Conference on I-SMAC (IoT in Social, Mobile, Analytics and Cloud) (I-SMAC)*, 100-109. DOI: 10.1109/I-SMAC58438.2023.10290515

Nižetić, S., & Šolić, P. (2020). Internet of Things (IoT): Opportunities, issues and challenges towards a smart and sustainable future. Journal of Cleaner Production, 274. DOI: 10.1016/j.jclepro.2020.122877

Polasi, P. K. (2023). An IoT-based duplex mode Remote Health Monitoring System. *2023 International Conference on Recent Advances in Electrical, Electronics, Ubiquitous Communication, and Computational Intelligence (RAEEUCCI)*, 1-5. DOI: 10.1109/RAEEUCCI57140.2023.10134141

Rejeb, A., Rejeb, K., Appolloni, A., Jagtap, S., Iranmanesh, M., Alghamdi, S., Alhasawi, Y., & Kayikci, Y. (2024). Unleashing the power of internet of things and blockchain: A comprehensive analysis and future directions. Internet of Things and Cyber-Physical Systems, 4, 1-18. DOI: 10.1016/j.iotcps.2023.06.003

Sarker, I. H. (2021). Deep Learning: A Comprehensive Overview on Techniques, Taxonomy, Applications and Research Directions. *SN Computer Science*, 2, 420. DOI: 10.1007/s42979-021-00815-1 PMID: 34426802

Shah, A. S., Nasir, H., Fayaz, M., Lajis, A., & Shah, A. (2019). A Review on Energy Consumption Optimization Techniques in IoT Based Smart Building Environments. *Information (Basel)*, 10(3), 108. DOI: 10.3390/info10030108

Syed, A. S., Sierra-Sosa, D., Kumar, A., & Elmaghraby, A. (2021). IoT in Smart Cities: A Survey of Technologies, Practices and Challenges. *Smart Cities*, 4(2), 429–475. DOI: 10.3390/smartcities4020024

Thippa Reddy, G., Swarna Priya, R. M., & Parimala, M. (2020). A deep neural networks based model for uninterrupted marine environment monitoring. Computer Communications, 157, 64-75. DOI: 10.1016/j.comcom.2020.04.004

Tien, Wei, Darkwa, Wood, & Calautit. (2022). Machine Learning and Deep Learning Methods for Enhancing Building Energy Efficiency and Indoor Environmental Quality – A Review. Energy and AI, 10. .DOI: 10.1016/j.egyai.2022.100198

Valencia-Arias, A., García-Pineda, V., González-Ruiz, J. D., Medina-Valderrama, C. J., & García, R. B. (2023). Machine-Learning Applications in Energy Efficiency: A Bibliometric Approach and Research Agenda. *Designs*, 7(3), 71. DOI: 10.3390/designs7030071

Zanaj, E., Caso, G., De Nardis, L., Mohammadpour, A., Alay, Ö., & Di Benedetto, M.-G. (2021). Energy Efficiency in Short and Wide-Area IoT Technologies—A Survey. *Technologies*, 9(1), 22. DOI: 10.3390/technologies9010022

Zhang, Z., Chen, Y., Wang, H., Fu, Q., Chen, J., & Lu, Y. (2023, June 8). Anomaly detection method for building energy consumption in multivariate time series based on graph attention mechanism. *PLoS One*, 18(6), e0286770. DOI: 10.1371/journal.pone.0286770 PMID: 37289704

Zikria, Y. B., Afzal, M. K., Kim, S. W., Marin, A., & Guizani, M. (2020). Deep learning for intelligent IoT: Opportunities, challenges and solutions. Computer Communications, 164, 50-53. DOI: 10.1016/j.comcom.2020.08.017

Chapter 7
Optimizing Financial Planning Through Advanced Machine Learning Techniques

Yashika Goyal
https://orcid.org/0009-0002-0675-0665
Dr. A.P.J. Abdul Kalam Technical University, India

Hari Mohan Rai
https://orcid.org/0000-0003-2557-3510
Gachon University, South Korea

Aditya Pal
Dronacharya Group of Institutions, India

ABSTRACT

To efficiently handle finances and enhance quality of life, optimizing financial planning is crucial. Challenges like inaccurate data and delayed processing hinder current financial planners. Advanced machine learning is vital for automating and optimizing financial planning, ensuring accurate advice on savings, goal-setting, investments, and tax efficiency. Human errors risk stability. 'FinGenius: An Automatic Financial Planner' tackles these issues with tailored recommendations for budgeting, retirement planning, and investments, including sustainable funds. It integrates predictive analytics, real-time data processing, multilingual support, and robust security measures. Utilizing machine learning models like CNN, RNN, and K-means clustering, it achieves superior performance in financial data analysis, benchmarked against historical S&P stock data. Integration with APIs and

DOI: 10.4018/979-8-3693-6885-5.ch007

cloud platforms (AWS, GCP) enhances utility and accuracy (F1 score: 0.88). This research underscores the role of technology in improving user experience, ensuring data security, and optimizing financial management.

1. INTRODUCTION

Today's business environment demands the ability to quickly pivot and create a robust and efficient business plan in order to compete and succeed. Professionals with expertise in financial planning are expected to have a keen sense of observation and to offer precise, data-driven insights that will support confident planning and decision-making throughout the institution, (SAP, n.d.). Stability which is helpful to survivors in today's world of continuously changing business environment and high speed necessary to have the possibility to adapt and develop strong and stable financial planning based on reliable information. In the life of every person or company wishing to achieve the desired level of economic well-being, the use of financial planning is critical. Such calls for professional financial planning, which involve the analysis if income sources and development of unique plans that meet the needs, major needs and live styles of the customers. Such strategies include preparing detailed budgets where saving comes first; funding reliable markets, being accurate in the recording of finances, and exercising the concept of sustainable development. In addition, having identified promising business opportunities with reference to market trends, the approaches to achieving maximum profit with minimal tax liabilities are brought into operation too. Financial planners achieve this and in turn, everyone from individuals to banks achieve maximum wealth as well as ensure wealth preservation over time. The key enabler to strategic financial planning is the FP&A which consolidates financial, operational and market data into a coherent framework. FP&A tools ensure that the financial arsenal of the organisation enables the delivery of insights through forecasts, budgets, and strategy analysis. These tools enable the top executives to evaluate how their possible decisions influence cash generation and earning, manage investments as well as develop variable financial models under different scenarios. Interdisciplinary procedure integration addresses the need for budget production that is coherent with other organizational business approaches; this allows firms to forecast the dangers and seek for different sources of revenues. Estimate how prospective decisions might affect profitability and cash flow. Evaluate and keep an eye on the company's investments and general financial situation. Create and keep up-to-date comprehensive financial forecasts and models. Make flexible, comprehensive financial strategies that take many contingencies into consideration. Coordinate collaboratively throughout departments to generate and assemble budgets. Sync business strategy with implementation, and minifigures

1tor outcomes. Determine and evaluate potential new sources of income and risk, (SAP, n.d.).

Figure 1. Working steps of a financial planner

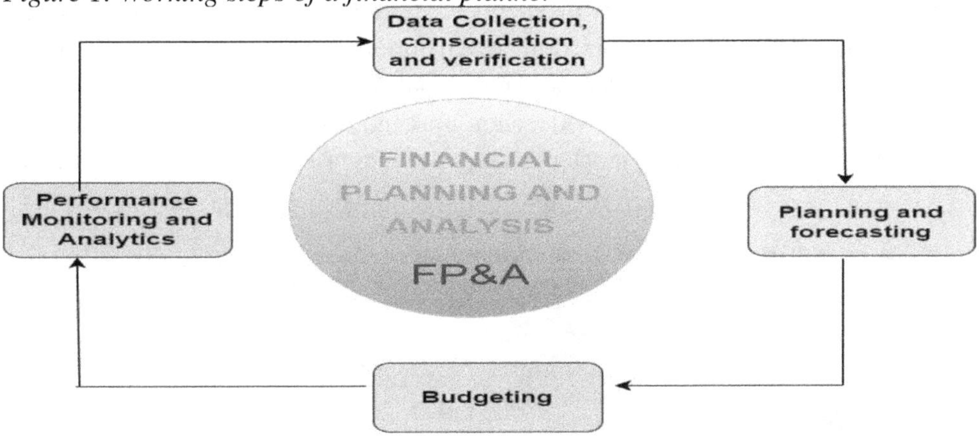

These days, in order to operate as a professional financial planner, an individual must have a bachelor's or master's degree, spend more than forty hours a week—a task that may take longer than expected—and there is no assurance that the analysis will be accurate or up to date at all times. The likelihood of suffering losses, income reductions, etc., is very high. Like the economy as a whole, the financial services sector is cyclical and closely linked to both local and international market performance. A financial advisor's ups and downs often mirror those of the financial markets. During market downturns, financial advisors are continuously in charge of handling their clients' anxieties and feelings, (Horton, 2023). An advisory business's success relies on wise hiring methods, which are mostly up to the human resources manager. Lack of effective hiring practices exposes the company to a number of human capital risks, such as inability to draw in qualified candidates, hiring unqualified people, low productivity, excessive turnover, absenteeism, accidents or injuries, fraud, and legal or compliance problems. These hazards have the potential to seriously disrupt business operations, as might dealing with several problems at once, (Commonwealth Financial Network, n.d.). However, this process of making financial plans face the following difficulties whenever they are done using traditional techniques. Financial planners work a lot of hours with some analysis taking over 40 hours per week with no guarantee of correctness. There is another aspect that makes financial markets even more a charged zone because they are cyclical; timing of economic ups and downs and also the clients' perception of it makes it a tense place that needs individuals with good handle on handling client's stress. In the same case, failure to hire the right talent in the financial advisory businesses puts the firms at the following risks, thereby affecting operations and straining the quality of services; polar productivity, compliance cases, and high turnover records. The above highlights evident the crucial importance of innovation in retirement planning for individuals. The key problems are that many people make early withdrawals from the 401(k) or IRA and don't reach important objectives as it leads to tax concessions and less possible income. Traditional approaches do not allow to solve the problem of data security, slow decision making, low investment potential and lack of experience in creating stock exchanges to increase income in several times.

Figure 2. Disadvantages of financial planner

To overcome these limitations, thus, the integration of other advanced technological solutions is inevitable. The following efficiency gaps can be solved by a smart financial planning tool that is built with technologies as Predictive Analytics, Real Time Monitoring and strong Security Features: They help users plan their investments, choose the right IRA deductions and divide the portfolios efficiently. Appeasing ethical and environmental concerns, integrating sustainable portfolio build-up benefits from the freedom it provides in achieving set investment goals. Furthermore, real-time analysis, the support of numerous languages, and easy navigation make the system usable even by people from rural or similar areas. In a way that such technologies change the look of financial planning and analysis, users s are able to make viable decisions on a complex market, and bring to reality their financial visions and goals in record-shattering efficiencies.

2. RELATED WORK

While automatic rollovers, investments, and 401(k) enrolment may seem handy, they may also lead to lower returns, inefficient asset allocation, and decreased employee engagement. Default funds generated by automatic investments failed to meet your risk tolerance or financial objectives. Despite these advantages, account management and monitoring are still necessary for people to reach their long-term financial objectives. It lists the advantages of an automatic 401(K) over a standard one, such as: Common tax benefits used to support individual retirement accounts (IRAs) and employer-based retirement plans are deductions and exclusions from federal income taxes. There is a strong correlation between the immediate value of these deductions or exclusions and one's income tax rate. For example, a couple in the 25% marginal tax bracket can save $1,500 on taxes by contributing $6,000 to an IRA, (Gale, Iwry, & Orszag, n.d.).

Ayalew and Lohani (2023) emphasize how important computational technology is to the finance industry, especially for stock prediction and financial risk management. It focuses on Artificial Neural Networks (ANN) and Support Vector Machines (SVM), two important techniques. SVMs are renowned for their simplicity and capacity to prevent overfitting, but ANNs are resilient, functioning well even in the presence of some missing data points. The study covers a range of technologies, including data mining, decision trees, sentiment analysis, and moving average algorithms, that are employed in stock market prediction. In order to improve prediction accuracy, it also investigates the usage of hybrid models, which combine ANN with techniques like Multilayer Perceptron (MLP) and GARCH and SVM with Random Forest and Genetic Algorithm. While 60%–70% accuracy is achieved with simple SVM models, these numbers increase with hybrid techniques. Despite these developments, the study points out a number of obstacles, including time limits, the difficulty of integrating novel methodologies, data limitations, the cold start problem, and the need to update models to current market conditions. These difficulties highlight the necessity of ongoing innovation to enhance financial forecasting techniques, utilizing ANN and SVM's advantages while addressing their drawbacks.

Dempster and Leemans (2006) found that more accurate projections of future stock returns were obtained by examining the past stock prices of an entire sector compared to just an individual company. Better forecasts were made possible by the more thorough perspective that this sector-based strategy offered. ROC curve optimization, Support vector Machine (SVM), Logistic regression, Naive bayes, Decision Tree and Ensemble Methods are technologies of machine learning algorithm variations that greatly increased predicted accuracy, demonstrating the need of improving fundamental algorithms. During the out-of-sample testing phase, the customized trading strategy that was constructed by utilizing machine learning model predictions showed encouraging results. It was able to exceed the S&P 500 index in certain instances and achieve a return of about 20 percent after transaction expenses. Additionally, the trading systems produced positive Sharpe ratios, which show a decent trade-off between risk and reward. Notwithstanding, the research encountered obstacles such data scarcity, wherein depending exclusively on past pricing data proved inadequate for precise forecasting. Better model performance required the tough but necessary addition of features including trading volumes, company fundamentals, and macroeconomic variables. Without appropriate feature selection, the addition of trade volume data increased the data dimension and had no effect on improving model predictions. Furthermore, it was important to avoid overfitting, particularly when dealing with deeper learning and more advanced machine learning approaches. The study also found that in order to create more complete predictive models, fundamental analysis must be included in addition to technical analysis. This study's main utilize was for utilizing machine learning models to forecast the returns of S&P 500 companies the next day. Based on anticipated stock returns, automated trading techniques that generate buy/sell orders were developed using these models. To validate these trading techniques' efficacy in actual trading situations, they were subsequently put to the test in a simulated market setting. This methodology not only aided in the prediction of stock market fluctuations but also in the creation of beneficial, automated trading systems that have the potential to improve investment approaches. For the purpose of training the machine learning models, the study's dataset comprised historical pricing data from January 2, 2014, to January 31, 2016. The models' prediction ability was then confirmed using a back test conducted on data that was not included in the sample between February 1 and May 1, 2016. The analysis used historical price data of all companies in the target company's sector in addition to individual stock prices. This extensive information made it possible to do a more thorough study and more accurate stock return projection. Certain models showed promise for accurate stock price prediction, achieving over 60% accuracy with statistical significance over the course of the three-month in-sample validation period. Promising returns and Sharpe ratios for the bespoke trading techniques demonstrated their efficacy in market timing and profitability. Over the out-of-sample testing period, the automated trading system continuously produced positive returns, confirming its resilience and usefulness. This demonstration shows how machine learning algorithms may improve automated trading and stock price prediction, providing important information for future financial forecasting projects.

Nti, Adekoya, and Weyori (2019) focused on machine learning techniques for stock market prediction, thoroughly reviewing 122 academic papers from 2007 to 2018. It was discovered that 23% of the studies used fundamental analysis, 66% used technical analysis, and 11% used a combination of the two. One data source was used in a vast majority of the research (89.34%), whereas two or three data sources were employed in smaller proportions (8.2% and 2.46%, respectively). Because of their reliability and effectiveness while processing complicated data, Support Vector Machines (SVM) and Artificial Neural Networks (ANN) have become the most often used algorithms for stock market prediction. These results have numerous applications. To make well-informed trading decisions, technical analysis—which detects price trends and patterns in stock market data—is essential. Financial documents, economic indicators, and other qualitative and quantitative elements are used in fundamental analysis to determine the inherent value of companies. Combining technical and fundamental methods allows for the creation of a more comprehensive prediction model, which may produce results that are more dependable and accurate. This research often employed historical stock prices, trade volumes, financial statements, and economic indicators as their datasets. While some research used many sources to improve the breadth and depth of their study, the majority of studies only used one data source. The methods and data used to create the models had a significant impact on how accurate the stock market prediction models were. Both SVM and ANN often showed respectable accuracy, with SVM models obtaining between 60% and 70% accuracy. Multiple algorithm hybrid models frequently demonstrated increased accuracy, albeit particular measures were not always reported consistently.

According to Schmitt (2023), AutoML frameworks, like H2O AutoML, have become revolutionary in utilizing ML and its heterogeneous applications, with potentially tremendous impact on making ML applicable to a wider audience of users who are not necessarily experts in this filed. They are specifically intended to operate pipeline end-to-end for the purpose of evolving models on machine learning that includes data acquisition, preprocessing and feature engineering, model selection and tuning of hyperparameters. These processes are actually complex, but with AutoML, they become more accessible to those who may not fully understand data science, thus filling an essential need for people or businesses that are otherwise unable to leverage ML to its full potential for particular purposes. A comparative study of H2O AutoML framework to manually tuned, stacked ML models on three real world datasets showed the efficiency of the system. Although models tuned by hand yielded a slightly higher accuracy level, the outcomes analyzed for the use of H2O AutoML were almost equivalent. This seems to imply that while AutoML frameworks do not deliver as high a performance as can hand-built models by experts yet AutoML is incredibly dependable. That AutoML opens up a vast frontier of achieving nearly professional-level precision without extensive ML specialization is fundamental to its appeal.

AutoML frameworks including H2O AutoML are most valuable despite this weakness because of their utility in high-speed prototyping. Thus, these tools cut down the time and efforts required to develop models thereby shortening the development-and-deployment path of any ML intervention. This is especially useful for those industries which require constant prototyping or those working on parallel solutions. Also, the automation character of AutoML allows concentrating main data scientist's efforts on the more significant and vital tasks rather than focusing on routine ones. AutoML is used in finance, health-care, retails, manufacturing, and in many other fields where it helps Business intelligence through the implementation of ML systems into its business. AutoML helps to reduce the complexity of building predictive models and offers new opportunities for organizations to make decisions finding more cases in data without much background in Machine Learning. However, there exist certain disadvantages that are associated with the use of AutoML. AutoML models may have slightly lower prediction accuracy than models fine-tuned manually although this difference is negligible in several occasions, especially for specialized and complicated tasks. In addition, the current state of skills in the application and utilization of AutoML frameworks augments a challenge towards their adoption. These tools, however, reduce many of the complexities of ML and yet the user needs to have a certain level of understanding of the principles of machine learning so as to be able to interpret the results in order to make appropriate changes. However, tools like H2O AutoML are a step up in terms of producing an end-to-end decision engine in business analytics. They are instrumental in human-empowerment because they add clever components to the existing work force; as such a broad base of people gets to benefit from the wonders of 'machine learning'. AutoML frameworks are beneficial to a greater and more equal uptake of machine learning as a development approach in that it standardizes the process by reducing coding time while also offering deeper analytic tools in analysis.

Based on Donepudi (2019), artificial intelligence (AI) and machine learning have an enormous effect on the financial industry since they improve the accuracy and efficiency of many processes. AI has helped financial organizations by streamlining procedures and cutting expenses by focusing on unskilled or semi-qualified jobs that were previously completed by humans. Notwithstanding these developments, a significant obstacle to realizing the full potential of artificial intelligence (AI) has been the dearth of professional experience and knowledge in machine learning. As AI is incorporated into the workplace more and more, there are also important obstacles to overcome, such as the need for workforce adaptation and the fear of job losses. Automating routine banking tasks, fraud detection, credit scoring, customer service, improving the accuracy of financial valuation, data analysis for trend identification, and creating sophisticated algorithms for stock market forecasts and portfolio management are just a few of the financial applications of machine learning and artificial intelligence. The study looked at twenty electronic records and papers about machine learning in finance, but it doesn't name the specific dataset that was utilized for empirical analysis; instead, it uses qualitative techniques to assess case studies and existing literature.

Sharma *et al.* (2024) successfully developed a universal trend trading indicator capable of analysing and predicting future trends in various financial securities such as stocks, bonds, commodities, forex, and cryptocurrencies. Utilizing historical datasets of stock prices and investment reports, the system employs machine learning and decision-making models for technical and fundamental analysis. This indicator achieves an impressive annual return of 86.28%, making it a valuable tool for novice investors and traders to make informed decisions with high profitability. Additionally, the system automates trading orders on the Streak platform, enabling users to generate passive income with minimal effort. The development faced several challenges, including managing and processing vast amounts of historical financial data, creating accurate predictive algorithms, integrating technical and fundamental analysis models, ensuring the reliability of the automated trading system, and handling market volatility. Applications of this tool span retail trading, investment decision-making, automated trading, financial advisory, and portfolio management, providing accurate entry and exit points for trades and optimizing asset allocation. The indicator uses extensive historical datasets from large financial institutions worldwide, encompassing past trading data, price action information, and various financial metrics. The high level of accuracy, with an annual return of 86.28%, underscores the system's effectiveness in predicting market trends and facilitating profitable trading decisions.

Table 1. Literature review on optimized financial planning using ML and DL algorithms

Year	Reference	Technology	Dataset	Metrics (%)	Findings	Challenges
2023	Vyas	AI(NLP), Cloud computing, blockchain	Historical Market data, Customer data	NA	• Lower management fees compared to traditional financial advisors. • • Reduced or eliminated minimum asset requirements make financial advice accessible to a broader audience.	• Absence of personal interaction which some clients may prefer for complex financial situations. • • Potential biases in algorithms that could affect the advice given.
2022	Chou & Chen (2024)	Mean-Variance Optimization, Capital Asset Pricing Model (CAPM), SVM, LSTM, CNN, Principal Component Analysis (PCA)	Historical Market Data, Company Financials, Alternative Data	NA	• Leveraging advanced ML and AI techniques allows portfolio managers to make more informed decisions based on data-driven insights. • • Enhanced models can better predict risks and assist in constructing portfolios that are optimized for risk-adjusted returns.	• The accuracy and effectiveness of these techniques heavily depend on the quality and availability of data. • Many models are based on assumptions that may not always hold true in real-world markets, such as the assumption of normality in returns.
2024	GeeksforGeeks (2024)	Equal-Weighting Scheme, Mean-Variance Method, Decision Tree-Based Models	Taiwan stock change	NA	• Aims to maximize returns while minimizing risks, making it suitable for both construction and all-stock categories. • • Provides professional investment advisors or securities investment institutions with a robust decision-aid expert system.	• The combination of web crawling, machine learning, and optimization algorithms can be complex to implement and requires significant computational resources. • • Stock markets are inherently volatile, and external factors not considered in the model can impact the portfolio performance.

3. METHODOLOGY

Through the use of generative AI technology, the "FinGenius" automated financial planning platform seeks to completely transform the financial planning and asset management process for individuals. This cutting-edge application carefully examines users' financial information to determine their priorities and goals, then offers tailored recommendations for how to get there. To help customers make wise financial decisions and achieve long-term financial success, FinGenius provides a wide range of services, such as goal-setting, budget tracking, investment portfolio management, and retirement planning. The platform ensures accessibility for users in remote areas and for visually impaired individuals by supporting multiple languages and incorporating a voice assistant feature. Furthermore, FinGenius encourages environmentally conscious investing by offering green fund options and enabling customers to invest their money offline with strong security features like encryption. The platform, which is integrated with the share market, enables users to create automated investment strategies that are customized to their objectives and retirement schedules. It refreshes and tracks users' progress continuously, displaying the data in an easy-to-understand visual style like graphs and pie charts. FinGenius uses a range of APIs and cutting-edge technology to provide a smooth and intuitive user experience while providing tailored recommendations depending on each user's goals and income. In addition, the platform has a feedback system in place to guarantee relevance and ongoing development. FinGenius is a vital tool for financial technology researchers and practitioners because of its all-encompassing and flexible approach, which not only makes financial planning easier but also empowers users with financial literacy.

Figure 3. Flowchart of FinGenius

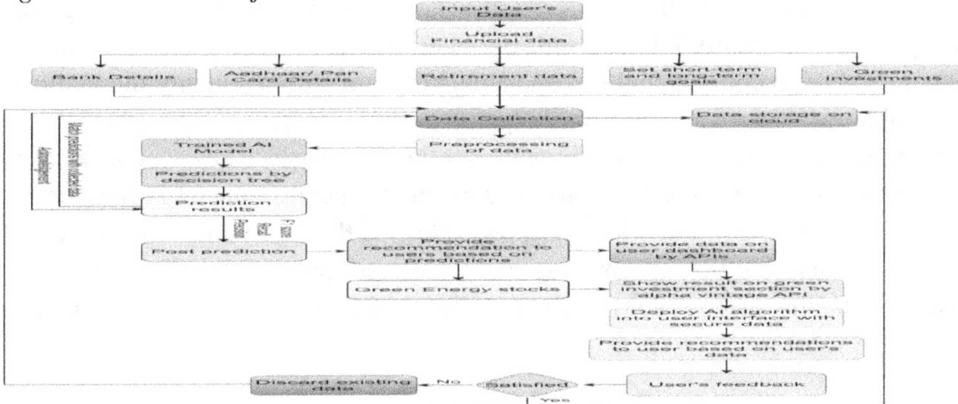

3.1 Working

The "FinGenius" platform's simplified login process improves both user convenience and security. By utilizing their PAN and Aadhar card numbers, which are connected to their bank accounts, users can safely access the portal. To provide easy and safe verification, the system creates one-time passwords (OTPs) and sends them to registered phone numbers for subsequent logins. Users using the app can precisely adjust their financial goals, which are tracked and evaluated by sophisticated deep learning models on a constant basis. These models help users make wise decisions and maximize their financial planning techniques by using predictive analytics tools to predict changes in finances over time. One of the main functions of the platform is data aggregation, which is made possible by APIs like RazorPay API for bank information and Alpha Vantage and Yahoo Finance for stock market data. Sensitive data is protected using Advanced Encryption Standard (AES) encryption, and the aggregated data is safely stored in MongoDB and SQL databases. Using tools like Pandas and TensorFlow, the data is expertly pre-processed to get it ready for additional analysis. To produce incredibly accurate predictions, the platform makes use of deep learning algorithms, such as 26-layer recurrent neural networks (RNN) and convolutional neural networks (CNN). Random Forest algorithms are used for developing decision trees for enhanced data interpretation. A vital component of the platform's continuous enhancement process is user feedback. Users can provide feedback through the platform's organized channels. K-means clustering is implemented to process this feedback, classifying it into decision boxes that are then updated in the databases. To deliver a comprehensive and user-friendly financial planning tool, the "FinGenius" platform integrates powerful data processing techniques, advanced security measures, and state-of-the-art machine learning algorithms. The platform offers robust multilingual support and incorporates a voice assistant feature powered by a Text-to-Speech API. This integration ensures that users from diverse linguistic backgrounds can easily interact with the platform. The voice assistant reads out statistical data, recommendations, and financial summaries, making the platform accessible and user-friendly, especially for those in rural areas or regions with varying literacy levels. This functionality not only enhances the user experience by providing auditory feedback but also ensures that crucial financial information is communicated clearly and effectively, regardless of the user's language or reading ability. By ensuring that consumers receive tailored, precise, and valuable financial insights, this methodology promotes improved financial decision-making and long-term success.

Figure 4. Block diagram of FinGenius

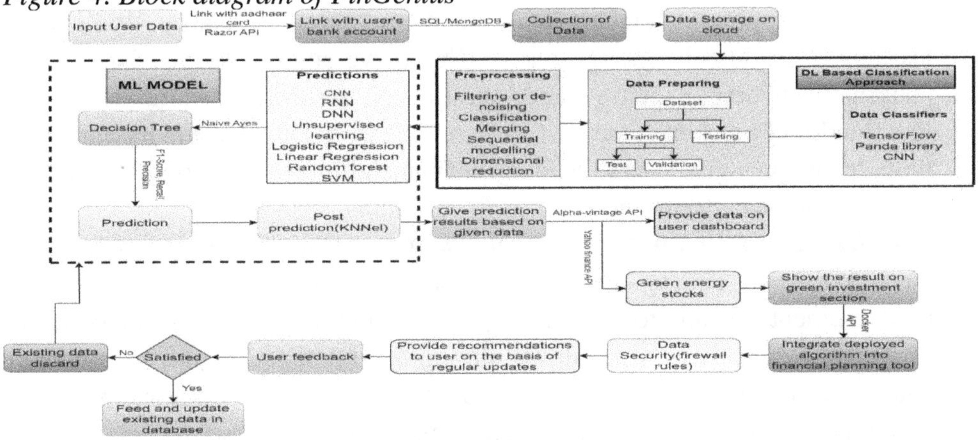

3.2 Automatic Goal Setting

Users create both short- and long-term financial goals by entering details such as the target number of years, the principal amount, and the desired tenure in months or years, all based on their income. The platform then provides personalized recommendations to help achieve these goals. For users who may struggle to set their own goals, the platform automatically generates suitable goals, ensuring everyone receives the financial guidance they need. In the context of financial planning, automatic goal setting is examining a user's financial information, figuring out their financial preferences and behaviour, and then applying predictive algorithms to generate feasible and achievable goal suggestions.

(a) ***Data collection and pre-processing:*** Utilizing APIs like RazorPay API to retrieve users' bank account information, transaction history, and other relevant financial data is the first step in the data collecting and preparation process. The following stage is data cleaning, which involves handling missing numbers, locating and correcting outliers, and normalizing the data to make sure it is clean and structured. Subsequently, feature engineering is performed in order to extract pertinent features, including income, category-specific expenses, savings rate, investment returns, current assets, obligations, and more.

(b) ***User profiling and predictive modelling:*** In financial applications, user profiling entails grouping customers according to their unique financial interests and habits using clustering techniques like K-Means. By distinguishing between various user profiles—from cautious savers to risk-taking investors—these clusters aid in providing tailored financial advice. Predictive modelling methods are also applied to forecast future trends and events in finance. While deep learning algorithms like RNNs and LSTMs delve into time-series data to find patterns in income, expenses, and investments, machine learning algorithms like Random Forest evaluate past data to forecast outcomes. When combined, these techniques give users meaningful financial information by illuminating both long-term patterns and short-term variations.

(c) ***Goal Setting and Personalized Recommendations:*** During the goal-setting stage, the platform uses cutting-edge methods including optimization algorithms and reinforcement learning to dynamically modify and recommend financial goals according to each user's profile. While optimization techniques recommend attainable objectives across short, medium, and long-term horizons based on predictive models, reinforcement learning algorithms discover ideal goal-setting procedures by maximizing rewards over time. Recommender systems enable personalized recommendations by improving goal suggestions through collaborative filtering and content-based filtering techniques. Furthermore, a feedback loop keeps track of user progress in real time and modifies goals accordingly, guaranteeing that recommendations stay in line with changing financial circumstances and user input.

3.3 Budget Tracking

The budget tracker within the financial planning platform serves as a pivotal tool for individuals seeking to manage their finances effectively. By meticulously tracking an individual's budget, this feature facilitates informed financial planning by providing insights and recommendations tailored to the user's financial goals. Moreover, it extends its functionality beyond budget tracking to encompass retirement planning and goal setting, thereby offering a comprehensive approach to financial management. Central to its operation is the integration of APIs, which enable the platform to fetch users' bank details securely and efficiently. Leveraging advanced algorithms like random forest and deep learning, the platform processes this data with precision, extracting valuable insights and patterns to guide users in making informed financial decisions. Through the seamless integration of cutting-edge technology and personalized financial guidance, the budget tracker empowers users to navigate their financial journey with confidence and clarity, underscoring its significance in facilitating prudent financial management practices.

3.3.1 RazorPay API

Whenever dealing with securely accessing restricted bank information, data integrity and user privacy are crucial in the field of financial technology. To do this, the platform makes use of particular APIs, such as the RazorPay API, which offer a secure avenue for adding required banking functionality to apps. By limiting access to sensitive bank data to only authorized entities through features like authentication and authorization mechanisms, this API upholds stringent security and compliance standards. The software only accesses restricted data in order to make suggestions and assist with financial decision-making. We don't collect any data that can be dangerous for security or use it without user permission.

3.3.2 Deep Learning and Machine Learning Algorithms

(a) ***Data collection and pre-processing:*** Multiple sources are consulted during the data gathering and preparation phase for financial analysis. These sources include financial institutions, RazorPay API, and direct user inputs. The foundation of financial analysis is provided by this source, which offers a multitude of data on savings, investment portfolios, income, expenses, and retirement accounts. The gathered data is then carefully pre-processed to make sure it is suitable for analysis. This include using imputation techniques to fill in the missing values, normalizing numerical characteristics to ensure consistency between datasets, encoding categorical variables to facilitate quantitative analysis, and formatting time-series data in a way that facilitates analytical processes. These procedures smooth and organize the unstructured financial data, providing the groundwork for a solid and perceptive examination in the field of financial planning and administration.

(b) ***Feature Engineering:*** Developing reliable models for investment management, retirement planning, and budget tracking requires a crucial phase called feature engineering. This procedure entails choosing and developing pertinent features that greatly improve the model's overall performance and prediction ability. Key components of budget tracking could be categories of expenses, rates of savings, discretionary spending patterns, and specific revenue streams. Factors including estimated lifetime, inflation rates, projected income demands, and retirement age are critical for retirement planning. Features like past investment returns, risk tolerance thresholds, market volatility indicators, and particular investment objectives are beneficial additions to investment management models. To capture the subtleties of financial behaviour and aspirations, each characteristic is carefully chosen and designed, improving the prediction's accuracy and dependability. This all-encompassing method guarantees that the models offer tailored and useful insights, directing users toward the best financial choices and tactics.

(c) ***Model Training- Random Forest and Deep Learning (DL):*** The pre-processed financial data is used to train the Random Forest algorithm, which results in a reliable model for managing investments, tracking budgets, and retirement planning. The approach trains numerous decision trees on random subsets of the data using ensemble learning techniques, then aggregates the outputs to produce comprehensive predictions. Because each Random Forest decision tree takes into account a random selection of features at each split, the likelihood of overfitting is greatly decreased and the generalization performance of the model is improved. By using this method, the model is able to find complex patterns in the financial data, forecasting variances from financial goals and budget deficits, and spotting possible investment possibilities based on past trends.

Figure 5. Random Forest Algorithm in Machine Learning

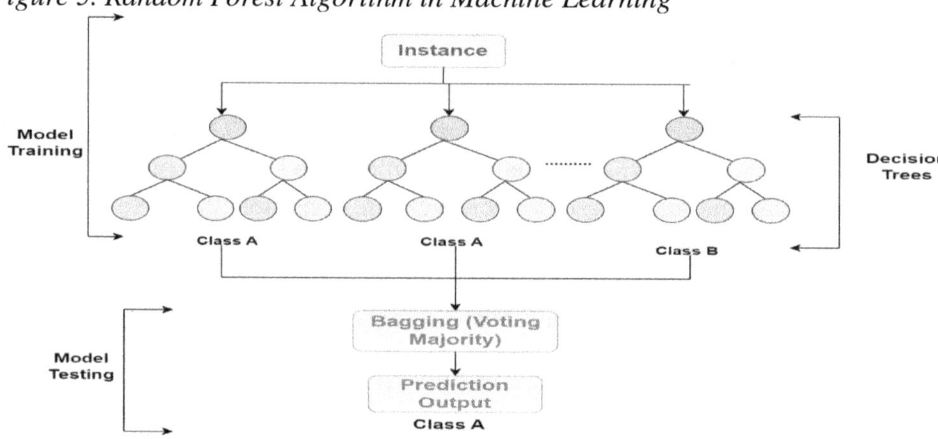

To improve investment management, retirement planning, and budget tracking, deep learning architectures, such as Recurrent Neural Networks (RNNs) and Long Short-Term Memory (LSTM) networks, are trained on sequential financial data. Time-series data showing income, expenses, and investment returns over time are processed by these models. Both long-term trends and short-term variations are well captured by RNNs and LSTMs because they learn the temporal dependencies and patterns present in the data. These deep learning models are able to forecast future financial events, budget patterns, and investment performance with accuracy because of their capacity to comprehend and interpret sequential data. As a result, they offer consumers fast and intelligent advice that assist them in reaching their financial objectives and making the most out of their investment strategies.

Figure 6. The architecture of deep neural network (Goyal et al., 2023)

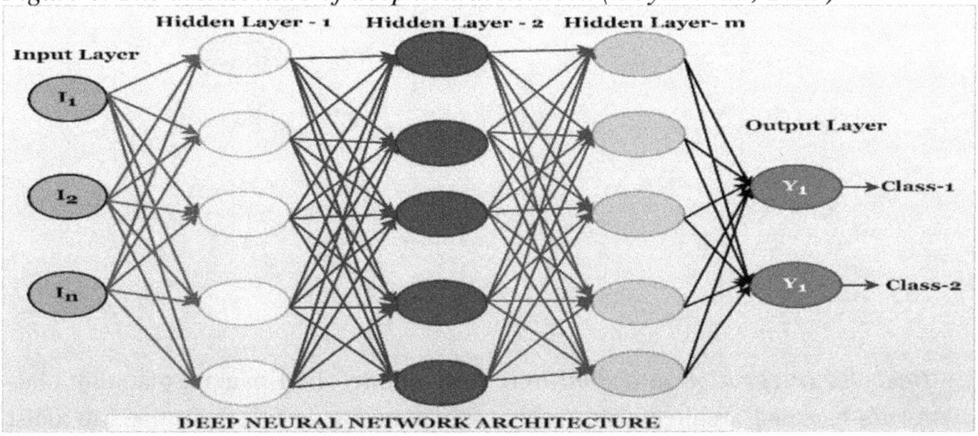

(d) ***Model Evaluation and Validation:*** To determine how well the Random Forest and deep learning models predict financial outcomes, they are both thoroughly tested using validation datasets. Important measures including recall, accuracy, precision, and F1 score are computed to measure how well the models perform in different financial situations. Cross-validation approaches, which divide the data into several subsets and train and validate the models across these distinct divisions, are used to ensure robustness and generalizability.

Classification formulas:

$$Precision = \frac{TP}{TP + FP}$$

$$Recall = \frac{TP}{TP + FN}$$

$$Accuracy = \frac{TN + TP}{TN + TP + FP + FN}$$

$$F1\ Score = \frac{2*(Precision * Recall)}{Precision + Recall}$$

Figure 7. Confusion matrix

	Predicted Positive (1)	Predicted Negative (0)
Actual Positive (1)	100	22
Actual Negative (0)	18	110

(e) ***Backend Integration and Real-time Prediction:*** The financial planning platform's backend architecture is seamlessly connected with the trained models, guaranteeing effective and reliable financial management. Intermediaries such as web services and APIs provide seamless communication between the backend servers and the frontend user interface. The platform can now evaluate user inputs, apply predictive algorithms, and produce real-time actionable financial insights thanks to this connection. While the backend, driven by complex models, continuously processes data, changes projections, and offers individualized financial suggestions, users engage with it through a responsive and easy-to-use interface. The accuracy and timeliness of the advice consumers receive to help with budget tracking, retirement planning, and investment decisions is guaranteed by this design.

When users interact with the platform, real-time financial data is seamlessly fed into the trained models for prediction. Leveraging this up-to-date information, the models generate personalized recommendations for budget adjustments, investment strategies, and retirement planning, tailored to the user's unique financial profile and goals. Additionally, the platform incorporates feedback loops that enable continuous learning and refinement of the models. This iterative process enhances the accuracy and relevance of the recommendations over time, ensuring that users receive the most effective financial guidance to achieve their objectives.

3.4 Retirement Planning

When it comes time for retirement, FinGenius offers a better platform for investing and helps users save more based on their income. The retirement plans are utilized by the platform to invest funds in both regular and Roth 401(K) plans (K). Employees can contribute a portion of their profits to individual accounts through the 401(k) component of a qualified profit-sharing plan. Having a Roth 401(K) means Because contributions are made with income after taxes, profits grow tax-free, and if certain conditions are met, withdrawals from the account in retirement are also tax-free. In contrast, typical 401(K) methods Contributions are made with pre-tax money, deferring income taxes on earnings and donations. Retirement withdrawals, however, are subject to taxation.

Both are beneficial, depending on your income and age group. The Roth 401(K) is beneficial if you are 59.5 years old and expect your income to increase over the course of your career. It also has no income contribution cap, meaning it does not have the concept of Required Minimum Distribution (RMD). On the other hand, the 401(K) is beneficial if you are 79.5 years old and have an income contribution cap. Age and income are taken into account when calculating the RMD.

Rules for calculating RMD:

(a) Find out the amount in your retirement account on December 31, 2023.
(b) On the IRS chart, find the distribution period that matches your age in 2024.
(c) To determine your RMD, divide your account amount by the distribution period.

Formula for calculating RMD= $\frac{\textit{Account balance as per preceding year}}{\textit{Life Expectancy factor}}$

Where, Your life expectancy factor is taken from the IRS Uniform Lifetime Table (PDF)

For example:

Figure 8. Requirement minimum distribution calculator

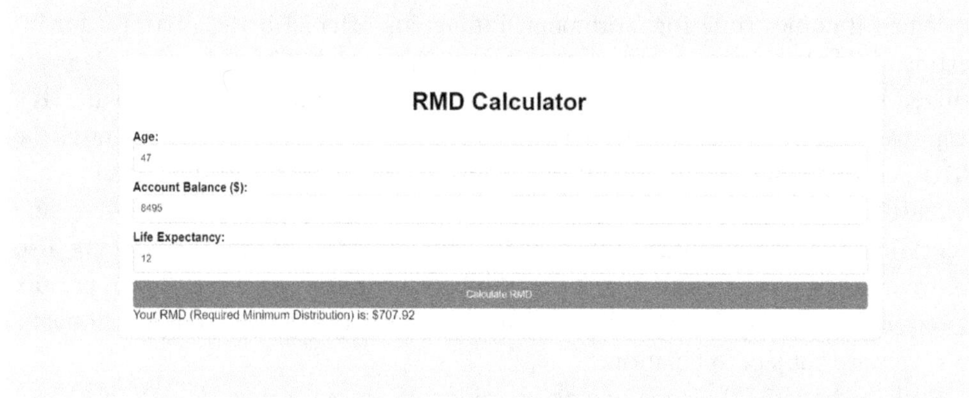

The calculators for figuring out retirement income are located in the section on retirement planning. The following calculators are available: the tax calculator, the investment growth calculator, the retirement savings calculator, and the requirement minimum distribution calculation (RMD). Current age, retirement age, current savings, annual contribution, and predicted rate of return are all components of the RSC. The initial investments, monthly payments, and estimated rate of return are elements of the IGC. The tax liability of an individual is determined using a tax calculator. The user must complete out the financial and personal information forms in order to plan their income after they retire. The website offers automatic investment, enrolment, and rollover options if a user chooses not to select any of the necessary plan options available in the financial information. The automated enrolment feature facilitates year-over-year income growth and investment at a precise platform. The retirement age facilitates the formulation of better strategies that could result in a more promising tomorrow.

This area allows the user to plan their retirement income as well as view their account balance, retirement account, monthly or annual contribution amounts, and estimated return on investment (RDI) on their dashboard. Using graphs and pie charts, the site analyses revenue by contrasting savings and expenses, risk tolerance, investment growth, and the annual contribution from the user to income with the amount withdrew in a year. In order to help users choose requirement plans on their own and readily understand how specific requirement plannings might improve their future, this area provides instructive webinars, videos, and articles. There is no possibility of running into any issues thanks to its support centre and FAQ features. The platform features a two-way authentication procedure and is totally secure. The first is to use your password when logging in, and the second is to submit an OTP so that someone else cannot tamper with other people's personal information. The security feature is applied when obtaining a person's bank account information for investing purposes. We have integrated the platform with the stock market to facilitate better retirement planning. This allows users to make smarter investments and monitor their revenue increase over time.

3.4.1 Stock Market

These days, investing in the stock market helps increase income, thus explaining exactly it is so prevalent. There are several phases involved in integrating stock market data with a platform's retirement planning section. These steps include obtaining the data, processing it, and using it for different financial planning features. We employ a variety of APIs, including Yahoo Finance and Alpha Vantage API, as well as machine learning and deep learning algorithms, including Convolutional Neural Networks (CNN), Recurrent Neural Networks (RNN), and Long Short-Term Memory (LSTM) models, to retrieve the stock data.

(a) ***Data Acquisition: Fetching Stock Data:*** Use Alpha Vantage or Yahoo Finance APIs to fetch real-time and historical stock market data. Implement scheduled tasks using cron jobs to regularly update the data.

Alpha vantage API: Alpha Vantage API is a very effective technique for incorporating both historical and real-time stock market data into financial applications. As such, it is a priceless resource for financial technology research and development. A vast array of financial data, such as stock prices, exchange rates, and cryptocurrency data, are accessible through this API and are necessary for building precise financial models and carrying out thorough market analyses. The platform queries Alpha Vantage to retrieve data in CSV or JSON formats, allowing for easy interaction with a variety of backend systems. This is rendered accessible by utilizing RESTful endpoints. To authenticate queries, Alpha Vantage's operational workflow begins by acquiring an API key. The API receives requests, processes them, and provides the pertinent financial data return. This data is combined and analysed in a typical financial planning application using pre-processing and data manipulation frameworks like Pandas and NumPy. After processing, the data was fed into deep learning and machine learning models, which were used to anticipate trends and stock prices. These models were constructed using frameworks such as TensorFlow, scikit-learn, and pandas. The platform's investment methods rely heavily on these forecasts.

Yahoo Finance API: The Yahoo Finance API is an invaluable resource for many applications since it offers a wealth of financial data, such as historical data, stock quotations, financial news, and market trends. With the use of the API's capability, users can obtain data for specific stocks, indexes, currencies, and commodities, facilitating in-depth research on international financial markets. We include the Yahoo Finance API into the platforms using basic HTTP requests. Through the use of this API, the platform is able to access a multitude of financial data for the purposes of doing market analysis, creating trading strategies, and learning about economic patterns. Furthermore, the Yahoo Finance API provides users with flexibility and customization choices so they adjust their data queries to meet certain needs.

(b) ***Data Pre-processing:*** For the purpose of preprocess stock market data for retirement planning applications, we suggest an original approach that combines Convolutional Neural Networks (CNN), Recurrent Neural Networks (RNN), and Long Short-Term Memory (LSTM) models. Our combined strategy makes use of each model architecture's advantages to efficiently capture temporal and spatial interdependence in the financial data. First, we take the raw stock market data and use CNNs to extract spatial patterns. Due to its ability to automatically learn hierarchical representations of input through convolutional layers, CNNs are a good fit for this task. CNNs are used in our preprocessing pipeline to extract pertinent features from the input data, including sentiment ratings, market trends, and technical indicators.

Figure 9. Combine approach of CNN and RNN

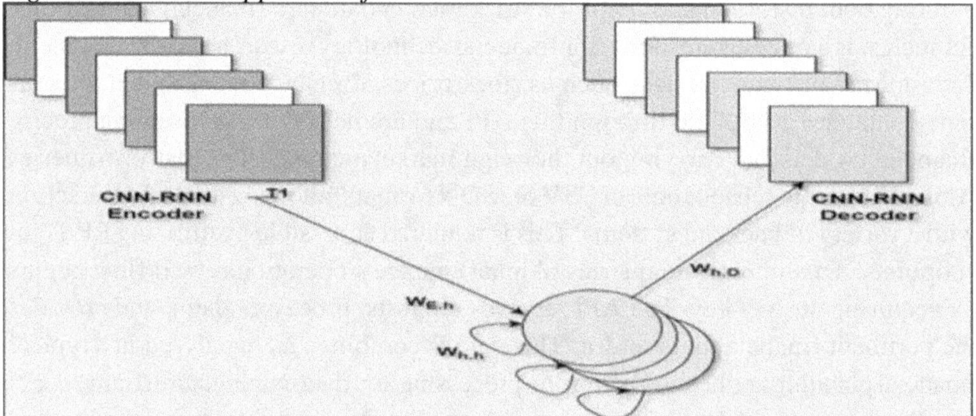

We afterwards apply the time-series stock market data to extract temporal dependencies using RNNs and LSTMs. Although algorithms have access to previous observations, RNNs and LSTMs are perfect for modelling sequential data. Our model can effectively capture the temporal dynamics of the financial markets, including trends, seasonality, and periodic patterns, by feeding the CNN layers' output into the recurrent layers. The output of the CNN-RNN-LSTM layers combined is then utilized to provide educational features for applications related to retirement planning. Historical stock prices, trading volumes, technical indicators, sentiment analysis scores, and economic indicators are a few examples of these elements. These components enable our model to offer individualized risk assessments, portfolio management plans, and investment recommendations based on each person's financial preferences and goals. The model is integrated into a comprehensive retirement planning framework. By means of comprehensive testing and verification on actual financial datasets, we exhibit the efficacy of our integrated methodology in preparing stock market data for retirement planning purposes.

(c) ***Data Storage:*** We are utilizing contemporary database technologies and frameworks that are effective in managing massive amounts of financial data to store the pre-processed stock market and retirement planning data. MongoDB, a NoSQL database that provides scalability and flexibility for storing both structured and unstructured data, is one such technology we take into consideration. Because of its customizable schema and document-oriented architecture, MongoDB is an excellent choice for storing a wide range of datasets, including user profiles, market prices, and technical indicators. Furthermore, relational data pertaining to user accounts, portfolio holdings, and transaction histories are stored in SQL databases. Because of their strong transaction support and query capabilities, relational databases such as SQL are well-suited for the management of structured data. In addition, we securely store and manage the databases using cloud-based storage solutions like Google Cloud Platform (GCP) and Amazon Web Services (AWS). With the scalability, dependability, and accessibility of cloud storage, we can store and retrieve financial data from any location with an internet connection.

(d) ***Security and Privacy:*** We deploy a variety of security technologies and procedures to safeguard sensitive financial data and reduce potential hazards to the data kept in the databases. Encryption is a crucial technique that we apply to convert data into a format that cannot be read without the right decryption key. Sensitive information kept in the databases is encrypted using Advanced Encryption Standard (AES), a popular encryption method renowned for its power and effectiveness. AES encryption guarantees sure that the encrypted data is safe and unreadable even in the event that someone gains illegal access to the database. We utilize access controls and authentication procedures in addition to encryption to limit who has access to the data and how they may employ it. Users are assigned particular roles and permissions according to their duties and responsibilities within the company through the usage of role-based access control, or RBAC. This guarantees that sensitive financial data is only accessible to authorized personnel and that access is limited in accordance with the least privilege principle. Finally, in order to find vulnerabilities and weaknesses in the database infrastructure, we regularly conduct security audits and assessments. We then swiftly install patches and updates to fix any security problems found. The availability, integrity, and confidentiality of the data kept in the databases are ensured by proactive security measures and ongoing monitoring, which also protect the data from cyberattacks, illegal access, and data breaches.

3.5 Investment Portfolio Management

The overall application encompasses key functionalities such as goal setting, retirement planning, budget tracking, feedback mechanism and risk assessment. Additionally, it provides personalized recommendations, monitors progress, and presents statistical data. Central to this application is investment portfolio management, which involves strategically handling a diverse array of investments to achieve specific financial goals while managing risk. Effective portfolio management includes crucial elements like asset allocation, diversifying investments across different asset classes (e.g., stocks, bonds, real estate) to balance risk and return. Risk assessment is vital, as it evaluates the investor's risk tolerance to determine the most appropriate investments. Continuous performance monitoring ensures investments remain aligned with financial goals, while periodic rebalancing maintains the desired asset allocation. Tax efficiency strategies are applied to minimize tax liabilities on investment gains, and cost management is essential to track fees and expenses associated with managing investments. Goal setting, both short-term and long-term, is a fundamental aspect of the process, guiding the overall strategy. Liquidity management ensures there is enough liquidity to meet short-term financial needs without disrupting the portfolio. The application visualizes data through pie charts, graphs, and comparative analyses. It features a multilingual interface and a voice assistant that reads statistical data and recommendations, enhancing usability, particularly in rural areas and diverse regions of India. All components are integrated into this section to effectively manage user profiles for optimal convenience and accessibility.

Figure 10. Overall wireframe of FinGenius

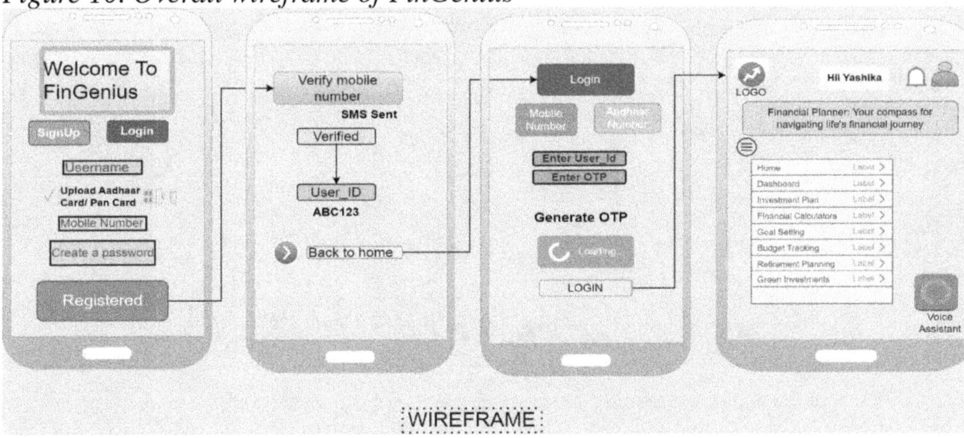

4. EXPERIMENTAL RESULTS

4.1 Stock Price Analysis

This study uses a complex model that combines the architectures of recurrent neural networks (RNN), convolutional neural networks (CNN), and long short-term memory (LSTM) to predict stock prices. The combined LSTM-CNN-RNN model makes use of each individual model's advantages to improve prediction accuracy. The method provides a strong comparison of forecast accuracy by using historical S&P stock data to benchmark the expected stock prices against actual market prices.

Sensitive information is secured during the prediction process thanks to sophisticated encryption algorithms that handle the security of financial data. This is accomplished by protecting the data integrity by encrypting and decrypting the model's keys. In order to optimize the model's parameters and boost prediction accuracy, the dataset is iterated over several times during the training and testing process, which spans 50 epochs. More accurate projections are produced as a result of this iterative method' assistance in identifying the complex patterns and trends in stock price movements.

Figure 11. Graph of actual vs predicted stock prices

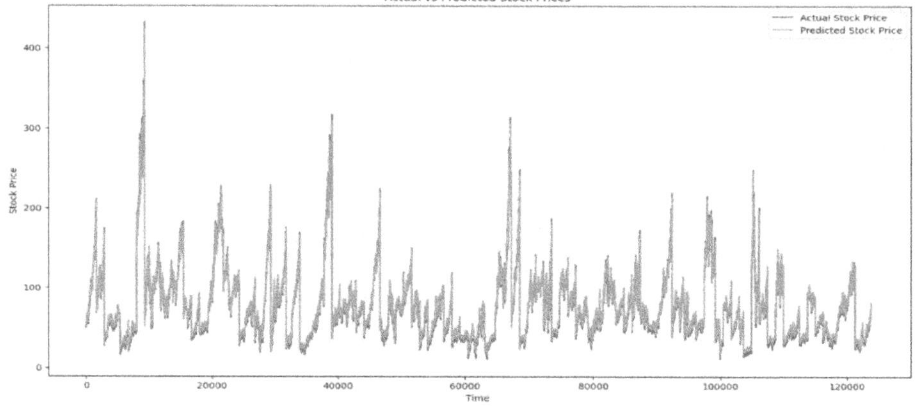

4.2 Budget Tracking Analysis

4.2.1 Model Training and Performance

Training Process: Sequences of past income, expenses, and investment returns were among the pre-processed financial data that were used to train the Random Forest and Deep Learning models. While the Deep Learning model used a combination of Recurrent Neural Networks (RNNs) and Long Short-Term Memory (LSTM) networks, the Random Forest model was set up with several decision trees.

Accuracy andperformance metrices: Validation datasets were used to assess the performance of the Random Forest and Deep Learning models, with an emphasis on important metrics including precision, recall, accuracy, and F1 score. With an F1 score of 0.83, accuracy of 0.84, recall of 0.82, and precision of 0.85, the Random Forest model performed well. By comparison, the RNN-LSTM, a Deep Learning model, performed better with an F1 score of 0.88, accuracy of 0.88, recall of 0.87, and precision of 0.89. These findings demonstrate how much better the Deep Learning model is than the Random Forest model at handling sequential financial data and forecasting financial outcomes. The enhanced metrics highlight the benefit of applying Deep Learning methods for accurate and trustworthy financial forecasts.

Table 2. Model performance metrics comparison

Model	F1 score	Accuracy	Recall	Precision
Random Forest Model	0.83	0.84	0.82	0.85
RNN-LSTM Model	0.88	0.88	0.87	0.89

4.2.2 Visualization and Interpretation

Loss Curves: Plotting the Deep Learning model's training and validation loss curves showed how the model converged during a 50-epoch period. The model successfully reduced loss and enhanced performance across the training period, as shown by the curves.

Figure 12. Loss curves using random forest and DL model

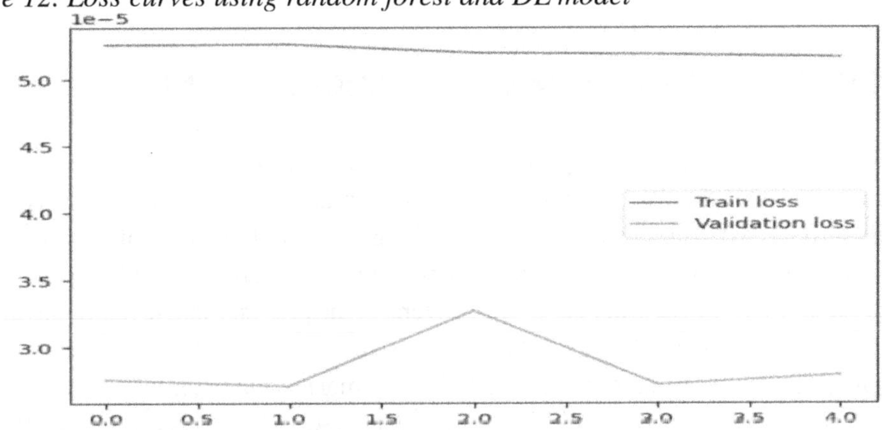

Actual vs. Predicted Values: Key financial indicator actual and predicted values were compared on graphs. These illustrations demonstrated how well the model anticipated financial events and gave clear insights into its predictive accuracy.

Figure 13. Actual and predicted graph of user's budget

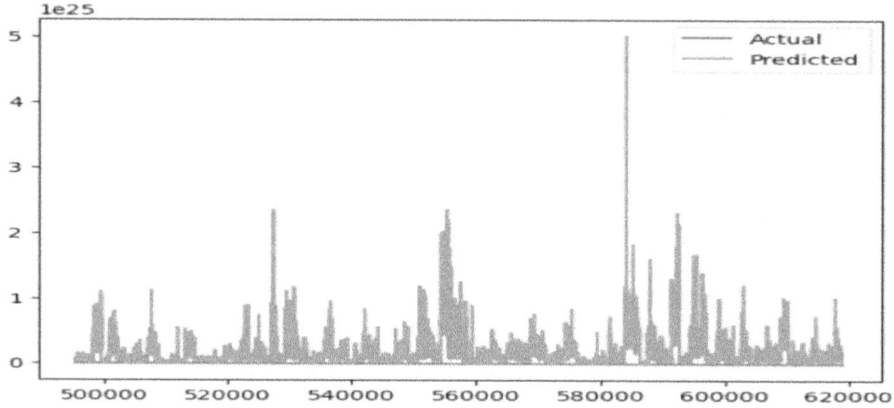

5. FEATURES OF AUTOMATIC FINANCIAL PLANNER

Voice Assistant: The integration of voice assistant into FinGenius is a step up in the right direction of making the best out of planning for the finances as a user, will converse with the assistant in naturals language. With the help of the commands for the financial operations, the customers can verify their account balance, get the desired savings or investment goals, and even get the professional investment advices all through the voice only. Also, the voice assistant will be able to convert statistics, graphs, and the so on and so forth, financial summaries and the like especially for the benefit of the Partially Sighted/Sight Impaired Persons. Such accessibility enhances the level of participation of the disabled persons in the platform hence improving the interlace of the service offered. Besides, the mid and far-field voice control does not only simplify the usage of the device but also increases the general comfort of users who can plan their finances without touching the device.

Multilingually: In the world where globalization is a trend, language could sometimes become the biggest problem when it comes to financial services. Multilingual support is still a challenge for many organizations that offer banking services and FinGenius is not an exception; to overcome this challenge, the platform supports multiple languages that clients can use while using the platform. This feature distances the platform from the realization that the ability to access financial planning service is hindered by language barriers, hence improving the versatility of the platform for its common users. In this case, FinGenius enables multiple language support promotes equality since people in different part of the world can use the platform in their own linguistic environment. This multicultural approach also improves the usability since users can interact with it personally and if a user feels that they cannot handle it due to their language ability challenges, they will find an easy way of handling it since other users may have used it assume it in various cultures, languages and interfaces.

Predictive Analysis: However, one of the most important components of FinGenius is based on machine learning which helps to predict the further trends and key events of the market. When analysing quantitative data as the basis for financial ratios and relating them to the context of previous years' financial statements, possible outcomes for investments, savings, or expenses can be determined. This arguably provides users with a unique ability to make analytical or managerial decisions based on data that improves the accuracy of their budgetary estimates. For example, FinGenius can give a definition on some likely market trends and assist users in how to best invest or save money based on the coming economic conditions. Since it involves the prediction of future financial behaviour using data, users are put in a position to correct their behaviour hence making it an important tool in improving financial planning to enhance future financial performance.

Real-time Data processing: With the use of real time data processing, FinGenius ensures that its users are provided with the latest information on the financial world. This feature makes it possible for the platform to capture, in real-time, movements in the financial activities so that insights can be generated in real-time. In financial data applications, real time processing is highly desirable since it enables users to work with current real time data on the circumstances in the market or the funds that have been shipped. For example, users can be notified regarding alterations of their investment portfolio, or whether market conditions are acceptable for given financial planning. Due to the timely speed of processing the financial data, it becomes a crucial solution for real-time money making or risk management opportunity that make or break the deal.

Feedback mechanism: The feedback mechanism included in the FinGenius architecture is a strong addition that allows the platform to improve itself by using previously collected information about user behaviour. Is will allow the platform to learn from the users' feedback and use it to enhance the recommendation algorithm, thus enhancing user experience as well as the improvement of the decision-making models on the platform. These advancements are achieved through an iterative development approach to continuously adapt to that of the users. For example, if users are always complaining to the effect that this piece of financial advice or that investment tip could be made more suitable for them, then FinGenius can adapt its programming codes to provide more client-centric solutions from the next time around. This improvement through feedback makes FinGenius flexible and confirms that it provides clients with unerring, timely, and customer-oriented guidance each time.

High security: There is always a major concern over data privacy especially when dealing with finances and FinGenius takes security into account. To ensure confidentiality of the users' financial data it uses methods such as encryption, cryptography and two-factor authentication. Because of strict security measures to follow, FinGenius avoids leakage of user data and consequently earns user trust especially those who depend on the application to manage their finances. Such a heightened level of security that is provided ensures that data including account details, and investment strategies, are safe from cyber criminals and thus giving users confidence when using the application to conduct their financial business.

Automation capabilities: Some of the most effectual elements of application are in the capability to address financial planning significance features including budgeting, investment and retirement systematically. In addition to decreasing the incidence of human error that often occurs when financial processes are performed manually, automation also helps facilitate financial activities, which take less time than when performed manually. For example, the user does not need to input the expenses to track them, set up new savings plan, or rebalance the investment portfolio depending on the current market rates all these events can happen without the user's interference and will be performed by FinGenius. It uses modern programmes, like CNN (Convolutional Neural Networks), RNN (Recurrent Neural Networks), and K-means clustering, all of which improve the accuracy and speed of financial choices. In this manner, FinGenius can help users save time for strategic plans for their financial life while the day-to-day financials are well managed. This increase in automation is not only time-saving but helps to keep users on budget and thus track their financial objectives.

6. CHALLENGES OF IMPLEMENTING AN AUTOMATED FINANCIAL PLANNER

FinGenius provides an effective solution to a number of financial planning problems, but creating and deploying such a sophisticated platform has its own set of troubles. Positively addressing these issues highlights the creative solutions and upcoming upgrades that can further boost the platform's effectiveness and user experience.

Data Privacy and Security: The first one is to ensure that information security and data privacy is well checked and upheld since some of the finances deal with critical information. To date, measures for the protection of user data include encryption, cryptography, and two-phase authentication at FinGenius. Nevertheless, the steady development of new threats requires constant investments in the growth of cybersecurity to restore users' trust in the platform.

User Adaptation and Learning Curve: The introduction of features such as predictive analytical tools and other forms of voice recognition require users who may not be very familiar with such technology to learn how the product works. To this, FinGenius responds with a user-friendly interface, as well as detailed user manuals that should make the process seamless. In addition, constant updates made with feedback from users should help lower the overall learning curve and give the platform a better chance of adapting to the expectations of its users.

Integration with External APIs: The integration of multiple APIs, for example, banking API provides via RazorPay and stock market via API from Alpha Vantage pose problems related to data compatibility issues and servicing. These problems are avoided by FinGenius by constantly engage with API providers and constantly vet the integration. In the future, one of the key development strategies of the platform is set on the growth of the API offering a wider range of extensive financial data to the users.

Accuracy of Predictive Models: The accuracy of financial predictions and recommendations depends on the quality and quantity of data available. *FinGenius* utilizes advanced machine learning and deep learning models to process and analyze data. Regular updates and model retraining with new data will help improve prediction accuracy, ensuring users receive the most reliable financial guidance.

Accessibility and Inclusivity: The issue of visibility for visually impaired and other users that are non-native in the English language will also continue to be an issue of concern with regards to FinGenius's accessibility. These and many more including a voice assistant and multilingual support form a strong foundation for inclusive solutions. subsequent releases will continue enhancing these features and adding more to allow the platform to serve as many users, as possible.

Real-time Data Processing: Handling and processing large volumes of financial data in real-time can be resource-intensive. *FinGenius* leverages cloud computing services such as AWS and GCP to manage this effectively. Ongoing optimizations in data processing algorithms and infrastructure will further enhance real-time capabilities, ensuring users receive timely and accurate insights.

Accuracy of predictive models: The quality and quantity of data incorporated in the platform play an important role in providing right financial forecasts and suggestions. Machine learning and deep learning concepts will initially be used while the enhancement of close-ended unconstrained models and their continued mass training with new data will be vital for FinGenius. These enhancements will continue through successive iterations to improve reliability of predictions and sustain user's confidence.

7. FUTURE SCOPE OF AUTOMATED FINANCIAL PLANNER: FINGENIUS

FinGenius has set a strong foundation in automated financial planning through advanced machine learning and deep learning techniques. Looking ahead, several exciting opportunities can further enhance its functionality, accessibility, and user engagement. These future developments promise to elevate *FinGenius* as a cutting-edge tool in financial management.

1. **Green Fund Investment:** Green Fund Investments may be considered one of the areas that should be further developed. Addressing the current trend towards ethical and sustainable investing, FinGenius is to expand its support of green funds by incorporating ESG factors into its suggestion engines. This addition will open a possibility for investing in the stocks that are in line with user's values and help support sustainable development goals. Thus, FinGenius can make sustainability as an accessible option by introducing the options like renewable energy funds or socially responsible investments.
2. **Gamification Features:** Gamification Features represent one more opportunity to extend the user engagement level. Financial planning can be a quite daunting and/ or repetitive task; the integration of game aspects will always impose a positive spin on the experience. Such components as budgeting, virtual savings reward system, quiz games, achievement to-do and save list, and challenges and goals established that can lure consumers to be persistent users. Thus, applying the principles relating to leaderboards and badges and such tangible incentives as pins, FinGenius will be able to enrich the users' experiences and make the process of financial existence more satisfying.
3. **Cloud Infrastructure:** Enhancing Cloud structures are necessary for operation enlargements and provision of uninterrupted real-time information analyses. Such opportunities for using the advanced services based on cloud computing technologies will allow FinGenius to avoid pointed problems and guarantee high availability, shorter response time and reliability even with high loads. Furthermore, cloud structures make it easy to release updates and new modules without interrupting demonstrations and improvements that will continue to be progressive.
4. **Blockchain Technology:** Blockchain Technology can be used to improve the operation of the given platform in terms of security and openness. The application of blockchain gives an opportunity to create a decentralized register of financial operations and prevalent manipulations, which provides reliability and adds confidence for users. It is possible to apply this technology in identity check,

payments monitoring and preventing frauds which will provide satisfaction with respect to the security of the personal information to the users.

5. **Augmented Reality (AR):** The use of Augmented Reality in developing financial applications holds the chance of changing how people perceive and manipulate the content. This way, intuitively presented in AR format, financial plans, investment portfolios or various budgeting scenarios become less complicated. A possibility to visualize the financial progress through the 3D models, to try out the results of investments, or to utilize Augmented Reality control panels for getting the real time data to improve decision making.
6. **Localization and Globalization:** As a result, Localization and Globalization will be the primary goals of FinGenius, as it targets clients all around the world. These will encompass issues to do with language, regulatory measures within the regions at large as well as culturally sensitive measures on financial advice. FinGenius can extend the framework's capability in understanding the context of users in different geographical locations to address the universal problem.
7. **Artificial Intelligence (AI)-Driven Personalization:** AI-Driven Personalization will be one of the key focal points in the development of FinGenius going forward. Through improving the methods of machine learning for the target prediction and understanding user characteristics, the platform can provide the best and more progressive product offers to the clients with proper changes in their financial activity. Everything from individualized investment services to interactive budgeting will be produced by AI – guaranteeing that the users receive the most valuable and useful recommendations.
8. **Integration with IoT Devices:** While we are on the topic, Integration with IoT Devices is another thrilling direction. Through activating the communication with wearable devices, smart home systems, and IoT sensors in financial trackers, FinGenius can deliver informative notifications. For instance, users may get spending notifications directly to their smart watch or monitor the progress of any saving goals through smart display within their homes.
9. **Educational Resources and Community Engagement:** Educational Resources and Community Engagement will be of high importance in the future development of FinGenius. Organizing free webinars, engaging tutorial sessions, and discussion groups or, even, financial help from one's friends and like-minded people can open the eyes of users and make them feel wanted. Also, with the help of AI, patterns with the user's questions and concerns could be detected and educational material could be provided in advance.

8. CONCLUSION

To summarize up, this study highlights how important it is to use cutting-edge machine learning methods to automate and optimize financial planning. The paper presents "FinGenius: An Automatic Financial Planner," a complex tool intended to overcome the drawbacks of conventional financial planning techniques, including problems with real-time processing, delayed management, and erroneous data. FinGenius improves the overall accuracy and effectiveness of financial management by using cutting-edge technologies to deliver customized financial recommendations.

FinGenius's primary strength is its capacity to forecast stock prices and manage budgets using sophisticated machine learning and deep learning models, including CNN, RNN, and LSTM. The stock price prediction model outperformed other models by catching intricate patterns and trends in historical S&P stock data. It does this by combining the LSTM, CNN, and RNN architectures. The model parameters were optimized through an iterative training procedure spanning 50 epochs, yielding exceptionally accurate stock price forecasts. This forecast accuracy highlights the robustness of the model and is essential for making well-informed investment decisions. FinGenius's interface with numerous APIs, including RazorPay for banking data, Twilio for authentication, and Alpha Vantage for real-time stock market data, enhances its all-inclusive approach to financial planning. The platform's usefulness and scalability are further increased by its utilization of Google Cloud Platform (GCP) and Amazon Web Services (AWS) for data retrieval, storage, and predictive modelling.

FinGenius utilizes Deep Learning and Random Forest models to evaluate financial data in the budget tracking domain. Using validation datasets, the models' performance metrics—precision, recall, accuracy, and F1 score—were assessed. With an F1 score of 0.83, accuracy of 0.84, recall of 0.82, and precision of 0.85, the Random Forest model performed well. Compared to the Random Forest model, the Deep Learning model—which merged RNN and LSTM networks—performed better, achieving an F1 score of 0.88, accuracy of 0.88, recall of 0.87, and precision of 0.89. These results highlight the superior capability of Deep Learning models in handling sequential financial data and predicting financial outcomes with higher accuracy.

REFERENCES

8 . Strategic risks in your financial advisory practice. (n.d.). Commonwealth Financial Network. https://www.commonwealth.com/insights/8-potential-risks-in-your-financial-advisory-practice

Ayalew, A. T., & Lohani, T. K. (2023). Prediction of Crop Yield by Support Vector Machine Coupled with Deep Learning Algorithm Procedures in Lower Kulfo Watershed of Ethiopia. *Journal of Engineering*, 2023, 1–8. DOI: 10.1155/2023/6675523

Chou, J., & Chen, K. (2024). Optimizing Investment Portfolios with a Sequential Ensemble of Decision Tree-Based Models and the FBI Algorithm for Effective Financial Indicator Analysis. *Applied Soft Computing*, 158, 111550. DOI: 10.1016/j.asoc.2024.111550

Dempster, M., & Leemans, V. (2006). An automated FX trading system using adaptive reinforcement learning. *Expert Systems with Applications*, 30(3), 543–552. DOI: 10.1016/j.eswa.2005.10.012

Donepudi, P. K. (2019). Automation and machine learning in transforming the financial industry. *Asian Business Review*, 9(3), 129–138. DOI: 10.18034/abr.v9i3.494

Gale, Iwry, & Orszag. (n.d.). The Automatic 401(k): A Simple Way To Strengthen Retirement Saving. Available: http://www.retirementsecurityproject.org

GeeksforGeeks. (2024, July 12). *Random Forest algorithm in machine learning*. GeeksforGeeks. https://www.geeksforgeeks.org/random-forest-algorithm-in-machine-learning/

Goyal, Y., Raj, Rai, H. M., Aggarwal, M., Saxena, K., & Amanzholova, S. (2023). *Revolutionizing Skin Cancer Detection: A Comprehensive Review of Deep Learning Methods*. DOI: 10.1145/3647444.3647885

Gunjan, A., & Bhattacharyya, S. (2022). A brief review of portfolio optimization techniques. *Artificial Intelligence Review*, 56(5), 3847–3886. DOI: 10.1007/s10462-022-10273-7

Horton, M. (2023, May 3). *Practice Management Guide for Financial Advisors*. Investopedia. https://www.investopedia.com/articles/professionals/080515/pros-cons-financial-advisor-career.asp

Lee, S. Y., Tama, B. A., Choi, C., Hwang, J., Bang, J., & Lee, S. (2020). Spatial and sequential deep learning approach for predicting temperature distribution in a Steel-Making continuous casting process. *IEEE Access : Practical Innovations, Open Solutions*, 8, 21953–21965. DOI: 10.1109/ACCESS.2020.2969498

Nti, I. K., Adekoya, A. F., & Weyori, B. A. (2019). A systematic review of fundamental and technical analysis of stock market predictions. *Artificial Intelligence Review*, 53(4), 3007–3057. DOI: 10.1007/s10462-019-09754-z

Schmitt, M. (2023). Automated machine learning: AI-driven decision making in business analytics. *Intelligent Systems with Applications*, 18, 200188. DOI: 10.1016/j.iswa.2023.200188

Sharma, G., Vidalis, S., Mankar, P., Anand, N., Minakshi, N., & Kumar, S. (2024). Automated passive income from stock market using machine learning and big data analytics with security aspects. *Multimedia Tools and Applications*. Advance online publication. DOI: 10.1007/s11042-024-19340-3

Vyas, A. (n.d.). *Robo-advisors as Automatic Personal Financial Advisors: Opportunities and challenges based on recent results and case studies - ProQuest*. https://www.proquest.com/openview/236788025e86a6c976475586ce751cf8/1?pq-origsite=gscholar&cbl=6447394

What is Financial Planning and Analysis (FP&A)? (n.d.). SAP https://www.sap.com/products/financial-management/what-is-financial-planning-and analysis-fpa.html

Chapter 8
Optimizing Theoretical Foundations and Implications of Time Travel:
From Relativity to Higher Dimensions and Beyond

Siddharth Rana
https://orcid.org/0009-0007-7542-7446
Dronacharya Group of Institutions, India

Hari Mohan Rai
https://orcid.org/0000-0003-2557-3510
International Information Technologies University, Kazakhstan

ABSTRACT

This chapter explores the theoretical foundations along with the vast implications of time travel from the theory of relativity to the concepts of higher dimensions. Derived from the Einstein's words embedded within the concept of relativity, this chapter provides a profound overlook upon the space-time continuum, allowing forward time-travel, while studying the multiple theoretical possibilities of backward time-travelling. This chapter provides a visualizations of the object approaching the speed of light and embarking beyond, unlocking the un-explored branches of the cosmos. Multiple visualization aspects to contemplate the lived-past and to-be-lived future have been visualized, connecting dots to every possibility of the entire cosmos. A unique aspect to understand the flow of the 4th dimension—time—has been overlooked from the 5th dimension, providing a complete access over the 4th

DOI: 10.4018/979-8-3693-6885-5.ch008

dimension, unfolding all-past and all-future simultaneously, while going beyond the conventional scope of human thinking. It addresses multiple aspects of time aiming to understand cosmos.

INTRODUCTION

Time-Travel consists of two words, 'Time' and 'Travel', meaning – to travel in Time. The movement of an individual travelling in Time can be compared to travelling on a Road (Banister, 2005). This journey involves transcending into the future, leaving all the lived moments behind in the past, at the unchanging rate of 1 second per second. Humans are, in essence, constantly time-travelling to the future, with every lived moment moving forward from the past. Remarkably, this movement through time does not require spatial movement; everyone is already moving in time regardless of any physical activity (Jha et al., 2023; Verma et al., 2022). On a larger scale, however, nothing in the universe is ever truly still – everything exists in a constant state of motion within the fabric of space-time (Bauer & Tulic, 2018).

Humans, as 3-dimensional beings, have the capacity to comprehend the 4th dimension – time – and experience its flow. While we are free to move in the 3 spatial dimensions in any direction (x, y, or z axis), we are restricted in our interaction with time, unable to move forward or backward at will. Humans are, as it stands, prisoners of the time dimension (Al-Khalili, 2003). Despite this limitation, we live with the perception of time constantly moving forward, into the future, without even being fully aware of its passage. Time Travel is a fascinating concept that allows us to question and contemplate the nature of reality and the lifespan of the universe itself, from its origins 13.8 billion years ago to its vastness, nearly 93 billion light-years in diameter (Du, 2022; Holtorf & Petersson, 2018). The scientific exploration of time travel traces back to 1905, when Albert Einstein introduced the world to a revolutionary idea of time as more than just a stubborn illusion. His paper, "On the Electrodynamics of Moving Bodies," laid the groundwork for the Special Theory of Relativity, where he explored the relationship between space, time, and motion (Saito, 2023). This landmark work opened the door to deeper discussions on time travel and its implications for the universe. Figure 1 presents a conceptual visualization of time travel based on Einstein's Special Theory of Relativity.

Figure 1. Conceptual framework of relativity and time travel

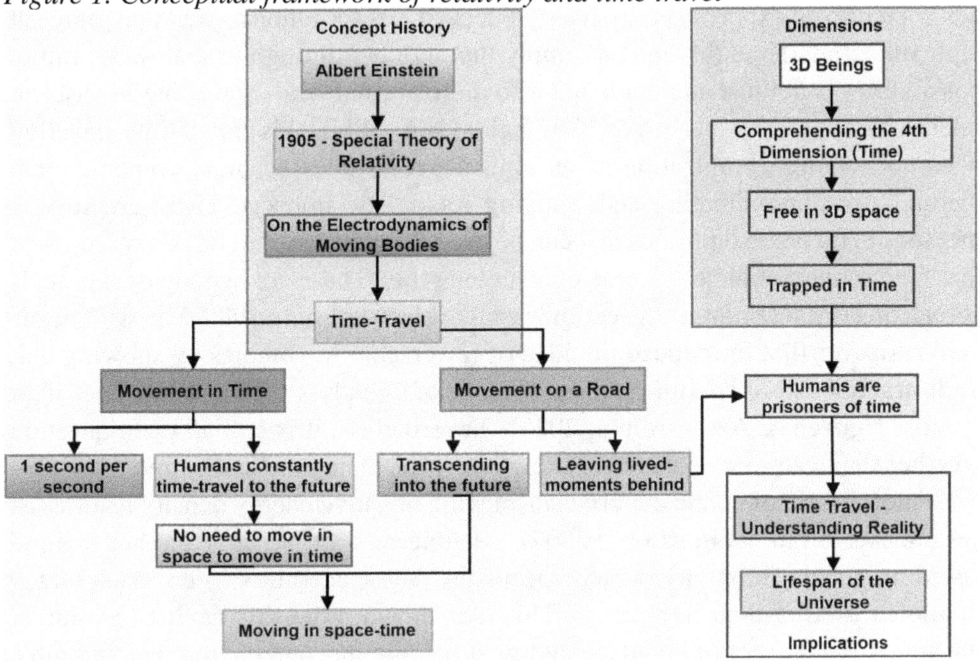

LITERATURE REVIEW

The concept of time travel has continuously caught people's attention in both literature and science. Numerous researchers have investigated many hypotheses and concepts to determine how time travel may function. This research shaped our knowledge of the potential and problems of time travel. Time travel has been a thrilling theme in science fiction and theoretical physics since the history of science. When it comes to the theory of relativity, time travel is a concurrent discussion affected by Albert Einstein's (Einstein, 1916) prediction of the space-time continuum which overturned our perception of space and time. Thus, according to the general theory of relativity suggested by Einstein, space and time are said to be existing as one four-dimensional continuum called spacetime. Besides, this concept also brought about the idea that massive objects could distort spacetime making "closed timelike curves" (CTCs) possible thereby enabling time travel as an example(Serdahely, 1990).

The theory of relativity is fundamental to understanding time travel in terms of modern physics. Special relativity, on the other hand, introduces time dilation as a concept whereby moving objects' clock slows down with respect to stationary observers at speeds close to that of light (Bergmann, 1962; Einstein, 1916). This has been proved experimentally like the decay rates for muons when they move at high velocities. Time dilation can imply that moving through time towards future possibilities is not just attainable but also quite normal while travelling in space at relativistic speeds(Misner et al., 1973; Wald, 1984). While this part of time-traveling does not require optimization as an aim, it necessitates accurate computational methods for approximating and studying relativistic impacts. There are several methods in theoretical physics that can be used for time travel. It has been proposed that wormholes could be one way of achieving this. These are hypothetical tunnels connecting distant points in spacetime just like black holes. In 1988, Morris, Thorne and Yurtsever first introduced the idea of traversable wormholes by showing that such structures would permit time travel if one of its ends is accelerated to near-light speeds (Nguyen & Azreg-Aïnou, 2023). Nevertheless, it is still an open question whether they can ever exist since the creation of their practical counterparts necessitates the use of exotic materials displaying negative energy density features as yet unobserved in nature (Lobo, 2007). Alcubierre warp drive is another method based on general relativity, which speculates that spacetime can be manipulated to allow for faster-than-light travel. This idea includes the ship having to contract the spacetime in front of it and expanding it behind thus making it move through a "warp bubble". Even though these suggestions push our knowing edge, they also impose massive requirements for computing power when modelling and optimizing the dynamics of such systems (Thorne et al., 1994).

The concept of parallel universes and other dimensions is another very important area in time travel literature. Many worlds interpretation (MWI) propounded by Hugh Everett III in 1957 suggests that all quantum events result into the universe splitting into many different timelines. Thus, this interpretation allows for the possibility of time travel without paradoxes, as actions done by a time traveler can cause him to form an entirely new timeline rather than transform the past of his own timeline(Haba et al., 2022). Moreover, the concept of time travel has been considered in various theories involving higher dimensions such as string theory. The theory of strings proposes that instead of point particles as fundamental building blocks of the universe, they are one-dimensional strings which vibrate in multidimensional spaces. Higher than four unobservable dimensions may offer new channels for time travel; but is speculative and requires complex mathematical models to test(Aguirre & Tegmark, 2011). Time travel research is computationally intensive, especially within the frameworks of general relativity and quantum mechanics. In order to solve Einstein's field equations which describe how matter-energy determines space-time curvature, an enormous amount of computational power and advanced numerical methods are required. Enhancing computational efficiency by applying Optimization techniques is critical for these simulations. Such approaches like parallel computing, algorithmic optimizations, and machine learning algorithms have been increasingly used in dealing with complex mathematical models that are involved in time-travel research (Haba et al., 2022). A good example is how in recent times the use of machine learning has gained support to refine the search for solutions to Einstein field equations(McKenzie, 2020). This can be achieved through training models on known solutions thereby making it possible to predict and generate new ones more quickly that may shed light on possibilities of time travel. Also, quantum computing based on the principles of quantum mechanics seems an excellent approach to optimize time travel simulations, such as modelling quantum states and investigating the effects of quantum entanglement in time travel scenarios(Y. Wang, 2012). In the research, understanding and optimizing causal models are essential for time travel. For instance, causality is one of the basic principles that any viable theory of time travel must reconcile (Deutsch, 1991a). The development of computational models that accurately simulate and optimize causal interactions in potential time travel scenarios is an ongoing area of research. Some techniques used to model causal relationships in time travel include causal inference and Bayesian networks which help avoid paradoxes and inconsistencies in theoretical models(-Deutsch, 1991b). Although time travel is still a theoretical concept, the meeting point of time travel research with computational optimization offers an exciting future potential. Advances in computational power, algorithmic efficiency, and quantum computing could eventually facilitate a greater appreciation for temporal transportation possibilities as well as their implications. The integration of optimization techniques will continue to be important as researchers refine these models in order to push the boundaries of what can be feasibly computed thus drawing us closer to making time travel a reality. Overall, time travel research lies at the intersection of various disciplines including theoretical physics, computational mathematics and optimization techniques. The review is made on the literature points out the immense challenges and prospects faced in this area mainly relating to improving computational efficiency. As much as time travel may sound speculative in nature; the development of ongoing optimization tools and techniques will be essential in understanding this incredible theory better than it was before.

THE CONCEPT OF TIME DILATION

Special Theory of Relativity presented a special case of moving bodies relative to the speed of light; The time of a moving body ticks slower, relative to a stationary observer, as measured from the rest frame – and called as *Dilated Time*. It does not mean that the clocks on the moving body only "appear" to slow down – the clock "actually" gets slow – The mechanical hands of the clock, and the biological processes of an individual, on the moving body and even the perception of time as well, all gets slow down with the motion, more noticeable when approaching the Speed of Light (Ma et al., 2021; Verma et al., 2022). Later in the year 1915, Albert Einstein generalized the concept of slowing time by introducing the effect of gravity, in his paper – "The Field Equation of Gravity", famously known as the General Theory of Relativity; He mentioned that, time slows down with gravity, in other words, as an object comes in the vicinity of a higher gravitational potential, its time slows down with respect to the other objects present in relatively lower gravitational potential (Trakas, 2023). Humans comprehend the perception of time by witnessing the causality (cause-and-effect), and since photons are the fastest known particles that allow us to perceive the causality, this makes them the very first medium to initiate the sense of seeing, and thus perceive the causality, and comprehend the perception of time (Al-Khalili, 2003; X. Wang et al., 2021). If a photon covers a longer distance, to reach the eyes of an observer, thus taking a longer time, this makes the perception of time slow down, relative to the other photon, covering a shorter distance and thus arriving earlier. In the case of an object in motion, the light from the event (accounting for the motion), travels relatively a longer distance, thus taking more time to reach the eyes of an observer, thus time slows down for an object in motion, as measured from the rest frame (Deutsch, 1991a; Topcu & Hirst, 2022). It should be noted that time measured inside the moving frame (by an observer), will tick at a normal rate, as the object would not be moving "inside" the frame of reference – the object would be at rest with respect to the moving frame. In other words, every object inside the moving frame would account for the motion, and with respect to the moving frame, every object inside, will be at rest, and thus the time, as measured inside the moving frame will tick at a normal rate – and called as *Proper Time*. In the moving frame, the photon will cover a normal distance, and thus there wouldn't be such a Time Dilation factor at all. Visualize two mirrors bouncing off a ball of a photon, up and down, placed inside a spaceship, consisting of a window so that this arrangement can be seen from outside. The complete motion of this photon going up and then coming back down (tick and tock) is registered as 1 second in the clock. *(Let us consider, it is possible to see the bouncing ball of a photon.)* You are on Earth, with a powerful telescope you are constantly observing this spaceship undergoing motion. Your friend Elon is present inside that spaceship, waving at you. From the perspective (or frame of reference) of Elon, who is sitting inside the moving space-ship, he would see the photon taking a straight up-down path, registering 1 second (tick and tock) in his clock (inside the moving space-ship) (Read & Le Bihan, 2021). On the other hand, from your perspective, observing the space-ship from Earth, you would see the photon taking a longer "diagonal" path instead of a straight up and down path – the upward velocity will slightly be translated to the horizontal velocity, resulting in a

Diagonal path, as this whole arrangement is in motion along with the whole moving space-ship, this would make the arrangement carry-forward with the forward motion of the space-ship, thus photon will take a longer diagonal path, accounting for the motion, instead of the straight up and down the path (Bauer & Tulic, 2018; Gupta et al., 2021). Due to this, the photon will take a longer time to complete its movement to register time (tiiick and tooock) – you would observe that the photon is taking longer than 1 second to complete its motion (up and down) (Lobo, 2007; Nguyen & Azreg-Aïnou, 2023). Therefore, the time registered in your clock, of the bouncing photon (-event), will be more than the time registered by Elon sitting inside the moving space-ship. In other words, the time of the moving body slows down as measured from a rest frame. This is the Special Theory of Relativity. Note that, the faster the space-ship moves or the closer it moves to the speed of photons (or light), the more the diagonal path will shift to the horizontal path, and moving at the speed of the photons, will completely translate the motion in the horizontal direction, and thus the photon will not move at all, therefore, there will be no perception of time, measured from a rest frame (Bergmann, 1962; Saito, 2023). What would happen if the speed is further increased? In the above discussion, we have ignored the other factors having a significant effect on the moving bodies such as *Length Contraction* and *Mass Dilation*.

- Length Contraction: The Length of an object contracts with speed.
- Mass Dilation: The observed Mass (or the Energy) of an object increases with speed.

From the above discussion, it is presented that one can travel to the Future by travelling relatively faster than others or being in a higher gravitational potential zone. However, travelling to the Past, more importantly, the past that one lived, is a No-Go. Many physicists have concluded that – "It is quite impossible to travel to the Past" and "There might be a physical law, yet to be discovered, that would prevent travelling to the past." Some physicists came up with the limitations to travelling to the past – You would require negative energy (or negative mass) to bend the space-time fabric in a reverse direction, allowing you to move backwards in time, however, even thinking about the negative mass (or energy) is beyond the scope of Human Understanding (Al-Khalili, 2003). Albert Einstein, in his General Theory of Relativity, presented a profound understanding and visualization of Gravity. Newton discovered Gravity, sitting under a tree (as they say), however, he wasn't quite sure what initiates gravity. He did know that there exists some mysterious force between two bodies in space that is attracting them towards each other, however, he didn't know how does that happen. Albert Einstein didn't come up with much new, however, he built from where Newton ended his work, in other words,

Einstein's theory is an expansion of Newton's laws; Newton's laws work precisely for the object experiencing a lesser speed or in under lower gravity, and Einstein's work expanded the laws of Newton, allowing them to work beyond. When you put lower speed and lower gravity in Einstein's equation, they become Newton's Law (Verma et al., 2022).

The Twin Paradox

It is a thought experiment in physics that validates the words of Einstein – *"Moving clock ticks slower as observed from a rest frame, thus are in the future"*. It shows that the time of one of the twin brothers, who travel on a spaceship, moving near the speed of light, would tick slow with respect to the time of the other brother who stayed on Earth. When the brother returns from space to Earth, he will age younger than his brother who stayed on Earth. Only a few years would have passed for the brother in space, however, many years would have passed for the brother (and for the people) on Earth (Banister, 2005; Younus et al., 2023). They would no longer be of the same age as they were before. Table 1 presents the Key concepts and mathematical formulas in relativity with respect to time travel.

Table 1. Key concepts and mathematical formulas in relativity with respect to time travel

Concept	Description	Mathematical Formula	Implications
Time Dilation	Time measured on a moving body (relative to a stationary observer) ticks slower.	$\Delta t = \frac{\Delta t_0}{\sqrt{1 - \frac{v^2}{c^2}}}$	Time on the moving body slows down relative to the stationary observer as velocity v approaches c.
Proper Time	Time measured inside the moving frame ticks at a normal rate.	Δt_0	No time dilation effect is observed within the moving frame itself.
Length Contraction	The length of an object contracts with speed.	$L = L_0\sqrt{1 - \frac{v^2}{c^2}}$	Objects appear shorter in the direction of motion as velocity v increases.
Mass Dilation	The observed mass (or energy) of an object increases with speed.	$m = \frac{m_0}{\sqrt{1 - \frac{v^2}{c^2}}}$	The mass of an object increases as its velocity v approaches c.
Twin Paradox	A thought experiment where one twin travels near the speed of light and returns younger than the twin who stayed on Earth.	$\Delta t_{Earth} = \gamma \Delta t_{space}$	Shows the time dilation effect, where the traveling twin ages slower relative to the stationary twin.

continued on following page

Table 1. Continued

Concept	Description	Mathematical Formula	Implications
General Theory of Relativity	Time slows down in a stronger gravitational field; higher gravitational potential means slower time.	$\Delta t = \Delta t_0\sqrt{1-\frac{2GM}{rc^2}}$	Time passes slower closer to a massive object compared to a location farther away.
Photon Path in Moving Frame	In a moving spaceship, the photon takes a diagonal path due to the ship's motion, making it appear to take longer from the stationary frame.	Path Length= $\sqrt{(c\Delta t)^2 - (v\Delta t)^2}$	Observers see the photon travel a longer path due to the combination of vertical and horizontal motion.

Where v is the velocity of the moving object, c is the speed of light, Δt is the time measured by the stationary observer, Δt_0 is the proper time measured inside the moving frame, L is the length measured in the moving frame, L_0 is the proper length of the object at rest, m is the relativistic mass, m_0 is the rest mass, γ is the Lorentz factor given by $\gamma = \frac{1}{\sqrt{1-\frac{v^2}{c^2}}}$, $\left(\text{Path Length}\right)$ is the diagonal path length of the photon as observed from the stationary frame, G is the gravitational constant, and M is the mass of the gravitational source. r is Radial coordinate (distance from the center of the gravitational source).

We can calculate the ages of brothers using the Time Dilation formula. Figure 2 shows the Flow Diagram for age calculation using the time dilation formula. There are twin brothers named – Albert and Newton (aged 30 years); Newton has always been fascinated by the never-ending space while Albert wondered upon the Mathematics of the Universe to comprehend the voices of the Universe. Newton got a chance to live his dream of leaping beyond Earth's atmosphere and travelling across space, he hopped onto a spaceship and later realized it to be a conspiracy to test what would happen to a living-being travelling at a faster rate. The spaceship traveled at 80% of the speed of light for 5 years. Newton measured 5 years at his clock while in the spaceship and returned back to Earth to meet and expose the conspiracy. Let us calculate the age of both the brothers. Newton's age: 30 + 5 = 35 years (No change would be here). Albert's age: He wouldn't tell his age, but he would show the age by using the formulas of his own creations – the Time Dilation formula.

$$t' = \frac{t^*}{\sqrt{1-\frac{v^2}{c^2}}}$$

Where, t' is the Time of the brother who stayed on Earth (Time of Albert) – measured from Earth (at rest) – (*To be calculated),* t * is the Time of the brother who is travelling on the space-ship (Time of Newton) – measured within the space-ship (in motion), v is velocity with which the space-ship is travelling, and c is the speed of light. Newton measured his time to be 5 years while moving on the spaceship for the span of 5 years. So, here (t*) would correspond to 5 years, i.e., t* = tN (Newton's Time on the Spaceship) = 5; Here, the velocity (v) would correspond to 0.80c (80% of c). Injecting all the values into the formulas, Einstein came up with his time. t' = tE (Einstein's Time on Earth) = 8.35; Einstein came up with an answer that his clock would show that almost 8 and a half years would have passed for him on Earth, whereas his brother Newton would only have experienced 5 years on the spaceship. In other words, 8.35 years of the Earth corresponds to 5 years of the moving spaceship. Newton has come 8.35 years into the future in 5 years – taking a shorter path "in-time" compared to everybody (including his brother Einstein) back on Earth. Thus, the Time Dilation.

Figure 2. Time dilation framework

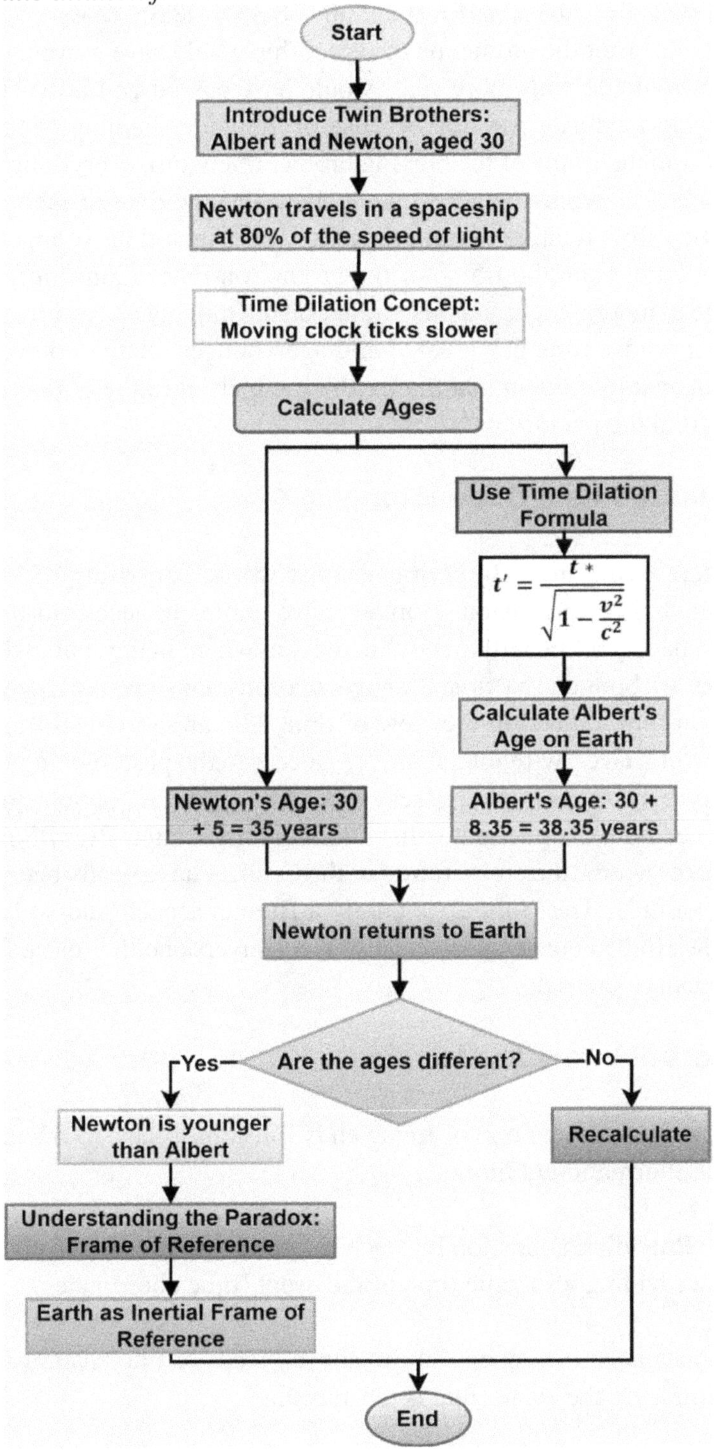

The age of both the brothers:

Newton: 30 + 5 = 35 Years; Einstein: 30 + 8.35 = 38.35 Years

Note that, the faster the brother on the spaceship would have moved, the extreme time dilation would be, thus more years would have passed on Earth. This thought experiment is termed as a paradox because of the understanding of the frame of reference – From the frame of the moving brother (Newton), everything else would be in motion and he would be at rest, so it should be the time of the whole world that should tick slow relative to him, thus the world should be younger than him. On the other hand, from the frame of the brother on Earth (Einstein), everything else would be in motion including his brother on the moving spaceship, so it should be his brother whose time gets dilated and age younger relative to everybody on Earth. It is taken into account that the Earth is an inertial frame of reference – thus coming out from the paradox.

Time Visualized as a Dimension

Humans are living in a (3+1) dimensional world, consisting of 3 spatial dimensions and 1 time dimension. Humans have complete access to the 3 spatial dimensions – having a free will to move across anywhere in the spatial dimensions, however, they are bounded by time, trapped in a constant flow, moving towards the future. Humans are trapped in the flow of time, like an individual trapped in the constant flow of a river, without having any access to the past, moving towards the unknown future. Humans might possess Free will – choosing options to live in the future, however, on a Cosmic scale, that doesn't really matter. Everything has been laid out, in other words, the entire future of the Cosmos has already been embedded within each particle. The "future" is purely a Human aspect (and so is time) that lies within the Human consciousness only. The Universe neither has a future nor a past – it just exists; eternal.

The Concept of When and Where

Imagine, if I must meet one of my friends Einstein, I have to mention at least two essential information to him-:

- Where: Providing a location in space (3 coordinates; X-Y-Z axes)
- When: Providing a specific time of the event (time coordinate)

The disappearance of any one of the above pieces of information will lead to failure in witnessing the event (that is our meeting).

- Without "When": We can be present at the mentioned location, however at different times.
- Without "Where": We can be present at the mentioned time, however at different locations.

Thus, it is quite mandatory to specify both space and time of an event, Space-time.

Visualizing Dimension-Travel

Humans are bound in time, most of the movements are dedicated to Time only, with almost negligible movement in space. This can be traced on a graph. Note that an object moving entirely in space, would have a horizontal line, parallel to the space-axis, i.e. there will be no movement in time, for that object. In other words, an object moving at the speed of light would leap beyond the boundness of time and might possess complete access over the time-dimension (Nguyen & Azreg-Aïnou, 2023; Y. Wang, 2012).

Humans are living in a (3+1) dimensional world, having complete access over the 3 spatial dimensions, and trapped in the flow of 1-time dimension. This can be generalized as: an individual living in a (n+1) dimensional world, would possess complete access over the nth dimension, and would be trapped in the $(n+1)^{th}$ dimension. In addition to that, the nth dimension would always be finite and the $(n+1)^{th}$ dimension would be infinite in nature. Currently, Humans possess a limited space (-3rd dimension) encompassed within the unlimited time (- 4th dimension). Based on this generalization, if an individual has to gain complete access over the 4th dimension (time), he/she must be in the (4+1) dimension or the 5th dimension. And in the 5th dimension, the 4th dimension – Time would become all-finite, thus providing complete access over the 4th dimension, while being encompassed within the in-finite 5th dimension (Banister, 2005; Debnath et al., 2013; Trakas, 2023).

Visualizing the 5th Dimension

If you were asked to point consistent object, you could point at it in space utilizing 3 spatial coordinates, however, if you were asked to point at a certain moment in time, you cannot point any-where (any-when), because a 'moment' consist of time coordinates and it is not possible to point any-when, while having access only till the 3rd dimension. However, once you leap to the 5th dimension, having all access to the 4th dimension, you would be able to point at any moment at any-when in your worldline (space-time line), from your 5th dimension (Bartlett, 2023). In the 5th dimension, an individual's flow to the future, in time, can be mapped to a collection of freeze frames, like a video broken down into multiple images. Where each image leads the flow or continuity to the next image carrying the continuity, thus being perceived as a video when observed together (FEDOSIN, 2012). In other words, in the 5th dimension, the complete flow of time from the past to the future would just exist eternally, there would neither be any beginning nor an end to it, quite similar to how we experience eternal space in the current 4th dimension. Note that, the frames of an individual cannot be experienced (or perceived) while being trapped in the constant flow of time, in the 4th dimension (as we are currently). This can only be experienced from a higher dimension – the 5th dimension (Bartlett, 2023; FEDOSIN, 2012). The faster an individual would move in space (or in the nth dimension), the lesser the frames (of time – the (n+1)th dimension) would be, as perceived from the 5th dimension [(n+1)+1] – here "n" is the dimension where the individual has complete access over. When an individual possesses a speed equivalent to the speed of light, there would exist only one still frame, as observed from the higher dimension, i.e. the movement in time would stop, as observed from the 5th dimension (Al-Khalili, 2003; Bartlett, 2023). When the individual takes a leap beyond the conventional speed of light, a higher dimension emerges and embraces the individual; the individual would then be in a 5-dimensional world, having complete access over the 4th dimension – able to perceive the frames that he/she left behind, present in an eternal temporal form, beyond the physical form of human (FEDOSIN, 2012; Verma et al., 2022).

Conventional Approach to Think About Time Travel

We have discussed that it is quite possible and almost feasible to travel to the future, by going relatively faster, and travelling to the past is not possible. However, in many science-fictions, time travelling has been depicted in a quite feasible manner, allowing an individual to meet and greet his/her past-self or the future-self while having no severe impact on him/herself.

Figure 3. Depiction of a timeline

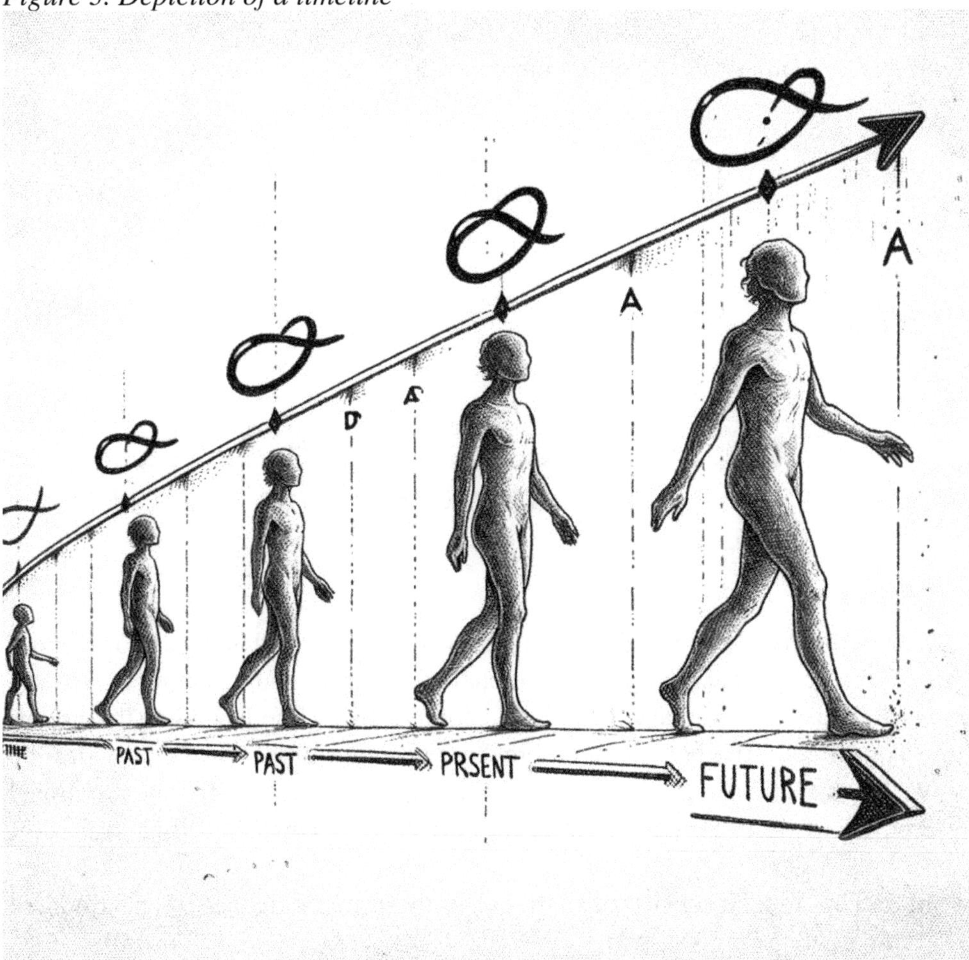

Most the science-fiction, Time is demonstrated as a single-line – TimeLine, consisting of the Past and the Future, where the causality leads into the future, maintaining the flow of the TimeLine, as shown in Figure 3. In those fictions it is assumed that there will exist a past-self or the future-self, to be greeted and meet in the past or the future, profoundly manifesting Time Travelling (Al-Khalili, 2003).

Alternate TimeLine: Allowing Time Travelling to the Past

Figure 4. Depiction of the alternate timeline

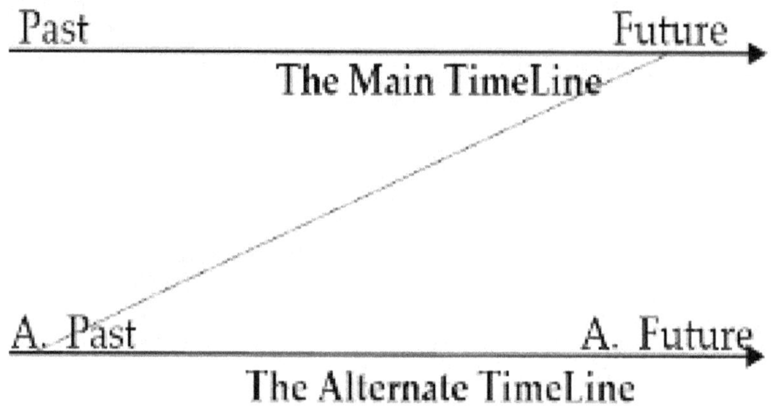

Most of the Paradoxes (or all) of Time Travelling are associated with Time Travelling to the Past, breaking the cause of chains of events, thus creating a two-way loop – Möbius strip. Alternate TimeLine is a loop-hole in Time Travelling that allows Time Travelling to the Past, without breaking any causality Figure 4 provides the pictorial representation of the main time vs alternate timeline based on the time travel concept. There are two types of TimeLines involved in Time Travelling scenario:

1. Main TimeLine: It consists of all the events that are experienced by an individual throughout his/her life span.
2. Alternate TimeLine: It is a replica of the Main TimeLine, copy-pasting all the significant events from the Main Timeline, however, it wouldn't exist initially. Its creation will take place only when there is an attempt made, to time travel to the past, running parallel to the Main TimeLine.

It should be noted that any event that occurred on the Alternate TimeLine, would have no effect on the Main TimeLine, they would have a separate flow and exist in different realities (or in different Universes). Both the TimeLines cannot run simultaneously – If there exists an Alternate TimeLine, the flow of the Main TimeLine must be stopped. In other words, when there is a break on the Main TimeLine (breaking Causality), there would be a creation of an Alternate TimeLine. Every event that shouldn't be supposed to happen on the Main TimeLine (as it already happened in the Past or the Future) will get mapped to an Alternate TimeLine. This approach provides us with an explanation to think about the major Time Travel paradoxes, specifically associated with Time Travelling to the Past [Fig.4] (Bauer & Tulic, 2018).

The Grandfather Paradox

It's not specifically about the Grandfather, the simpler version for this goes as follows: If an individual travelled to the past and prevented his/her parents from meeting each other, he/she would never born, and so does, never time travel to the past in the first place – and since, there was no time travel to the past, that would mean that there was no one to prevent the meeting of the parents, and since they met, the traveler would be born only to time travel to the past, and later on carrying the whole events in a "sort-of" a Loop. – This is the Paradox – until there's only one Main TimeLine. Introduction of Alternate TimeLine to paradoxes involving Time Travelling to the past, allows an individual to take a leap to a completely different reality and prevents any past-event in that reality would not have any effect on the individual itself, as the events would belong to a different TimeLine Reality (or different Universe). In the above case, when the individual travels to an Alternate Past (in a different reality), and prevents his/her parents from meeting each other, this would be carried forward in the Alternate TimeLine. In the Alternate Future, there will be no traveler, as the parents never met each other. However, the original travel will still remain to exist, as he/she belongs to the Main TimeLine (Banister, 2005; Younus et al., 2023). It should be noted that, when the traveler moves to the Alternate TimeLine, this would stop the flow of the Main TimeLine, i.e. there will be no future for the traveler on the Main TimeLine, the only future at that point will exist on the Alternate TimeLine. In other words, the Main TimeLine and Alternate TimeLine cannot flow simultaneously, if there exists an Alternate TimeLine – the Main TimeLine has to stop flowing and if the Main TimeLine is flowing – there exists No Alternate TimeLine.

The traveler may return back to the Main TimeLine, after accomplishing his/her mission, at the point when he/she previously time traveled back, continuing the flow of the Main TimeLine, and later to live happily afterwards (Saito, 2023; Younus et al., 2023). Concepts, implications, and corresponding examples of time travel and alternate timelines is presented in Table 2.

Table 2. Concepts, implications, and corresponding examples of time travel and alternate timelines

Concept	Description	Implications	Examples
Conventional Time Travel	Theoretical possibility of traveling to the future by moving faster; traveling to the past is considered impossible. Science fiction often depicts time travel as feasible, allowing interaction with past or future selves without severe consequences.	Suggests a future where time travel could be a reality; raises questions about causality and the nature of time.	Movies like “Back to the Future” where characters interact with their past or future selves.
TimeLine	A single line representing the continuum of time, consisting of the Past and the Future. It maintains causality and the flow of events.	Ensures a consistent progression of events; changes in the past affect the future in a linear fashion.	The classic depiction of time as a straight line in various science fiction narratives.
Alternate TimeLine	A secondary timeline created when traveling to the past, running parallel to the Main TimeLine. It replicates significant events from the Main TimeLine but does not affect it.	Allows for the possibility of altering past events without disrupting the original timeline; avoids paradoxes.	“The Butterfly Effects” where small changes in the past create different outcomes in an alternate timeline.
Main TimeLine	The primary timeline containing all events experienced by an individual throughout their life.	Represents the primary sequence of events and experiences for an individual; changes to this timeline have broad impacts.	The original storyline in a time travel narrative, such as in “Doctor Who” where the main timeline is followed.
Alternate TimeLine Creation	Occurs when someone attempts to travel to the past, creating a parallel timeline that does not affect the Main TimeLine. Events in this timeline exist separately in a different reality or universe.	Enables the exploration of “what if” scenarios without altering the established history of the Main TimeLine.	In the “Avengers: Endgame,” time travel creates alternate realities, separate from the main timeline.
The Grandfather Paradox	A time travel paradox where an individual traveling to the past and altering events (e.g., preventing their parents from meeting) creates a loop: the traveler would not exist to perform the action, thus creating a logical contradiction.	Highlights the complexities and contradictions inherent in time travel; suggests that altering the past may create logical inconsistencies.	Classic example in “Back to the Future” where Marty McFly prevents his parents from meeting, risking his own existence.

continued on following page

Table 2. Continued

Concept	Description	Implications	Examples
Resolution via Alternate TimeLine	The introduction of an Alternate TimeLine resolves paradoxes by separating events into different realities. An individual can alter events in an Alternate TimeLine without impacting their own Main TimeLine.	Provides a way to avoid paradoxes by ensuring that changes in one timeline do not affect another; supports the concept of multiple realities.	In "Rick and Morty," characters often create and interact with alternate realities where different outcomes occur.
Interaction with Alternate TimeLine	When a traveler moves to an Alternate TimeLine and changes events, it affects only that timeline. The original traveler continues to exist in the Main TimeLine. The Main TimeLine stops when the traveler is in the Alternate TimeLine and resumes when they return.	Indicates that while traveling in an Alternate TimeLine, the original timeline is in a state of suspension; traveler's actions have consequences only in the alternate reality.	In "The Terminator," actions taken by characters in the past affect an alternate future while the original timeline progresses.

Alternate TimeLine within an Alternate TimeLine

Figure 5. Alternate timeline(s) within the alternate timeline

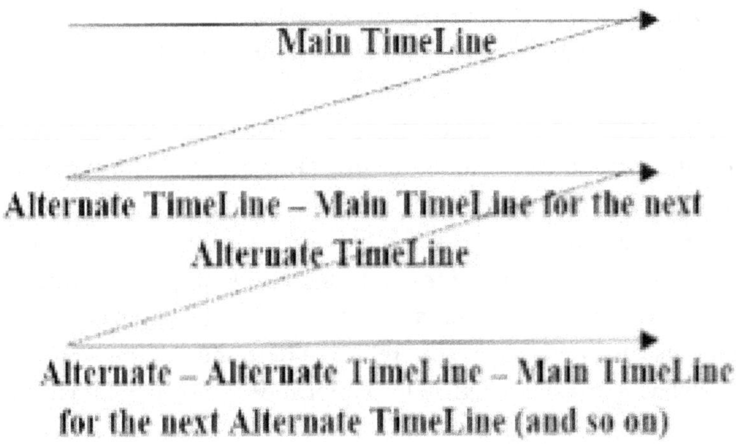

If an individual Time Travels, from an existing Alternate TimeLine, there would be a creation of yet another Alternate TimeLine (of the Alternate TimeLine), where the existing Alternate TimeLine will act as a Main TimeLine for the very next Alternate TimeLine. In this way, there can be a series of Alternate TimeLines – Alternate TimeLines within Alternate TimeLines as shown in Figure 5, or different Universes within Universes(Deutsch, 1991b). The individual may keep jumping to these series of Alternate TimeLine, existing in a completely new realm, each time he/she travels to the Past. And the event happening in the later Alternate TimeLines would have no impact over the previous TimeLines. There would remain Causality. (It should be noted that there would lie different causality for different TimeLines or Universes.) Note that, there will be no creation of Alternate TimeLine on Time Travelling to the Future, as in this model, the future is yet to be created – and even if it exists – exist in the Future that will lead the Causality instead of breaking it (Aguirre & Tegmark, 2011).

Fixing the Flow of the Main TimeLine: Returning Back to the Main TimeLine

It has been discussed that once there is creation of an Alternate TimeLine takes place, the flow of the Main TimeLine will stop, in other words, there will be no Future for the Main TimeLine, and everything that ever existed on the Main TimeLine will now be existing in an Alternate form, on the Alternate TimeLine. This can be put forward in the following manner: Every possibility of an event already exists in the form of *Many-TimeLines*, instead of existing in Alternate TimeLine(s), and in the Future, there exists only one outcome among the Many-TimeLines; while other gets switched OFF and the one which exists in the Future gets switched ON [Fig.5] (Nguyen & Azreg-Aïnou, 2023; Topcu & Hirst, 2022).

If an individual prevents his/her parents from ever meeting each other – he/she didn't prevent it, instead the traveler switched ON this possibility among Many-TimeLines at the Past, in other words, the event where the Parents were prevented from ever meeting each other, already exist in a "Turned-OFF" form until the traveler arrives a switch it ON. Thus, the TimeLine gets pruned on self (like self-healing or self-creating), every time there is Time Travel. In a nutshell, every possibility for an event exists in *Many-TimeLines*, yet only one makes the Future. And every attempt made to change the past or break the causality will switch ON, the respective TimeLine(s), thus turning on to a new reality where the 'change' would lead to a new Future (lead by a new switched – ON TimeLine). The other TimeLine(s) would have no causality – these would be *Dead TimeLine(s)*, where the event doesn't lead to any further Future, every event would lie there as a Constant eternal-reality. When the traveler returns to the original TimeLine, this would switch ON the original flow of TimeLine, and the other TimeLine would become *Dead TimeLine(s)* again, thus leading to the original flow of the TimeLine. "All-Past" exist yet there exists only one-Future. Table 3 summarizes the key concepts and mathematical formulations associated with TimeLine dynamics, such as alternate timeline creation and management, causality preservation, flow transitions, activation functions, event mapping, self-healing mechanisms, and multi-timeline probability distributions.

Each notion is discussed together with its ramifications and related mathematical formulae, offering a full overview of how temporal interactions are handled in a multi-timeline framework.

Table 3. Framework of timeline dynamics and temporal interactions

Concept	Description	Mathematical Formulas	Implications
Alternate TimeLine Creation	Creation of a new Alternate TimeLine (AL_n) when traveling within an existing Alternate TimeLine (AL_{n-1}).	$AL_n = AL_{n-1} + \Delta T$ Where ΔT represents the time shift or action causing the creation of AL_n.	Each new Alternate TimeLine branches off from a previous one, creating a new parallel reality.
Causality Preservation	Ensuring events in one TimeLine do not affect others, maintaining causality within each separate timeline.	$C_{AL_i} \cap C_{AL_j} = \emptyset$ Where C_{AL_i} and C_{AL_j} represent causality sets in TimeLines AL_i and AL_j.	Causality is preserved independently within each TimeLine, preventing paradoxes across parallel realities.
Flow Transition Between TimeLines	Transitioning between Main TimeLine and Alternate TimeLine, where only one TimeLine is active at a time.	$Flow_{Active} = \sum_{i=1}^{n} Status_{AL_i}$ Where $Status_{AL_i}$ is 1 if TimeLine AL_i is active, 0 otherwise.	Ensures that only one TimeLine is active or "ON" at any given time, with others being inactive.
TimeLine Activation Function	Function representing the activation or deactivation of TimeLines based on temporal events.	$A_i(t) = \begin{cases} 1 & if\ t \in Active\ Period \\ 0, & Otherwise \end{cases}$	Determines the current state of each TimeLine, whether it is active or deactivated based on time *t*.
Event Mapping and Reality Shifts	Mapping events to either the Main TimeLine or an Alternate TimeLine based on changes made during time travel.	$E_{AL_n} = f(E_{Main}, \text{Change})$ Where E_{AL_n} is the event in Alternate TimeLine AL_n, E_{Main} is the event in Main TimeLine, and Change is the modification introduced.	Events modified in one TimeLine result in equivalent events in the corresponding Alternate TimeLine.
Self-Healing and TimeLine Pruning	The process of reinstating the original TimeLine flow upon return and deactivating alternative TimeLines.	$H_{\text{Main}} = \text{Repair}(T_{\text{Main}}, R)$ Where, H_{Main} Healed Main TimeLine. T_{Main}: Main TimeLine. R: Action of returning to the Main TimeLine.	The original timeline resumes as if no changes were made, while alternate realities become inactive.
Multi-Timeline Probability	Probability distribution of events across multiple TimeLines, reflecting the likelihood of various outcomes.	$P_{AL} = \frac{1}{N}\sum_{i=1}^{N} P_i$ Where P_{AL} is the probability of an event in TimeLine *AL*, *N* is the number of TimeLines, and P_i is the probability of the event in TimeLine *i*.	Provides a probabilistic view of events across multiple timelines, influencing the likelihood of outcomes.

Travelling With Respect to the Speed of Light (299792458 m/s)

Before diving into unfolding the future of the Universe from the past, let us first understand yet another concept from Relativity – "Relativity of Simultaneity". It states that:

"Events that are simultaneous in one frame, need not be simultaneous in every frame (or moving frame)"

Visualize there is a photon emitter in between two detectors (mirror for example) – the photon emitter emits two photons towards the detectors at the same time, and the photons will hit the detectors and get detected at the same time – Preserving Simultaneity. However, if an observer from a moving frame (moving car) would be observing this, for her, this wouldn't be simultaneous. This is because, from the frame of reference of the observer, the detector close to her would appear to move towards her than the detector away from her (as she would be at rest "relative" to the environment – this would be the same as seeing trees passing by from a window on a moving Bus). Thus, the detector away from the observer would move towards the photons – moving towards it, and the detector closer to the observer would be moving away from the photons – This would all be taking place from the frame of reference (moving frame) of the observer only. Thus, the detector away from the observer would reach and detect the photons before the detector moves away from the photons and towards the observer. This has been shown in Figure 6. (Einstein, 1916; Lobo, 2007).

Figure 6. Relativity of simultaneity

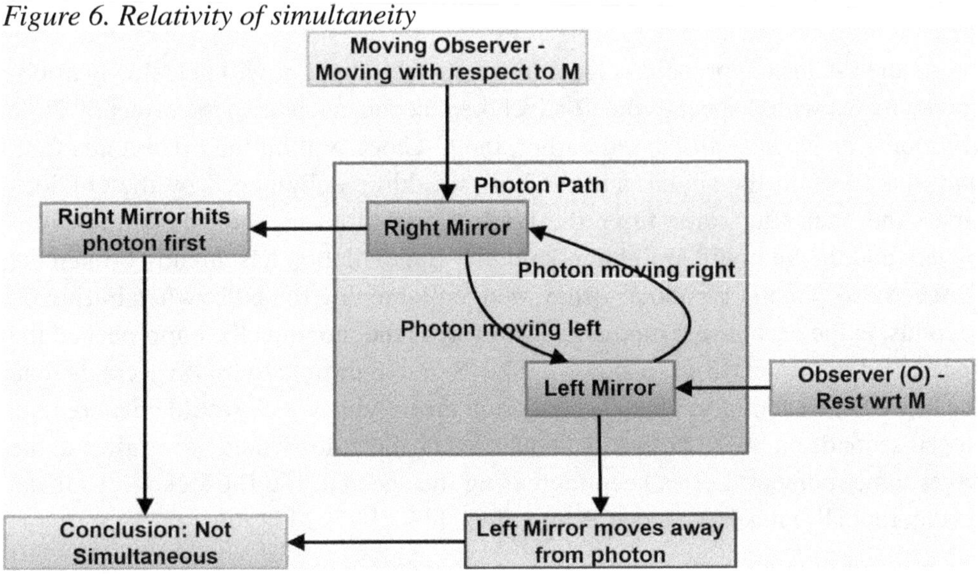

Let us now dive into the approach to unfolding the future from the living past. In Special Theory of Relativity, Albert Einstein described that, as a clock approaches the Speed of light, it slows down, as measured from a rest frame. It means, that as an object approaches the speed of light, its clock gets dilated (as measured by a stationary observer), and it comes closer to witnessing the future.

Visualize there are two clocks: P-Clock and Q-Clock, perfectly synced; The P-Clock is moved from point A (source) to point B (destination) with increasing speed in every scenario, approaching near the speed of light and beyond the speed of light (theoretical). While the Q-Clock stays with us – the observers, to note the time difference, registering Time Dilation. Let us assume we observed 60 seconds (seeing the moving P-Clock) when the P-Clock is moved at a normal rate from point A to point B. There exists no noticeable time difference measured between the two clocks; the Q-Clock kept with us also showed 60 seconds. A mechanism has been constructed that allows a light bulb to shine at the exact same moment when the clock hits 60 seconds. Each clock has its own light bulb – assuming that the signal that would enlighten the bulb, travels at the speed of light, and wouldn't account for Time Dilation, as the Speed of Light stays the same in every inertial frame of reference. Initially, both the bulb would shine at the exact same moment, as the P-Clock only travelled at a normal rate. Now, as the P-Clock is moved at a faster rate approaching the speed of light its "observed time" would slow down (or dilate), exceeding the time of the rest clock – Q-Clock, complying with the principle of Special Relativity, Validating Time Dilation.

Travelling Closer to the Speed of Light

As the P-Clock approaches closer to the speed of light, it will tick slowly as observed by us, with respect to the Q-Clock kept beside us. Due to the effect of Time Dilation – as we have discussed earlier, the Q-Clock will hit the 60 seconds first, and thus transmit the signal, and the bulb would be enlightened by the Q-Clock first. And later after some time, the P-Clock would hit 60 seconds (as observed by us), and the bulb will enlighten the bulb. Time Dilation has already broken the synched time among the clock – they were enlightening the bulb, when hitting 60 seconds, at the exact same moment. However, as the moving clock approached the speed of light, it ticked more slowly and took a longer time to hit 60 seconds than the clock kept stationary. The 60 seconds on the moving Clock would be more than the 60 seconds on the rest clock, and due to this, the bulbs would never glow at the exact same moment. Let us keep increasing the speed of the P-Clock – let's make it (theoretically) reach the exact Speed of Light – 299792458 m/s.

Travelling at the Speed of Light

As the moving clock approaches the speed of light, it gets slower, and at the speed of light, the time of the moving clock as measured from a stationary frame, would come to a complete halt – the time would no longer tick. The hands of the P-Clock would stop moving as observed by us (theoretically, ignoring the length contraction), thus when the P-Clock hits 60 seconds – we would never know, as it will no longer tick. We cannot observe a clock-ticking, moving at the speed of light. In this case, the Q-Clock will hit 60 seconds (normal time), and switch-ON the bulb, however, on the other hand, the P-Clock will never make it to 60 seconds, as observed by us, and thus never be able to switch-ON the bulb. The bulb will never glow by the P-Clock, as observed by us.

Travelling Beyond the Speed of Light

This is where the "apparent" Causality breaks. It wouldn't be possible to make any object accelerate to and beyond the speed of light as it goes beyond practicality; It would require an infinite amount of energy to make an object move to the speed of light, and theoretically, it would require negative energy to make an object go beyond the speed of light. An object may exist at a speed faster than the speed of light, without violating any laws of physics, however, making an object reach the speed of light or beyond, wouldn't be possible, even on paper. Particles travelling at the speed of light – Photons do not accelerate to reach at a speed of 299792458 m/s, instead they "exist" at the speed – their minimum speed is the speed of light, in a similar way a particle may exist at the speed faster than the speed of light, in other words, the minimum speed of such a particle would be the speed of light faster than the speed of light.

As the P-Clock goes beyond the speed of light, it hits 60 seconds and glows the bulb even before any light reaches the clock to bounce off, into our eyes to see the cause of the event. In other words, we would notice the bulb glowing even before the clock hits 60 seconds – theoretically. This would flip the cause-and-effect of the event, in this case, the effect would come before the cause itself. In the above experiment, the effect is the glowing of the bulb, which should only take place after the cause which is the clock hitting 60 seconds and initiating the signal to glow the bulb. The clock moving at a speed faster than the speed of light itself, would hit 60 seconds before we observe the clock hitting 60 seconds, and this would initiate the mechanism to enlighten the bulb before we register 60 seconds of that moving clock. Thus, the bulb would light first, and then we would see the clock hitting 60 seconds – the effect would come before the cause initiating it. Figure 7 presents the time dilation and causality effects in special relativity: Analysis of P-Q Clocks scenarios

Figure 7. Scenario of P-Q clock with respect to the speed of light

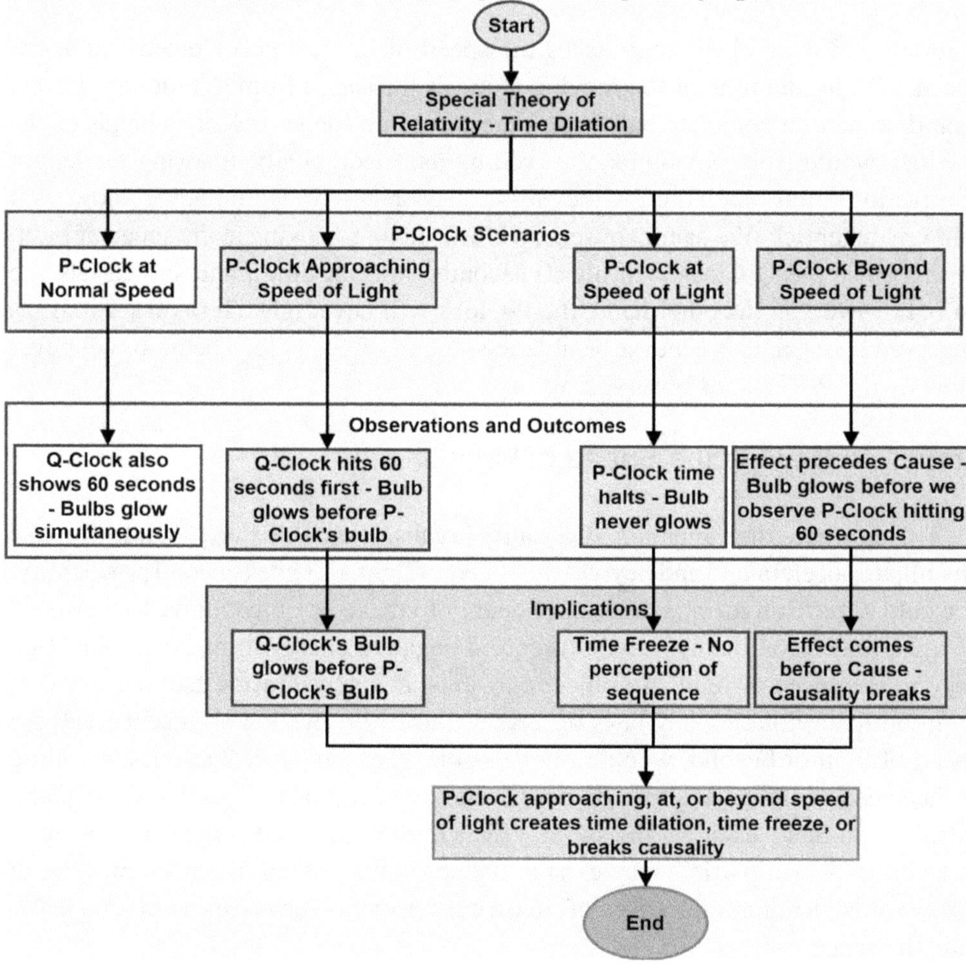

What would an object (capable of perceiving) perceive when travelling with respect to the speed of light – Hypothetical case?

1. Approaching the Speed of Light

As an object approaches the speed of light, it comes closer to the photons carrying the moments of the Future (reflected from the Future), and it would witness the Future before anybody else does, due to travelling closer to the photons, and thus the object would be in the Future.

2. Moving at the Speed of Light

Although relativity describes that an object having mass cannot travel to the speed of light, as it would require an infinite amount of energy. Photons are massless particles that travel at the speed of light and don't have a rest frame to perceive any event. They do not experience time the same way as we do. However, within the scope of Time Dilation, as an object approaches the exact speed of light, time would completely freeze for that object, it wouldn't be able to comprehend the sequence of Time – Time would freeze for the object.

"The moment a photon was born or emitted by any light source, the precise same moment, it would get absorbed by its destination."

An object travelling at the speed of light or "with" the speed of light wouldn't receive a change in receiving photons, as it would be travelling along with the photons, thus there would only be one single information of the Future receiving to the object, and no sequence of time or causality would be there. Therefore, an object moving at the speed of light would perceive a frozen future with no time-tick.

3. Leaping beyond the Speed of Light

The Human-understanding of the entire Cosmos comes to a stop at this point. Yet humans are obliged to make sense out of the entire cosmos and beyond. An object travelling beyond the speed of light would be travelling ahead of all the photons or ahead of the Future, leaving all photons behind, thus outrunning all the future-information about the entire Universe contained within the photons. The object wouldn't perceive anything while travelling at a speed faster than the medium to perceive reality. To witness the future, the object needs to come to a stop, to allow photons to reach to it, and assuming that it would be possible for the object to reduce its speed from an exceptional speed beyond the speed of light to a speed much lesser than the speed of light, to come to a halt, and the moment the object would come to a rest, it would start receiving the photons that it missed earlier during its outrun, thus witnessing a future that it missed earlier – a Delayed Future. Note that the delayed future (a moment from the past) wouldn't be a "lived" past for that object, it would be yet another future from the past. It should be noted that it wouldn't be possible for the object moving at a speed faster than the speed of light to witness anything (or the future), as it would constantly be missing photons carrying the information about the future, so to perceive any information about the future, the object must come to a halt, to come within the Horizon of photons, and to perceive the future, yet would only witness the moment that it missed earlier – Delayed Future. It might be possible that a whole new realm emerges beyond the speed of light that requires no photons to comprehend, constantly existing beyond our Horizon, in the Higher-dimensional-future. The photons wouldn't be there in the other-higher dimensions.

CONCLUSION

This chapter thoroughly explored the scientific basis of time travel, measuring its development from Einstein's landmark work to the speculative regions of higher dimensions. By investigating the interaction of space and time, we looked into the paradoxical nature of time travel and its possible consequences for the understanding of the cosmos. From relativity dilation of time to the possible presence of many dimensions, this research has aimed to improve our understanding of the fundamental principles regulating time travel. While actual time travel remains a distant prospect, our work has helped to deepen our understanding of the theoretical challenges and potential connected with this unidentified concept. This chapter attempts to encourage more investigation into the intricacies of time travel and its possible effects on our sense of reality by analysing the gaps in our present understanding and suggesting possible directions for future study.

Future Scope

Time travel research is still very much underway. In order to resolve the seeming paradoxes related to time travel, future study should concentrate on improving the theoretical models that are already in place and investigating novel concepts. Novel comprehensions of the nature of time and space might be gained via the development of innovative technologies like those connected to quantum physics and gravity. More research is required to fully understand the philosophical consequences of time travel. Developing a thorough understanding of this complex phenomenon will require taking into account the possible effects on cause-and-effect, free will, and the framework of reality embedded within the Cosmos.

REFERENCES

Aguirre, A., & Tegmark, M. (2011). Born in an infinite universe: A cosmological interpretation of quantum mechanics. *Physical Review. D*, 84(10), 105002. DOI: 10.1103/PhysRevD.84.105002

Ahmed, H., Shukla, S., & Rai, H. M. (2014). Static handwritten signature recognition using discrete random transform and combined projection based technique. *International Conference on Advanced Computing and Communication Technologies, ACCT*, 37–41. https://doi.org/DOI: 10.1109/ACCT.2014.76

Al-Khalili, J. (2003). Time travel: Separating science fact from science fiction. *Physics Education*, 38(1), 14–19. DOI: 10.1088/0031-9120/38/1/302

Banister, D. (2005). *Time and Travel*. DOI: 10.1007/3-540-28550-4_17

Bartlett, R. (2023). The 5th Dimension and its Implications for the String Theory, Conservation of Energy and Heisenberg Uncertainty Principle. *IPI Letters*, 1, 41–55. DOI: 10.59973/ipil.29

Bauer, D., & Tulic, M. (2018). Travel time predictions: Should one model speeds or travel times? *European Transport Research Review*, 10(2), 46. DOI: 10.1186/s12544-018-0315-7

Bergmann, P. G. (1962). *The General Theory of Relativity*. DOI: 10.1007/978-3-642-45973-3_3

Debnath, A., Rai, H. M., Yadav, C., & Bhatia, A. (2013). Deblurring and Denoising of Magnetic Resonance Images using Blind Deconvolution Method. *International Journal of Computer Applications*, 81(10), 7–12. DOI: 10.5120/14046-2209

Deutsch, D. (1991). Quantum mechanics near closed timelike lines. *Physical Review. D*, 44(10), 3197–3217. DOI: 10.1103/PhysRevD.44.3197

Du, M. (2022). *The Theoretical Basis and Feasibility of Time Travel*. DOI: 10.2991/assehr.k.220105.048

Einstein, A. (1916). *Relativity: The Special and General Theory*. Methuen & Co Ltd.

Fedosin, , S. (2012). Scale dimension as the fifth dimension of spacetime. *Turkish Journal of Physics*. DOI: 10.3906/fiz-1110-20

Gupta, S., Sharmila, & Rai, H. M. (2021). IoT-Based Automatic Irrigation System Using Robotic Vehicle. In D. Goyal, V. E. Bălaş, A. Mukherjee, V. H. C. de Albuquerque, & A. K. Gupta (Eds.), *Information Management and Machine Intelligence. ICIMMI 2019. Algorithms for Intelligent Systems. Springer* (pp. 669–677). Springer, Singapore. DOI: 10.1007/978-981-15-4936-6_73

Haba, R., Ohzeki, M., & Tanaka, K. (2022). Travel time optimization on multi-AGV routing by reverse annealing. *Scientific Reports*, 12(1), 17753. DOI: 10.1038/s41598-022-22704-0

Holtorf, C., & Petersson, B. (2018). Archaeology and Time Travel. In *Encyclopedia of Global Archaeology* (pp. 1–11). Springer International Publishing. DOI: 10.1007/978-3-319-51726-1_2793-1

Jha, K., Pasbola, M., Rai, H. M., & Amanzholova, S. (2023). Utilizing Smartwatches and Deep Learning Models for Enhanced Avalanche Victim Identification, Localization, and Efficient Recovery Strategies: An In-depth Study. *Proceedings of the 5th International Conference on Information Management & Machine Intelligence*, 1–5. DOI: 10.1145/3647444.3652483

Lobo, F. S. N. (2007). *Exotic solutions in General Relativity: Traversable wormholes and "warp drive" spacetimes.*

Ma, S., Chen, J., Zhang, Y., Shrivastava, A., & Mohan, H. (2021). Cloud based Resource Scheduling Methodology for Data-Intensive Smart Cities and Industrial Applications. *Scalable Computing: Practice and Experience*, 22(2), 227–235. DOI: 10.12694/scpe.v22i2.1899

McKenzie, A. (2020). Reality and Super-Reality: Properties of a Mathematical Multiverse. *Axiomathes*, 30(4), 453–478. DOI: 10.1007/s10516-019-09466-7

Misner, C. W., Thorne, K. S., & Wheeler, J. A. (1973). *Gravitation*. W. H. Freeman and Co. New York.

Nguyen, H. K., & Azreg-Aïnou, M. (2023). Traversable Morris–Thorne–Buchdahl wormholes in quadratic gravity. *The European Physical Journal C*, 83(7), 626. DOI: 10.1140/epjc/s10052-023-11805-3

Read, J., & Le Bihan, B. (2021). The landscape and the multiverse: What's the problem? *Synthese*, 199(3–4), 7749–7771. DOI: 10.1007/s11229-021-03137-0

Saito, S. (2023). Special theory of relativity for a graded index fibre. *Frontiers in Physics*, 11. DOI: 10.3389/fphy.2023.1225387

Serdahely, W. J. (1990). A brief history of time: From the big bang to black holes. *Journal of Near-Death Studies*, 9(2), 123–131. DOI: 10.1007/BF01074212

Thorne, K. S., Braginsky, V., & Ginzburg, V. (1994). Black Holes and Time Warps: Einstein's Outrageous Legacy. *Physics Today*, 47(11), 85–86. DOI: 10.1063/1.2808700

Topcu, M. N., & Hirst, W. (2022). *Collective mental time travel: Current research and future directions* (pp. 71–97). DOI: 10.1016/bs.pbr.2022.06.002

Trakas, M. (2023). Journeying to the past: Time travel and mental time travel, how far apart? *Frontiers in Psychology*, 14. Advance online publication. DOI: 10.3389/fpsyg.2023.1260458

Verma, S., Warrier, L., Bolia, B., & Mehta, S. (2022). Past, present, and future of virtual tourism-a literature review. *International Journal of Information Management Data Insights*, 2(2), 100085. DOI: 10.1016/j.jjimei.2022.100085

Wald, R. M. (1984). *General Relativity*. University of Chicago Press. DOI: 10.7208/chicago/9780226870373.001.0001

Wang, X., Zhang, X., Gong, H., Jiang, J., & Rai, H. M. (2021). A flight control method for unmanned aerial vehicles based on vibration suppression. *IET Collaborative Intelligent Manufacturing*, 3(3), 252–261. DOI: 10.1049/cim2.12027

Wang, Y. (2012). Quantum Computation and Quantum Information. *Statistical Science*, 27(3). DOI: 10.1214/11-STS378

Younus, M., Nurmandi, A., & Suswanta, S. (2023). Concept of Time Travel and The Different Theories for Making It Possible and The Implications of Time Travelling. *Journal of Wood Science*, 2(4), 576–582. DOI: 10.58344/jws.v2i4.268

Chapter 9
Quantum Computing for Optimization and Its Applications

Poornima Pandian
https://orcid.org/0000-0002-5751-0859
Sri Sai Ram Engineering College, India

Chithra Selvaraj
Anna University, Chennai, India

R. Yugha
Sathyabama Institute of Science and Technology, India

ABSTRACT

Quantum computing is a novel kind of computation that solves very complicated problems rapidly by applying concepts from basic physics. Concepts like quantum mechanical computing and quantum algorithms are included in the field of quantum computing study. Researchers have imagined quantum computing as a revolutionary idea among emerging technologies in terms of concepts, methods, and techniques. These are cross-pollinated. Hence, quantum computing becomes more and more multidisciplinary. Quantum computing leverages quantum mechanical phenomena like superposition and quantum interference to deal with some kinds of problems more precisely than conventional computing. Because of its unique characteristics, which set it apart from conventional computers in terms of functionality and operation, quantum computing has grown in popularity. There are possibilities of creating hybrid models, namely approaches for large-scale mixed-integer programming issues, that effectively combine the strengths of quality control techniques with deterministic algorithms to handle combinatorial challenges.

DOI: 10.4018/979-8-3693-6885-5.ch009

INTRODUCTION

Quantum computing utilizes quantum physics to store and perform computations. This can be significantly beneficial for some activities, outperforming even the best supercomputers. Computing power has been transformed by the development of quantum computing. In recent years, the field has made great strides, beginning with its early 20th century origins, the priorities were set on realizing qubits, or the quantum equivalents of classical bits, during the 1990s and the first half of the 2000s. A number of noteworthy innovations, including Shor's algorithm for factoring big numbers laid the foundation for quantum computers exponential speedup. The interest in quantum computing has increased as a result of this finding, and there are now many scientific issues that need to be resolved before quantum computers can be implemented. The foundation of quantum computing is quantum mechanics, which describes how matter behaves at the minuscule scale. It constitutes the basis of quantum computing, an endeavor to solve complicated computational problems by manipulating quantum processes. The recent research works have introduced novel idea of utilizing the quantum-inspired Acromyrmex evolutionary algorithm as a powerful global optimization tool for complex systems. The review of quantum-inspired population-based metaheuristics is performed to identify which metaheuristics might be applied to existing quantum computers using the circuit model programming paradigm.

Quantum computing utilizes quantum physics to store and perform computations. This can be significantly beneficial for some activities, outperforming even the best supercomputers. The performance of quantum computers and classical computers are studied in terms of capacity and computational complexity. The authors (Pathak *et al.,* 2022) suggested a quantum computing algorithm for the COVID-19 pandemic. This work covers fundamental quantum phenomena like superposition and entanglement, as well as quantum programming tools like Qiskit (IBM) and pyQuil (Google). The researchers (Potempa & Porebski, 2022) compare the concepts of quantum and classical neural network models for image classification. The results of comparing classical and quantum neural networks with similar training parameters show that the quantum network outperforms the classical network in terms of convergence, training accuracy, and time complexity. However, there is an intriguing proposal to improve security with quantum computing. This leads to the development of the quantum algorithms that run faster than classical algorithms, reduce time complexity, and prevent attacks. It is found that reinforcement learning methods outperformed traditional machine learning methods and utilization of the genetic algorithm is proposed to generate quantum circuit programs for the Open Quantum Assembly Language. The researchers have presented a quantum version of classical neurons, resulting in quantum feedforward neural networks capable of universal quantum computation (Valdez & Melin, 2023).

A Bayesian optimization framework for stochastic quantum program synthesis is proposed for performing complex computations. Quantum computers and algorithms outperformed Von Neumann computing for NP-complete programs, resulting in exponential performance gains. The efficiency of the quantum optimization is measured by using neural network focuses on states important to the Quantum Approximate Optimization Algorithm by analyzing several qubit wave functions. This gives a classical simulation of the Quantum Approximate Optimization Algorithm. The fundamental phases involved in Quantum Computing is given in Figure 1.

Figure 1. Fundamental phases of quantum computing (Sood & Chauhan, 2024)

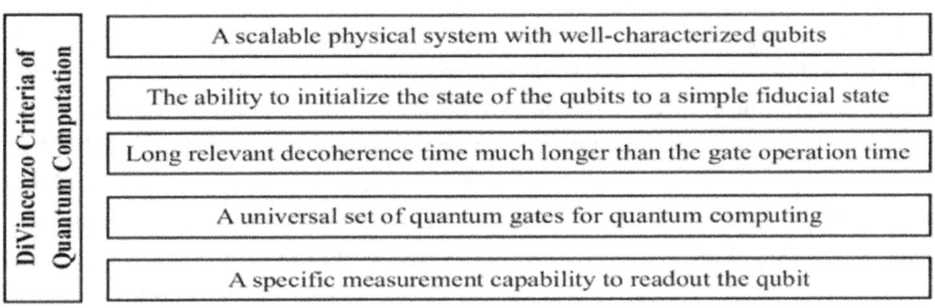

QUANTUM COMPUTING-INSPIRED OPTIMIZATION

Quantum computing-inspired optimization (QCiO) offers new strategies to achieve optimal behavior, in addition to other optimization techniques. QCiO was a significant innovation in computing during the 20th century. Researchers worldwide have investigated this revolutionary idea to achieve best results in various applications. The global market for quantum computing is expected to exceed $10,000 million by 2030. QCiO utilizes qubits to represent several data states simultaneously, similar to quantum computers. QCiO approaches for decision-modeling in IoT applications. It is suggested to incorporate quantum-resistant access authentication and data allocation system for large-scale IoT networks. The suggested paradigm minimizes network traffic while providing maximum security and privacy against quantum assaults. The proposed model was tested in real-time and produced ideal results. On the other hand, the QCi model has been utilized to optimize load distribution across fog nodes in IoT systems. The described solution uses a neural network formulation of QCiO to forecast optimal fog node deployment in real time. The experiment simulated the distribution of 600 random tasks among ten fog nodes. After doing a comparison examination, the authors found that their model outperformed other cutting-edge models. Based on the importance of IoT, it is crucial to perform data accuracy (DA) analysis for this further processing. The DA analysis focuses on the accuracy and optimal behavior of data segments collected by widely distributed IoT devices. When several devices are integrated in the environment to achieve a shared goal, data mistakes, missing segments, and false perceptions can make the IoT environment less dependable. The present research focuses on optimizing accuracy in real-time IoT environments by limiting sensor space (a subset of sensor sets). In the IoT sensor space, DA is classified as either physical or immaterial. The tangible accuracy of an IoT sensor refers to manufacturing faults and the time it takes to repair. Intangible accuracy considers sensor displacement, data collecting time, and sensory capability in a stochastic environment. The current work aims to improve intangible accuracy in real-time IoT environments. Minimizing IoT sensor space is a dynamic challenge influenced by traditional sensor placement problems.

In quantum computing, a qubit is the minimal quantity of information that can be processed. It is a two-dimensional quantum-mechanical system that encodes classical bits 0 and 1 in its basic states ($|0\rangle$ and $|1\rangle$). This system can be in a combination of states $|0\rangle$ and $|1\rangle$. This is the first crucial attribute of quantum systems: they can be in all of the system's states simultaneously. In practice, it is challenging to achieve the conditions needed for adiabatic quantum computing in a quantum annealing process. It might be challenging to ensure that a system's development is totally adiabatic or that it starts in the correct ground state of the initial Hamiltonian. Thus, quantum annealing is an approximation of adiabatic computing. The works have demonstrated that approximation adiabatic computing can achieve near-optimal solutions for a known issue NP-hard: polynomial time.

This characteristic enables quantum computers to execute parallel computations on a vast scale. Given a two-qubit system, it is possible that the states of each qubit cannot be defined separately. The state cannot be factored as a tensor product of two distinct states. Another important distinction between classical and quantum computing is the core set of operations. Classical computing relies on binary operations, including the NOT and AND gates. NOTs and ANDs are universal operations that can replicate any other boolean operation. They are also non-reversible: given the output of an AND gate, one cannot determine the input variables. The Schroedinger equation indicates that quantum evolution is reversible. Measurements and other events that disrupt reversibility result in loss of quantum behavior. To achieve quantum gain, only reversible, unitary gates should be used. It can be demonstrated that a subset of these gates is also universal. The details of available Quantum Computing software are shown in Figure 2.

In general, a quantum algorithm consists of five steps:

1. Convert the input data to the state of a set of qubits.
2. Put the qubits in superposition over multiple states.
3. Use quantum entanglement to apply an algorithm (oracle) to all states at once. At the end of this phase, one state will have the correct answer.
4. Increase the likelihood of measuring the proper state (e.g., by quantum interference).
5. Measure one or more qubits.

Figure 2. The details of quantum computing simulators, software, and processors (Bhatia & Sood, 2020)

Quantum Simulators	**Quantum Programming Languages**	Quantum Processors
•QDK (Microsoft) •Cirq(Google) •Strawberry Fields(Xanadu) •QX Simulator	•QCL •Quantum pseudocode •Q# •Q language	•Google Bristlecone •IBM Q 5 Tenerife •Rigetti 8Q Agave • D-Wave 2000Q

Quantum Optimisation in Internet of Things

Internet of Things (IoT) technology has enabled novel applications in industries such as healthcare, logistics, and agriculture. The future of the industry is focused on enhancing automation and efficiency through the use of IoT. By 2025, the world is estimated to have approximately 50 billion networked IoT devices. In recent years, IoT has emerged as an interesting study topic. Researchers worldwide have proposed frameworks for incorporating IoT into many service sectors. A modified deep residual network model is proposed for human activity recognition using IoT technologies. Smartphone sensors identified and processed human body signals on a cloud computing platform. The authors also presented a cloud-based function-as-a-model for real-time activity analysis. A secure IoT-based network infrastructure for hybrid industrial deployment with block chain technology is demonstrated. The authors highlighted the cost-effectiveness and accuracy of IoT-based service delivery. Blockchain technology enabled real-time data extraction and transparency for industrial users. The trial implementation yielded improved outcomes, with an 89% success rate. The authors (Thigale *et al.*, 2019) proposed a secure IoT platform for data exchange. The authors presented an IoT communication protocol that is immune to cross-layer attacks. The framework addresses both time-sensitive and ubiquitous service delivery challenges. Several frameworks have been proposed to incorporate (Li *et al.*, 2019) introduced a wireless sensor-based routing algorithm based on the quantum version of the ant colony multi-objective technique. The suggested technique monitors the computing environment to optimize routing. The node pheromone was designed using q-bits and quantum gates to optimize data load. The best path was determined considering transmission latency, network load balancing, and energy usage. The exponential increase in quantum inspired optimization applications is given in Figure 3.

Figure 3. Increase in quantum inspired optimization applications (Bhatia et al., 2023)

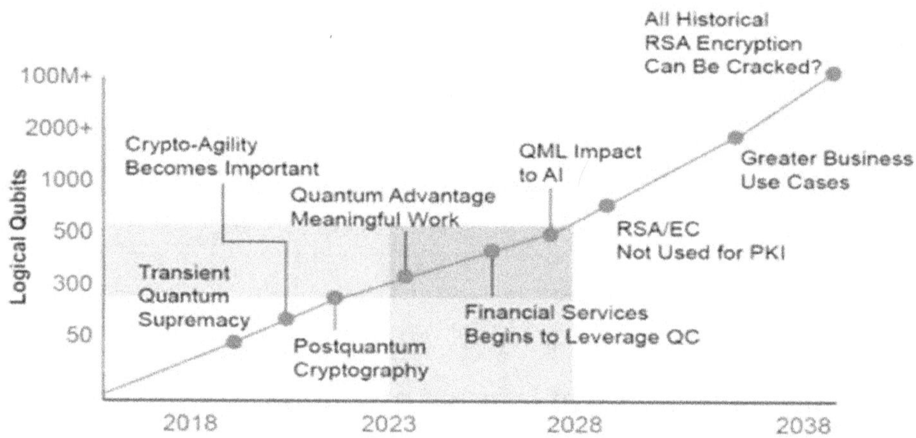

Quantum Optimisation in Finance

Many financial troubles are rooted in optimization issues. Classical computers cannot efficiently find the best portfolio due to the NP-Hard problem. Quantum optimization can be implemented in a variety of ways. Quantum annealing is the most well-known algorithm on a quantum computer. The method of adiabatic quantum computation (Farhi *et al.*, 2000) is central to quantum optimization methods can be considered. To minimize the cost function, there is a need to first transfer the optimization problem to the physical problem of determining the ground state of a Hamiltonian H_0. The system is prepared in the ground state of an initial Hamiltonian H_P. The H_0 was chosen since its ground state is well understood and easy to manufacture. Then adiabatically deform H_0 to H_P over a long time (T). According to the adiabatic theorem, a system will remain close to its instantaneous ground state if its lowest energy levels are non-degenerate and evolution is gradual. In practice, selection of $T = \Delta^2$, where Δ is the lowest energy difference between the instantaneous ground and first exited states. When this is the case, measuring the system's state at the conclusion of its evolution has a high possibility of reverting to H_P ground state. This is the universal model of quantum computation, which means that it can theoretically execute any quantum algorithm. This model is very adaptable, allowing for the addition of intermediate Hamiltonians and the ability to meet local adiabatic requirements.

In practice, it is challenging to achieve the conditions needed for adiabatic quantum computing in a quantum annealing process. It might be challenging to ensure that a system's development is totally adiabatic or that it starts in the correct ground state of the initial Hamiltonian. Thus, quantum annealing is an approximation of adiabatic computing. The authors have demonstrated that approximation adiabatic computing can achieve near-optimal solutions to NP-hard problems in polynomial time (Orús *et al.,* 2019).

Quantum Optimisation in Logistics

In recent years, several studies have been conducted to address supply chain and logistics optimization issues linked to design and operation. Some research offers a real-time scheduling optimization model that focuses on operational energy efficiency, as well as a mathematical model of last-mile delivery difficulties such as scheduling and assignment challenges. A three-echelon supply chain network using particle swarm optimization is proposed for modeling and optimizing the supply chain in order to meet the demand unpredictability and restrictions posed by each echelon in supply chain design activities. The supply chain and logistics solutions are measured in order to quantify availability, flexibility, efficiency, and plasticity indicators. According to studies, unmanned aerial vehicles have the potential to reduce CO_2 emissions more effectively than traditional modes of transportation. Researchers presented two models (classical and Vendor Managed Inventory coordination) for a two-level closed-loop supply chain, taking into account three environmental factors: energy use in production processes, greenhouse gas emissions, and transportation activities. In today's competitive global market, enterprises rely heavily on their supply chain networks. Just-in-time production is a supply chain strategy that decreases inventory and improves business production efficiency. Frequent small-scale production necessitates quick response to transportation demands, resulting in significant environmental damage and expensive transport costs.

A multi-criterion decision model based on the just-in-time system is suggested to optimize product production, quality, pricing, cost, equipment, and technology. The model successfully satisfied customer demand and export quality standards.

The corporation implemented a just-in-time decision-making system to enhance sales, design, and manufacture of its products. Few researchers have constructed a multi-objective mathematical model based on a three-level distribution network to ensure timely delivery. However, the model did not incorporate environmental impact. Green supply chain management aims to consider the environmental impact of the process. Logistics play a significant role in environmental pollution, including greenhouse gas emissions. Despite increased awareness of green logistics, environmental constraints are rarely implemented in practical logistics operations. The multi-target fuzzy approach is the most effective tool for creating a green supply chain network. Multi-target fuzzy models aim for least cost and environmental impact, which may clash. An optimized closed-loop supply chain network integrates forward and reverse propagations to reduce the environmental effect of logistical operations (using CO_2 equivalent as an indication). To align with the objectives and limits of green logistics, a new combinatory optimization model is needed, as traditional production and distribution models frequently prioritize cost minimization.

In this work (Wu *et al.,* 2018) to optimize a three-echelon supply chain network, a mathematical model was built with constraints such as capacity, production cost, transportation cost, carbon emissions, and time window. The three-echelon supply chain considered for optimization is shown in Figure 4. The quantum-particle swarm optimization technique was used to solve the problem. The supply chain is divided into three tiers: suppliers, distribution centers, and retailers. It is determined by the number and location of suppliers, the mode of transportation, and the quantity of products to be transported.

Figure 4. The three-echelon supply chain model

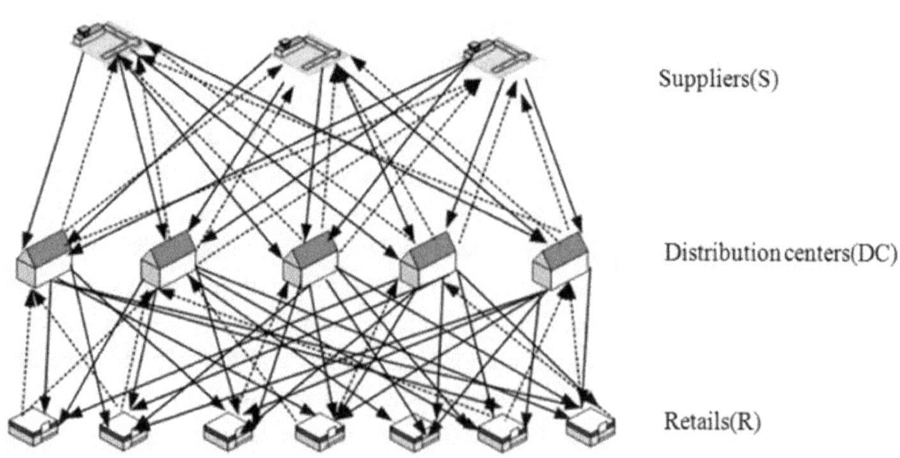

Quantum Optimization in Naturally Inspired Algorithms

Quantum Computing (QC) is a promising field for optimizing decision-making in various applications. Globally researchers have proposed QC-Algorithms (QCA) for real-time applications. The QC-inspired (QCI) approach to schedule jobs in fog computing settings. An experimental simulation was conducted to schedule 600 tasks across 10 computing nodes. The simulations yielded ideal results for energy efficiency, temporal delay, sensitivity, and precision. It is suggested to have a cooperative multiple-input, multiple-output technique in IoT systems to improve cluster lifetime.

The quantum-inspired particle swarm optimization (QPSO) is proposed to pick optimal sender and receiver, eliminating the need for cooperative coalitions. The researchers (Xiong *et al.,* 2018) examined various Quantum Rotation Gates (QRG) for the quantum-inspired evolutionary algorithm (QEA). The authors provide a detailed classification of QRGs based on their direction and rotation angle magnitude. 21 QRG groups were identified using predefined characteristics to compare their performance.

Four sophisticated optimization functions and a standard 0-1 Knapsack problem were used for implementation. The proposed system achieved effective outcomes for QEA applications. The authors (Jagatheesan *et al.,* 2018) used the QCA technique in time-sensitive thermal power systems to improve power supply stability and quality during fluctuating load demand. The suggested concept connects three area-specific single-stage thermal power systems within each region. The authors presented a hybrid QEA to adjust controller gain levels during uneven load demands. In experimental experiments, the proposed technique outperformed previous futuristic genetic algorithms. The researchers (Zhao *et al.,* 2018) have introduced a geometric-constrained multi-view image matching method that uses the semi-global optimization method to calculate the cost value of an energy function. The authors proposed using the homography transformation parameter computing technique to speed up cost calculations.

Furthermore, the practical simulation shows that the suggested framework outperforms current methods. In this work (Fiasché *et al.,* 2018), the authors have employed quality control techniques to optimize production unit scheduling in the manufacturing business. Minimization is a common optimization issue used in industries to improve production. The suggested approach uses QC mathematical computing to generate timely results. Experiments were conducted at two plants producing optoelectronics items. The offered solution improved productivity compared to manual production scheduling techniques. In this work (Chang *et al.,* 2018) used a convex optimization algorithm to identify the faulty picture area using pretreatment and otsu segmentation techniques. The authors suggested a methodology that extracts 5 parameters from the image's defective area for categorization. The authors determined that the segmentation strategy performed better. The authors (Han & Kim 2002) introduced a revolutionary QEA concept. The suggested approach uses basic mathematical functions such as Q-bit representation for probabilistic information, evaluation for population production, and dynamics. In this work (Rajpurohit *et al.,* 2017) used a Q-gate as a variation operator to derive an optimal solution. The suggested technique was validated by simulation experiments on the evolutionary knapsack problem, yielding optimal results when compared to previous genetic algorithms. The quantum computing based optimal solution selection flow diagram is given in Figure 5. The interconnection between I/O modules and quantum optimization shown in Figure 6.

Figure 5. Optimal solution selection using quantum computing

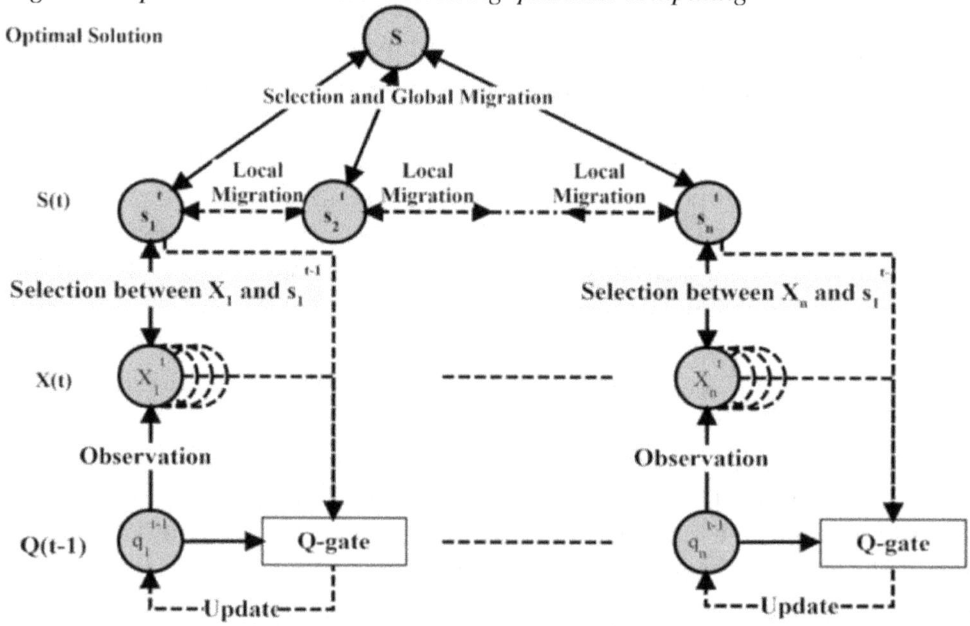

Figure 6. Interconnection between I/O modules and quantum optimization

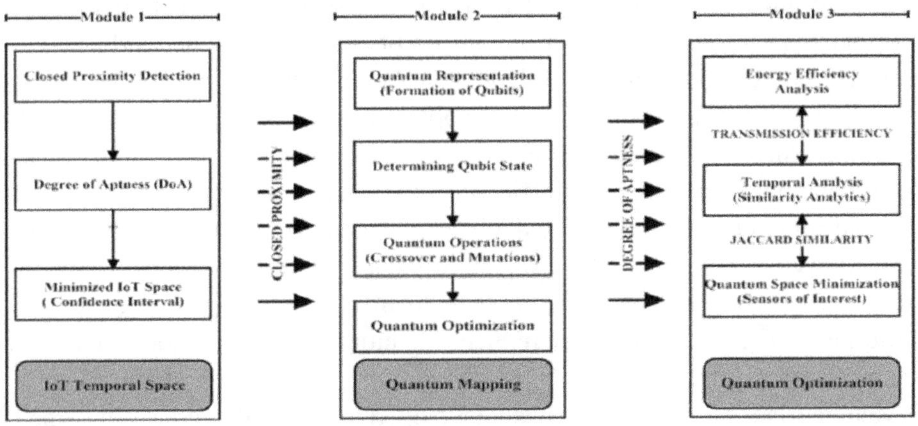

APPLICATIONS OF QUANTUM OPTIMISATION

• Industrial IoT (IIOT)

Industrial IoT (IIoT) applications improve operations by maximizing coverage, connection, energy efficiency, fault tolerance, and reliability. Various researchers have evaluated fault tolerance options for improving coverage and connectivity, including sleep schedules, relay node deployment, and node repositioning. The difficulties of homogeneous communication between IIoT nodes and developed a solution to improve auto-configuration by focusing on connectivity are identified. The zero message quality-based communication in industrial systems for various sensing applications was proposed.

Although the approach improves reliability, it may not be suitable for a large-scale IIoT framework. Sensor nodes near the gateway consume more energy and may experience temporal death due to forwarding packets from end nodes, affecting the network's lifetime.

The temporal death model for energy harvesting is based on a 3D stochastic technique that considers buffer queues and packet blocking probabilities to determine a dynamic strategy for harvesting. Topology control is a method for improving and maintaining connection between devices. Topology control strategies consider accessibility, accuracy, number of devices, transmission range, duty cycle management, and data clustering. A topology control approach using binary grey wolf optimization to achieve decreased topology while maintaining network connectivity is proposed. It utilizes binary scheduling for active and inactive sensor nodes. In addition, it introduces a fitness function to limit the number of active nodes while accomplishing the aim of lifetime expansion of the nodes and network.

An IIS-based IoT system for environmental monitoring, divided into four layers: perception, network, middleware, and application are proposed. The researchers suggested a direct and greedy search strategy to deploy the fewest number of sensor nodes while maintaining energy-efficient coverage and connection. A single-phase manifold initiator technique can calculate the link cover set to meet coverage and connectivity requirements. However, both techniques fall into local maxima due to inherited greedy behavior. To prevent local maxima in greedy algorithms, a nature-inspired genetic algorithm reduces the number of sensor nodes in a network with barriers.

Metaheuristic strategies have been developed to optimally address coverage and connectivity constraints in the IIoT framework. To prevent early swarm convergence, methods are suggested based on the concept of diversity. The attainable zone is configured with lower and higher constraints to ensure optimal search results for real-time applications. The duty cycle technique prioritizes scheduling the least number of sensor nodes into active mode. Various approaches, including localization, geometry, and hybridization of direct information methods, have been proposed to address k-connectivity in wireless sensor networks.

A local search genetic algorithm is used to reduce the number of sensor nodes required for maximum coverage in a 2D sensing area, resulting in a connected network. Quantum ant colony multi-objective routing to monitor complicated manufacturing environments, taking into account node energy consumption, transmission latency, and network load-balancing is devised. Few works propose a range-free localization approach using quantum particle swarm optimization (QPSO) to estimate node distances in heterogeneous wireless sensor networks.

Existing node deployment options rely on a basic disk coverage model, which is impracticable for industrial environments. These algorithms do not consider the spatial link of supervised physical attributes, sensor node association, or network fault tolerance. As a result, they fail to meet worldwide optimization standards. Metaheuristic algorithms performance can be improved due to their slower convergence rate to optimal solutions. Algorithms can be improved for better exploration and exploitation. To overcome these challenges, we present an upgraded PSO (EQPSO) algorithm for IIoT that incorporates quantum PSO, differential evolution, and crossover operators. Some other applications of quantum computing shown in Figure 7.

Figure 7. Applications of quantum computing

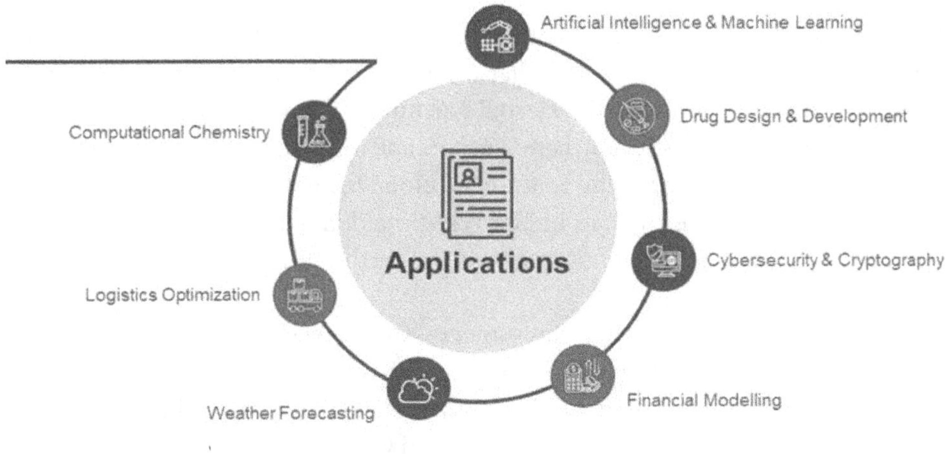

• Mobile Cloud Computing

The advancement of mobile networks and wireless technology will enable the deployment of various applications, including video games, facial identification, augmented reality, healthcare, and natural language processing. These applications and facilities require extensive and efficient processing, which cannot be met by tools with limited resources. Mobile cloud computing (CC) is seen to be the best approach for addressing the limits of mobile users. Mobile cloud computing (CC) addresses the limits of mobile users by offloading and centralizing processing to the cloud over wireless channels. This process improves battery life by reducing its burden. Centralized CC has a significant disadvantage in terms of maximum latency due to MU, which takes longer to transmit data and complicates real-time reporting. Furthermore, the CC mechanism poses a significant security problem as data and services are vulnerable to various dangers during cloud transmission. To address mobile CC difficulties, developers found that resource applications are more cost-effective and have shorter delays. This leads to the identification of a new concept known as Mobile Edge Computing (MEC). Furthermore, real-time solutions can be simplified by maximizing bandwidth and minimizing latency.

• Big Data

Internet research defines the evolution of user data in relation to Big Data. Big Data developers must master models that offer quick responses and user-friendly information when interacting with external machines. The Internet of Things (IoT) connects various sensors, including nano-sensors and high-definition video cameras. IoT data cannot be shifted from the centralized cloud to analytics due to latency and bandwidth constraints. Delays can hinder real-time demands such as surveillance and intelligent transportation management, as well as the ability to predict dangerous items on a consistent basis.

For informed decision-making, the subject issue necessitates extensive investigation. This paper presents GAN-QEHO, a generative adversarial network (GAN) that combines a quantum elephant herd optimization (QEHO) algorithm for MEC in IoT-enabled big data environments. The proposed GAN-QEHO technique involves two stages: feature selection (FS) and data categorization. The QEHO algorithm selects the most efficient feature subset for the FS procedure. Quantifying elephant individuals broadens the search scope and optimizes the balance between exploration and exploitation. Next, the GAN model is used to classify distinct labels. Validate the experimental results of the GAN-QEHO algorithm.

• Blockchain Technology

The existing works have demonstrated a secure IoT-based network infrastructure for hybrid industrial deployment with blockchain technology and highlighted the cost-effectiveness and accuracy of IoT-based service delivery. Blockchain technology enabled real-time data extraction and transparency for industrial users. The trial implementation yielded improved outcomes, with an 89% success rate with a secure IoT platform for data exchange. The authors presented an IoT communication protocol that is immune to cross-layer attacks. The framework addresses both time-sensitive and ubiquitous service delivery challenges. In addition to deepening the understanding of quantum phenomena, quantum computing research aims to usher in a speedier computer era and steer technological breakthroughs in the twenty-first century in terms of security aspects.

CHALLENGES IN QUANTUM COMPUTING

Quantum computing has been proposed as a solution for computationally intensive problems, particularly in machine learning, which requires analyzing large volumes of data. Currently, there is no quantum RAM (qRAM) that can efficiently encode and store this information for long periods. This is one of the major hardware problems for quantum computing (Orús et al.2019).

One of the most critical issues is decoherence, which refers to uncontrolled interactions between the system and its environment. This reduces quantum behavior in the processor, negating the benefits of quantum algorithms. The decoherence time limits the number of operations possible in a quantum algorithm. A significant designing greater fidelity qubit is a hardware problem. Qubits are incorporated in an open environment, making classical simulation software packages are useful. Decoherence can be corrected using error-correcting algorithms. Encoding the quantum state with redundancy over multiple qubits is only conceivable if individual quantum gates have a low error rate. These allow us to create quantum algorithms that last longer than the decoherence time. Operating a single fault-tolerant qubit requires thousands of physical qubits, which is a significant challenge. According to a recent study, quantum computing may have a large speedup in absolute time. However, this advantage is lost when error-correction techniques are implemented.

To overcome these challenges, researchers have adopted techniques for Noisy Intermediate-Scale Quantum (NISQ) processors. These are designed to function on malfunctioning quantum computers while producing good results despite decoherence. This branch of quantum computing is highly versatile and a promising option for achieving quantum dominance. Because this is a relatively new field of study, we do not yet have an important algorithm library for NISQ machines. Developing novel algorithms for near-term quantum computers to solve real-world problems is an exciting software challenge.

REFERENCES

Bhatia, M., Sood, S., & Sood, V. (2023). A novel quantum-inspired solution for high-performance energy-efficient data acquisition from IoT networks. *Journal of Ambient Intelligence and Humanized Computing*, 14(5), 5001–5020. DOI: 10.1007/s12652-020-02494-x

Bhatia, M., & Sood, S. K. (2020). Quantum computing-inspired network optimization for IoT applications. *IEEE Internet of Things Journal*, 7(6), 5590–5598. DOI: 10.1109/JIOT.2020.2979887

Chang, Z., Cao, J., & Zhang, Y. (2018). A novel image segmentation approach for wood plate surface defect classification through convex optimization. *Journal of Forestry Research*, 29(6), 1789–1795. DOI: 10.1007/s11676-017-0572-7

Cuomo, D., Caleffi, M., & Cacciapuoti, A. S. (2020). Towards a distributed quantum computing ecosystem. *IET Quantum Communication*, 1(1), 3–8. DOI: 10.1049/iet-qtc.2020.0002

Farhi, E., Goldstone, J., Gutmann, S., & Sipser, M. (2000). Quantum computation by adiabatic evolution. arXiv preprint quant-ph/0001106.

Fiasché, M., Liberati, D. E., Gualandi, S., & Taisch, M. (2018). Quantum-inspired evolutionary multiobjective optimization for a dynamic production scheduling approach. Multidisciplinary approaches to neural computing, 191-201.

Han, K. H., & Kim, J. H. (2002). Quantum-inspired evolutionary algorithm for a class of combinatorial optimization. *IEEE Transactions on Evolutionary Computation*, 6(6), 580–593. DOI: 10.1109/TEVC.2002.804320

Jagatheesan, K., Samanta, S., Choudhury, A., Dey, N., Anand, B., & Ashour, A. S. (2018). Quantum inspired evolutionary algorithm in load frequency control of multi-area interconnected thermal power system with non-linearity. Quantum computing: an environment for intelligent large scale real application, 389-417.

Li, F., Liu, M., & Xu, G. (2019). A quantum ant colony multi-objective routing algorithm in WSN and its application in a manufacturing environment. *Sensors (Basel)*, 19(15), 3334. DOI: 10.3390/s19153334 PMID: 31362459

Orús, R., Mugel, S., & Lizaso, E. (2019). Quantum computing for finance: Overview and prospects. *Reviews in Physics*, 4, 100028. DOI: 10.1016/j.revip.2019.100028

Pathak, N., Misra, N. K., Bhoi, B. K., & Kumar, S. (2022). Concept and algorithm of quantum computing during pandemic situation of COVID-19. *Smart Systems: Innovations in ComputingProceedings of SSIC*, 2021, 523–535.

Potempa, R., & Porebski, S. (2022). Comparing concepts of quantum and classical neural network models for image classification task. In Progress in Image Processing, Pattern Recognition and Communication Systems: Proceedings of the Conference (CORES, IP&C, ACS)-June 28-30 2021 12 (pp. 61-71). Springer International Publishing. DOI: 10.1007/978-3-030-81523-3_6

Rajpurohit, J., Sharma, T. K., & Abraham, A. (2017). Glossary of metaheuristic algorithms. *International Journal of Computer Information Systems and Industrial Management Applications*, 9, 25–25.

Sood, V., & Chauhan, R. P. (2024). Archives of quantum computing: Research progress and challenges. *Archives of Computational Methods in Engineering*, 31(1), 73–91. DOI: 10.1007/s11831-023-09973-2

Thigale, S. B., Pandey, R. K., Gadekar, P. R., Dhotre, V. A., & Junnarkar, A. A. (2019). Lightweight novel trust based framework for IoT enabled wireless network communications. *Periodicals ofEngineering andNatural Sciences*, 7(3), 1126–1137. DOI: 10.21533/pen.v7i3.624

Valdez, F., & Melin, P. (2023). A review on quantum computing and deep learning algorithms and their applications. *Soft Computing*, 27(18), 13217–13236. DOI: 10.1007/s00500-022-07037-4 PMID: 35411203

Wu, D., Huo, J., Zhang, G., & Zhang, W. (2018). Minimization of logistics cost and carbon emissions based on quantum particle swarm optimization. *Sustainability (Basel)*, 10(10), 3791. DOI: 10.3390/su10103791

Xiong, H., Wu, Z., Fan, H., Li, G., & Jiang, G. (2018). Quantum rotation gate in quantum-inspired evolutionary algorithm: A review, analysis and comparison study. *Swarm and Evolutionary Computation*, 42, 43–57. DOI: 10.1016/j.swevo.2018.02.020

Zhao, W., Yan, L., & Zhang, Y. (2018). Geometric-constrained multi-view image matching method based on semi-global optimization. *Geo-Spatial Information Science*, 21(2), 115–126. DOI: 10.1080/10095020.2018.1441754

Compilation of References

Abbas, R., & Graepel, T. (2024). Artificial Intelligence in Healthcare Supply Chains: Enhancing Resilience and Reducing Waste through Quantitative Forecasting. *ResearchGate*. DOI: 10.13140/RG.2.2.25337.28006

Abdullah-All-Tanvir, E. M., Mahir, S., Akhter, S., & Huq, M. R. (2019). Detecting fake news using machine learning and deep learning algorithms. *2019 7th International Conference on Smart Computing & Communications (ICSCC),* 1–5. DOI: 10.1109/ICSCC.2019.8843612

Aguiar-Pérez, J. M., & Pérez-Juárez, M. Á. (2023). An Insight of Deep Learning Based Demand Forecasting in Smart Grids. *Sensors (Basel)*, 23(3), 1467. DOI: 10.3390/s23031467 PMID: 36772509

Aguirre, A., & Tegmark, M. (2011). Born in an infinite universe: A cosmological interpretation of quantum mechanics. *Physical Review. D*, 84(10), 105002. DOI: 10.1103/PhysRevD.84.105002

Ahamed, , e. (2023). Design of an energy-efficient IOT device-assisted wearable sensor platform for healthcare data management. *Elsevier- Measurement. Sensors (Basel)*, 100928.

Ahmed, H., Shukla, S., & Rai, H. M. (2014). Static handwritten signature recognition using discrete random transform and combined projection based technique. *International Conference on Advanced Computing and Communication Technologies, ACCT*, 37–41. https://doi.org/DOI: 10.1109/ACCT.2014.76

Ahmed, H., Traore, I., & Saad, S. (2017). Detection of online fake news using N-gram analysis and machine learning techniques. In *Intelligent* (pp. 127–138). Secure, and Dependable Systems in Distributed and Cloud Environments. DOI: 10.1007/978-3-319-69155-8_9

Ahmed, H., Traore, I., & Saad, S. (2018). Detecting opinion spams and fake news using text classification. *Security and Privacy*, 1(1), e9. DOI: 10.1002/spy2.9

Al Asaad, B., & Erascu, M. (2018). A tool for fake news detection. *2018 20th International Symposium on Symbolic and Numeric Algorithms for Scientific Computing (SYNASC),* 379–386. DOI: 10.1109/SYNASC.2018.00064

Alexandru Rancea, E. (2024). Edge Computing in Healthcare: Innovations, Opportunities, and Challenges. *MDPI.* https://www.mdpi.com/1999-5903/16/9/329

Al-Khalili, J. (2003). Time travel: Separating science fact from science fiction. *Physics Education*, 38(1), 14–19. DOI: 10.1088/0031-9120/38/1/302

All data. (n.d.). Retrieved April 4, 2023, from https://drive.google.com/file/d/0B3e3qZpPtccsMFo5bk9Ib3VCc2c/view

Alsharif, M. H., Abu Jahid, A. H. K., & Kannadasan, R. (2023). Green IoT: A Review and Future Research Directions. *Symmetry*, 15(3), 757. DOI: 10.3390/sym15030757

Amir Mosavi, A. B. (2019). Energy Consumption Prediction Using Machine Learning: A Review. *Research Gate*. https://www.researchgate.net/publication/331638667_Energy_Consumption_Prediction_Using_Machine_Learning_A_Review

Anatomy, C. (2016). *Stanford Neurosurgical Simulation and Virtual Reality Center.* https://med.stanford.edu/anatomy.html

Angelos, I., & Stoumpos, F. K. (2023). Digital Transformation in Healthcare: Technology Acceptance and Its Applications. *International Journal of Environmental Research and Public Health*, 20(4), 3407. DOI: 10.3390/ijerph20043407 PMID: 36834105

Aniket, , Patil, & Patil. (2023). Analyzing the effect of Process Parameters on Amaranth Popping and Puffing in the Lahi Machine using the Taguchi Method. *Journal of Physics: Conference Series*, 2601012013.

Anindya Bose, S. R. (2024). Application of Cloud Computing in Healthcare – A Comprehensive Study. *International Journal of Future Computer and Communication*, 13(2), 8.

Antoun, W., Baly, F., Achour, R., Hussein, A., & Hajj, H. (2020). State of the art models for fake news detection tasks. In *2020 IEEE International Conference on Informatics, IoT, and Enabling Technologies (ICIoT)* (pp. 519–524). IEEE. DOI: 10.1109/ICIoT48696.2020.9089487

Aphiwongsophon, S., & Chongstitvatana, P. (2018). Detecting fake news with machine learning methods. *2018 15th International Conference on Electrical Engineering/ Electronics, Computer, Telecommunications and Information Technology (ECTI-CON),* 528–531. DOI: 10.1109/ECTICon.2018.8620051

Ayalew, A. T., & Lohani, T. K. (2023). Prediction of Crop Yield by Support Vector Machine Coupled with Deep Learning Algorithm Procedures in Lower Kulfo Watershed of Ethiopia. *Journal of Engineering*, 2023, 1–8. DOI: 10.1155/2023/6675523

Bahdanau, D., Cho, K., & Bengio, Y. (2015). Neural machine translation by jointly learning to align and translate. *3rd International Conference on Learning Representations, ICLR 2015.*

Banister, D. (2005). *Time and Travel.* DOI: 10.1007/3-540-28550-4_17

Barocas, S., Hardt, M., & Narayanan, A. (2019). Fairness and Machine Learning. fairmlbook.org.

Bartlett, R. (2023). The 5th Dimension and its Implications for the String Theory, Conservation of Energy and Heisenberg Uncertainty Principle. *IPI Letters*, 1, 41–55. DOI: 10.59973/ipil.29

Bauer, D., & Tulic, M. (2018). Travel time predictions: Should one model speeds or travel times? *European Transport Research Review*, 10(2), 46. DOI: 10.1186/s12544-018-0315-7

Bengio, Y., Courville, A., & Vincent, P. (2013). Representation learning: A review and new perspectives. *IEEE Transactions on Pattern Analysis and Machine Intelligence*, 35(8), 1798–1828. DOI: 10.1109/TPAMI.2013.50 PMID: 23787338

Bergmann, P. G. (1962). *The General Theory of Relativity.* DOI: 10.1007/978-3-642-45973-3_3

Berniak-Woźny, J., & Rataj, M. (2023). Towards Green and Sustainable Healthcare: A Literature Review and Research Agenda for Green Leadership in the Healthcare Sector. *MDPI, 20*(2). .DOI: 10.3390/ijerph20020908

Bhatia, M., & Sood, S. K. (2020). Quantum computing-inspired network optimization for IoT applications. *IEEE Internet of Things Journal*, 7(6), 5590–5598. DOI: 10.1109/JIOT.2020.2979887

Bhatia, M., Sood, S., & Sood, V. (2023). A novel quantum-inspired solution for high-performance energy-efficient data acquisition from IoT networks. *Journal of Ambient Intelligence and Humanized Computing*, 14(5), 5001–5020. DOI: 10.1007/s12652-020-02494-x

Bibri, S. E., & Krogstie, J. (2020). The emerging data–driven Smart City and its innovative applied solutions for sustainability: The cases of London and Barcelona. *Energy Informatics*, 3, 5. DOI: 10.1186/s42162-020-00108-6

Blum, C. (2021). *Hybrid metaheuristics in optimization: Combining different techniques*. Springer Nature Switzerland AG. DOI: 10.1007/978-3-030-60152-2

Bue, X. P. N. (2019). *Cloud Volumes ONTAP, Cloud Data Sense, Data Protection, Advanced.*https://bluexp.netapp.com/blog/data-compliance-regulations-hipaa-gdpr-and-pci-dss

Casper van der Zee, E. (2024). Assessing the Carbon Footprint of Telemedicine: A Systematic Review. *Health Services Insights*. Advance online publication. DOI: 10.1177/1178632924127 PMID: 39139395

Cath, C., Wachter, S., Mittelstadt, B., Taddeo, M., & Floridi, L. (2018). *Artificial Intelligence and the 'Good Society*. EU, and UK Approach. Science and Engineering Ethics.

César Morcillo Serra, E. (2022). Environmental impact of digital health. *Scientific Reports*. DOI: 10.21203/rs.3.rs-1262007/v1

Chang, Z., Cao, J., & Zhang, Y. (2018). A novel image segmentation approach for wood plate surface defect classification through convex optimization. *Journal of Forestry Research*, 29(6), 1789–1795. DOI: 10.1007/s11676-017-0572-7

Chen, Y., Conroy, N. J., & Rubin, V. L. (2015). Misleading online content: Recognizing clickbait as "false news." In *Proceedings of the 2015 ACM Workshop on Multimodal Deception Detection* (pp. 15–19). DOI: 10.1145/2823465.2823467

Chidolue, , E. (2024). Green data centers: Sustainable practices for energy-efficient IT infrastructure. *Engineering Science & Technology Journal*, 5(1), 99–114.

Choi, N. (2022). *Johns Hopkins Uses Augmented Reality to Deliver High-Quality, Low-Cost Pediatric CPR Feedback.*https://www.jhuapl.edu/news/news-releases/220331-johns-hopkins-augmented-reality-cpr-coach

Chou, J., & Chen, K. (2024). Optimizing Investment Portfolios with a Sequential Ensemble of Decision Tree-Based Models and the FBI Algorithm for Effective Financial Indicator Analysis. *Applied Soft Computing*, 158, 111550. DOI: 10.1016/j.asoc.2024.111550

Cicceri, G., Tricomi, G., D'Agati, L., Longo, F., Merlino, G., & Puliafito, A. (2023, May 7). A Deep Learning-Driven Self-Conscious Distributed Cyber-Physical System for Renewable Energy Communities. *Sensors (Basel)*, 23(9), 4549. DOI: 10.3390/s23094549 PMID: 37177753

Clinic, C. (2023). *The Role of Virtual Reality in Medical Education.*https://my.clevelandclinic.org/podcasts/meded-thread/the-role-of-virtual-reality-in-medical-education

Coello Coello, C. A. (2020). *Evolutionary multi-objective optimization techniques and applications.* Springer Nature Switzerland AG. DOI: 10.1007/978-3-030-52173-8

Conroy, N. J., Rubin, V. L., & Chen, Y. (2015, November). Automatic deception detection: Methods for finding fake news. In *Proceedings of the 78th ASIS&T Annual Meeting: Information Science with Impact: Research in and for the Community* (p. 82). American Society for Information Science.

Cuomo, D., Caleffi, M., & Cacciapuoti, A. S. (2020). Towards a distributed quantum computing ecosystem. *IET Quantum Communication*, 1(1), 3–8. DOI: 10.1049/iet-qtc.2020.0002

Davim, J. P., & Conceição António, C. A. (2001). Optimisation of cutting conditions in machining of aluminium matrix composites using a numerical and experimental model. *Journal of Materials Processing Technology*, 112(1), 78–82. DOI: 10.1016/S0924-0136(01)00551-9

Dean, J., et al. (2012). Large Scale Distributed Deep Networks. NeurIPS.

Deb, K. (2019). An efficient evolutionary algorithm for large-scale multi-objective optimization. *Journal of Optimization Theory and Applications.* Advance online publication. DOI: 10.1007/s10957-019-01670-2

Debnath, A., Rai, H. M., Yadav, C., & Bhatia, A. (2013). Deblurring and Denoising of Magnetic Resonance Images using Blind Deconvolution Method. *International Journal of Computer Applications*, 81(10), 7–12. DOI: 10.5120/14046-2209

Della Vedova, M., Tacchini, E., Moret, S., Ballarin, G., Di Pierro, M., & De Alfaro, L. (2018). Automatic online fake news detection combining content and social signals. *Proceedings of the 22nd Conference of Open Innovations Association FRUCT.* DOI: 10.23919/FRUCT.2018.8468301

Dempster, M., & Leemans, V. (2006). An automated FX trading system using adaptive reinforcement learning. *Expert Systems with Applications*, 30(3), 543–552. DOI: 10.1016/j.eswa.2005.10.012

Deng, L., & Yu, D. (2014). Deep learning: Methods and applications. *Foundations and Trends in Signal Processing*, 7(3-4), 197–387. DOI: 10.1561/2000000039

Deutsch, D. (1991). Quantum mechanics near closed timelike lines. *Physical Review. D*, 44(10), 3197–3217. DOI: 10.1103/PhysRevD.44.3197

Dewey, C. (2016). Facebook has repeatedly trended fake news since firing its human editors. *Washington Post*.

Divya, Raju, & Singaravel. (2019). A Review of TOPSIS Method for Multi Criteria.

Donepudi, P. K., Ahmed, A. A., & Saha, S. (2020). Emerging market economy (EME) and artificial intelligence (AI): Consequences for the future of jobs. *PalArch's Journal of Archaeology of Egypt/Egyptology, 17*(6), 5562-5574.

Donepudi, P. K. (2019). Automation and machine learning in transforming the financial industry. *Asian Business Review*, 9(3), 129–138. DOI: 10.18034/abr.v9i3.494

Donepudi, P. K. (2020). Crowd sourced software testing: A timely opportunity. *Engineering International*, 8(1), 25–30. DOI: 10.18034/ei.v8i1.491

Donepudi, P. K., Banu, M. H., Khan, W., Neogy, T. K., & Ahmed, A. A. (2020). Artificial intelligence and machine learning in treasury management: A systematic literature review. *International Journal of Management*, 11(11), 13–22. DOI: 10.34218/IJM.11.11.2020.002

Dorigo, M. (2023). Ant colony optimization for dynamic and multi-objective optimization. *Artificial Intelligence Review*. Advance online publication. DOI: 10.1007/s10462-022-10141-0

Du, M. (2022). *The Theoretical Basis and Feasibility of Time Travel*. DOI: 10.2991/assehr.k.220105.048

Einstein, A. (1916). *Relativity: The Special and General Theory*. Methuen & Co Ltd.

Elayan, E. (2021). Digital Twin for Intelligent Context-Aware IoT Healthcare Systems. *IEEE, 99*(1). DOI: 10.1109/JIOT.2021.3051158

Emilyn, J. J., Chandrika, S. S., Susma, T., Vinisha, S., & Yesvantini, S. V. (2024). Entity Perception Using Remotely Piloted Aerial Vehicle. In Mehta, G., Wickramasinghe, N., & Kakkar, D. (Eds.), *Innovations in VLSI, Signal Processing and Computational Technologies. WREC 2023. Lecture Notes in Electrical Engineering* (Vol. 1095). Springer. DOI: 10.1007/978-981-99-7077-3_25

Engelbrecht, A. P. (2023). *Particle swarm optimization in engineering and robotics*. Springer Nature Switzerland AG. DOI: 10.1007/978-3-030-75967-9

Evangelia Katsoulakis, E. (2024). Digital twins for health: a scoping review. *NPJ Digital Medicine*, *7*(77).

Fake news detection. (n.d.). Retrieved April 4, 2023, from https://www.kaggle.com/jruvika/fake-news-detection

Fake news samples. (n.d.). Retrieved April 12, 2023, from https://www.kaggle.com/pontes/fake-news-sample

Fake or Real News. (n.d.). Retrieved April 12, 2023, from https://www.kaggle.com/datasets/jillanisofttech/fake-or-real-news

Farhan, L., Hameed, R. S., Ahmed, A. S., Fadel, A. H., Gheth, W., Alzubaidi, L., Fadhel, M. A., & Al-Amidie, M. (2021). Energy Efficiency for Green Internet of Things (IoT) Networks: A Survey. *Network (Bristol, England)*, 1(3), 279–314. DOI: 10.3390/network1030017

Farhi, E., Goldstone, J., & Gutmann, S. (2014). A Quantum Approximate Optimization Algorithm. arXiv preprint arXiv:1411.4028.

Farhi, E., Goldstone, J., Gutmann, S., & Sipser, M. (2000). Quantum computation by adiabatic evolution. arXiv preprint quant-ph/0001106.

Fedosin, , S. (2012). Scale dimension as the fifth dimension of spacetime. *Turkish Journal of Physics*. DOI: 10.3906/fiz-1110-20

Fei, N. C., Mehat, N. M., & Kamaruddin, S. (2013). Practical Applications of Taguchi Method for Optimization of Processing Parameters for Plastic Injection Moulding: A Retrospective Review. ISRN Indust. Eng., 1–11.

Feurer, M., & Hutter, F. (2019). *Hyperparameter Optimization. Automated Machine Learning*. Springer.

Fiasché, M., Liberati, D. E., Gualandi, S., & Taisch, M. (2018). Quantum-inspired evolutionary multiobjective optimization for a dynamic production scheduling approach. Multidisciplinary approaches to neural computing, 191-201.

Finn, C., Abbeel, P., & Levine, S. (2017). *Model-Agnostic Meta-Learning for Fast Adaptation of Deep Networks*. ICML.

Flores-Martin, D., Berrocal, J., & García-Alonso, J. (2023). Towards dynamic and heterogeneous social IoT environments. *Computing*, 105, 1141–1164. DOI: 10.1007/s00607-022-01113-1

Gale, Iwry, & Orszag. (n.d.). The Automatic 401(k): A Simple Way To Strengthen Retirement Saving. Available: http://www.retirementsecurityproject.org

Gautam, G. D., & Mishra, D. R. (2019). Evaluation of geometrical quality characteristics in pulsed Nd: YAG laser cutting of Kevlar-29/basalt fiber reinforced hybrid composite using grey relational analysis based on genetic algorithm. *FME Trans.*, 47(3), 560–575. DOI: 10.5937/fmet1903560G

Gautam, G. D., & Mishra, D. R. (2019). Firefly algorithm based optimization of kerf quality characteristics in pulsed Nd:YAG laser cutting of basalt fiber reinforced composite. *Composites. Part B, Engineering*, 176, 107340. DOI: 10.1016/j.compositesb.2019.107340

GeeksforGeeks. (2024, July 12). *Random Forest algorithm in machine learning*. GeeksforGeeks. https://www.geeksforgeeks.org/random-forest-algorithm-in-machine-learning/

Glover, F. (2019). *Metaheuristic optimization algorithms: Tabu search*. Springer Nature Switzerland AG. DOI: 10.1007/978-3-030-65338-6

Goldberg, D. E. (1989). *Genetic Algorithms in Search, Optimization, and Machine Learning*. Addison-Wesley.

Gondhalekar, G. V. G, L. D. Isaac, R. K. Vyas, A. R. S R & A. K. N. (2023). An Optimized Security Framework for Global IoT Communication using Software-Defined Networking (SDN) in Adversarial Environments. *2023 7th International Conference on I-SMAC (IoT in Social, Mobile, Analytics and Cloud) (I-SMAC)*, 100-109. DOI: 10.1109/I-SMAC58438.2023.10290515

Goodfellow, I., Bengio, Y., & Courville, A. (2016). *Deep Learning*. MIT Press.

Gowda, B. M. U., Ravindra, H. V., Prakash, G. V. N., Nishanth, P., & Ugrasen, G. (2015). Optimization of Process Parameters in Drilling of Epoxy Si3N4. *Materials Today: Proceedings*, 2(4–5), 2852–2861. DOI: 10.1016/j.matpr.2015.07.300

Goyal, Y., Raj, Rai, H. M., Aggarwal, M., Saxena, K., & Amanzholova, S. (2023). *Revolutionizing Skin Cancer Detection: A Comprehensive Review of Deep Learning Methods*. DOI: 10.1145/3647444.3647885

Granik, M., & Mesyura, V. (2017). Fake news detection using naive Bayes classifier. In *2017 IEEE First Ukraine Conference on Electrical and Computer Engineering (UKRCON)* (pp. 900-903). DOI: 10.1109/UKRCON.2017.8100379

Gunjan, A., & Bhattacharyya, S. (2022). A brief review of portfolio optimization techniques. *Artificial Intelligence Review*, 56(5), 3847–3886. DOI: 10.1007/s10462-022-10273-7

Gupta, S., Sharmila, & Rai, H. M. (2021). IoT-Based Automatic Irrigation System Using Robotic Vehicle. In D. Goyal, V. E. Bălaş, A. Mukherjee, V. H. C. de Albuquerque, & A. K. Gupta (Eds.), *Information Management and Machine Intelligence. ICIMMI 2019. Algorithms for Intelligent Systems. Springer* (pp. 669–677). Springer, Singapore. DOI: 10.1007/978-981-15-4936-6_73

Haba, R., Ohzeki, M., & Tanaka, K. (2022). Travel time optimization on multi-AGV routing by reverse annealing. *Scientific Reports*, 12(1), 17753. DOI: 10.1038/s41598-022-22704-0

Han, K. H., & Kim, J. H. (2002). Quantum-inspired evolutionary algorithm for a class of combinatorial optimization. *IEEE Transactions on Evolutionary Computation*, 6(6), 580–593. DOI: 10.1109/TEVC.2002.804320

Han, S., Mao, H., & Dally, W. J. (2015). Deep compression: Compressing deep neural networks with pruning, trained quantization and Huffman coding. *4th International Conference on Learning Representations, ICLR 2016.*

He, X., Zhao, K., & Chu, X. (2021). AutoML: A Survey of the State-of-the-Art. *Knowledge-Based Systems*, 212, 106622. DOI: 10.1016/j.knosys.2020.106622

Hidayat Ullah, E. (2023). Exploring the healthcare metaverse: AR and VR applications in patient care. *Journal of Digital Health, 20*(2), 210-225.

Holtorf, C., & Petersson, B. (2018). Archaeology and Time Travel. In *Encyclopedia of Global Archaeology* (pp. 1–11). Springer International Publishing. DOI: 10.1007/978-3-319-51726-1_2793-1

Horne, B., & Adali, S. (2017). This just in: Fake news packs a lot in title, uses simpler, repetitive content in text body, more similar to satire than real news. *Proceedings of the International AAAI Conference on Web and Social Media, 11*(1), 759–766. DOI: 10.1609/icwsm.v11i1.14976

Horton, M. (2023, May 3). *Practice Management Guide for Financial Advisors.* Investopedia. https://www.investopedia.com/articles/professionals/080515/pros-cons-financial-advisor-career.asp

Hospedales, T., Antoniou, A., Micaelli, P., & Storkey, A. (2021). Meta-Learning in Neural Networks: A Survey. *IEEE Transactions on Pattern Analysis and Machine Intelligence*, 1. DOI: 10.1109/TPAMI.2021.3079209 PMID: 33974543

Hossein Omrany, A. M. (2024). Digital Twin Technology and Social Sustainability: Implications for the Construction Industry. *MDPI- Sustainability*, *16*(9). .DOI: 10.3390/su16198663

Huang, Y.-F., & Chen, P.-H. (2020). Fake news detection using an ensemble learning model based on self-adaptive harmony search algorithms. *Expert Systems with Applications*, 159, 113584. DOI: 10.1016/j.eswa.2020.113584

Jadhav, S. S., & Thepade, S. D. (2019). Fake news identification and classification using DSSM and improved recurrent neural network classifier. *Applied Artificial Intelligence*, 33(12), 1058–1068. DOI: 10.1080/08839514.2019.1661579

Jagatheesan, K., Samanta, S., Choudhury, A., Dey, N., Anand, B., & Ashour, A. S. (2018). Quantum inspired evolutionary algorithm in load frequency control of multi-area interconnected thermal power system with non-linearity. Quantum computing: an environment for intelligent large scale real application, 389-417.

Jamil, Khan, He, Li, Zhao, & Sarfraz. (2019). Multi-response optimisation of machining aluminium-6061 under eco-friendly electrostatic minimum quantity lubrication environment. Int. J. Mach. Mach. Mater., 21(5– 6), 459–479.

Jha, K., Pasbola, M., Rai, H. M., & Amanzholova, S. (2023). Utilizing Smartwatches and Deep Learning Models for Enhanced Avalanche Victim Identification, Localization, and Efficient Recovery Strategies: An In-depth Study. *Proceedings of the 5th International Conference on Information Management & Machine Intelligence*, 1–5. DOI: 10.1145/3647444.3652483

Kairouz, P., & McMahan, H. B. (2019). Advances and Open Problems in Federated Learning. arXiv preprint arXiv:1912.04977.

Kaiser. (2023). *Kaiser Permanente data center: continuous and innovative energy efficiency improvements.*https://www.energystar.gov/sites/default/files/asset/document/Kaiser_Permanente_case_study.pdf

Kaliyar, R. K., Goswami, A., Narang, P., & Sinha, S. (2020). FNDNet – A deep convolutional neural network for fake news detection. *Cognitive Systems Research*, 61, 32–44. DOI: 10.1016/j.cogsys.2019.12.005

Karla, . (2024). The Impact of Digital Health Solutions on Bridging the Health Care Gap in Rural Areas: A Scoping Review. *The Permanente Journal*, 28(3), 130–143. DOI: 10.7812/TPP/23.134 PMID: 39135461

Kaur, S., Kumar, P., & Kumaraguru, P. (2020). Automating fake news detection system using multi-level voting model. *Soft Computing*, 24(12), 9049–9069. DOI: 10.1007/s00500-019-04436-y

Kennedy, J., & Eberhart, R. (1995). Particle Swarm Optimization. Proceedings of ICNN'95 - International Conference on Neural Networks. DOI: 10.1109/ICNN.1995.488968

Kennedy, J., & Eberhart, R. (2021). Particle swarm optimization and its hybrid approaches in optimization. *IEEE Transactions on Evolutionary Computation*, 25(6), 1095–1105. DOI: 10.1109/TEVC.2020.3007312

Kesarwani, A., Chauhan, S. S., & Nair, A. R. (2020). Fake news detection on social media using K-nearest neighbor classifier. *2020 International Conference on Advances in Computing and Communication Engineering (ICACCE)*, 1–4. DOI: 10.1109/ICACCE49060.2020.9154997

Khalil, A., Jarrah, M., Aldwairi, M., & Jararweh, Y. (2021). Detecting Arabic fake news using machine learning. In *2021 Second International Conference on Intelligent Data Science Technologies and Applications (IDSTA)* (pp. 171–177). IEEE. DOI: 10.1109/IDSTA53674.2021.9660811

Khan, J. Y., Khondaker, M. T. I., Afroz, S., Uddin, G., & Iqbal, A. (2021). A benchmark study of machine learning models for online fake news detection. *Machine Learning with Applications*, 4, 100032. DOI: 10.1016/j.mlwa.2021.100032

Khezr, E. (2019). Blockchain Technology in Healthcare: A Comprehensive Review and Directions for Future Research. *MDPI- Applied Science*, *9*(9).

Kingma, D. P., & Ba, J. (2014). Adam: A Method for Stochastic Optimization.

Knibbe, E. (2022). Digital twins in the green life sciences. *NJAS: Impact in Agricultural and Life Sciences - T&F*, *94*(1). .DOI: 10.1080/27685241.2022.2150571

Kotteti, M. M., Dong, X., Li, N., & Qian, L. (2018). Fake news detection enhancement with data imputation. *2018 IEEE 16th International Conference on Dependable, Autonomic and Secure Computing (DASC)*, 187–192. DOI: 10.1109/DASC/PiCom/DataCom/CyberSciTec.2018.00042

Krishna, N. L. S. R., & Adimoolam, M. (2022). Fake News Detection system using Decision Tree algorithm and compare textual property with Support Vector Machine algorithm. In *2022 International Conference on Business Analytics for Technology and Security (ICBATS)* (pp. 1–6). IEEE. DOI: 10.1109/ICBATS54253.2022.9758999

Kudarvalli, H., & Fiaidhi, J. (2020). Experiments on detecting fake news over social media using machine learning algorithms. *International Journal of Advanced Nursing Education and Research*, 8(1), 15–26. DOI: 10.21742/ijriar.2020.8.1.03

Kumar, J., & Verma, R. (2020). Experimental investigations and multiple criteria optimization during milling of Graphene Oxide (GO) doped epoxy/CFRP composites using TOPSIS-AHP hybrid module. *FME Transactions*, 48(3), 628–635. DOI: 10.5937/fme2003628K

Kumar, K. R., Sreebalaji, V. S., & Pridhar, T. (2018). Characterization and optimization of abrasive water jet machining parameters of aluminium/tungsten carbide composites. *Measurement*, 117, 57–66. DOI: 10.1016/j.measurement.2017.11.059

Kumar, K. V., & Sait, A. N. (2017). Modelling and optimisation of machining parameters for composite pipes using artificial neural network and genetic algorithm. *International Journal on Interactive Design and Manufacturing*, 11(2), 435–443. DOI: 10.1007/s12008-014-0253-0

Kumar, V., Kumar, A., Singh, A. K., & Pachauri, A. (2021). Fake news detection using machine learning and natural language processing. *Proceedings of the International Conference on Technological Advancements and Innovations (ICTAI), 3878*(6), 547-552. DOI: 10.1109/ICTAI53825.2021.9673378

Kurasinski, L., & Mihailescu, R. C. (2020). Towards machine learning explainability in text classification for fake news detection. In *Proceedings of the 19th IEEE International Conference on Machine Learning and Applications (ICMLA)* (pp. 775-781). DOI: 10.1109/ICMLA51294.2020.00127

Lai, C. M. (2019). Integrating simplified swarm optimization with AHP for solving capacitated military logistic depot location problem. *Applied Soft Computing*, 78, 1–12. DOI: 10.1016/j.asoc.2019.02.016

Lee, S. Y., Tama, B. A., Choi, C., Hwang, J., Bang, J., & Lee, S. (2020). Spatial and sequential deep learning approach for predicting temperature distribution in a Steel-Making continuous casting process. *IEEE Access : Practical Innovations, Open Solutions*, 8, 21953–21965. DOI: 10.1109/ACCESS.2020.2969498

Levin, S. (2017, June 13). Pay to sway: Report reveals how easy it is to manipulate elections with fake news. *The Guardian*.

Li, F., Liu, M., & Xu, G. (2019). A quantum ant colony multi-objective routing algorithm in WSN and its application in a manufacturing environment. *Sensors (Basel)*, 19(15), 3334. DOI: 10.3390/s19153334 PMID: 31362459

Lili Wang, X. S. (2023). Foveated rendering: A state-of-the-art survey. *Computational Visualizations*, 9(2), 195–228.

Liu, S. Z. (2024). Enhancing User Experience in VR Environments through AI-Driven Adaptive UI Design. *Research Gate*, 8.

Li, Y. (2022). Swarm intelligence-based algorithms for complex scheduling problems. *IEEE Transactions on Systems, Man, and Cybernetics. Systems*. Advance online publication. DOI: 10.1109/TSMC.2021.3124661

Lobo, F. S. N. (2007). *Exotic solutions in General Relativity: Traversable wormholes and "warp drive" spacetimes.*

Lodwick, W. A., & Untiedt, E. A. (2012). *Fuzzy Optimization. In Computational Complexity*. Springer New York.

Luo, H. T. (2024). Recent Advances in Wearable Healthcare Devices: From Material to Application. *MDPI- Bio Engineering*, 11(4). .DOI: 10.3390/bioengineering11040358

Madry, A., Makelov, A., Schmidt, L., Tsipras, D., & Vladu, A. (2017). *Towards Deep Learning Models Resistant to Adversarial Attacks*. ICLR.

Magazine, I. (2019). *A Stroke of Genius: Neurorehabilitation through Virtual Reality*. https://illumin.usc.edu/about-us/

Marri, M. A. (2024). *Comparing Digital Twin and Metaverse Technologies: An In-Depth Analysis*.https://www.linkedin.com/in/mohamed-almarri/

Ma, S., Chen, J., Zhang, Y., Shrivastava, A., & Mohan, H. (2021). Cloud based Resource Scheduling Methodology for Data-Intensive Smart Cities and Industrial Applications. *Scalable Computing: Practice and Experience*, 22(2), 227–235. DOI: 10.12694/scpe.v22i2.1899

McKenzie, A. (2020). Reality and Super-Reality: Properties of a Mathematical Multiverse. *Axiomathes*, 30(4), 453–478. DOI: 10.1007/s10516-019-09466-7

McMahan, H. B. (2017). *Communication-Efficient Learning of Deep Networks from Decentralized Data*. AISTATS.

Meel, P., & Vishwakarma, D. K. (2021). HAN, image captioning, and forensics ensemble multimodal fake news detection. *Information Sciences*, 567, 23–41. DOI: 10.1016/j.ins.2021.03.037

Mehrotra, N. (2024). *How sustainable practices can drive inclusive growth in modern business*.https://www.ey.com/en_in/insights/climate-change-sustainability-services/how-sustainable-practices-ensure-a-green-healthcare-ecosystem

Misner, C. W., Thorne, K. S., & Wheeler, J. A. (1973). *Gravitation*. W. H. Freeman and Co. New York.

Mosallanezhad, , E. (2023). An IoMT platform for an integrated sustainable energy-efficient disaster relief supply chain to prevent severity-driven disruptions during pandemics. *Journal of Industrial Information Integration*, 100502, 35. DOI: 10.1016/j.jii.2023.100502

Muguthu, Dong, & Ikua. (2015). Optimization of machining parameters influencing machinability of Al2124SiCp (45% wt) metal matrix composite. J. Compos. Mater.

Mukherjee, I., & Ray, P. K. (2006). A review of optimization techniques in metal cutting processes. *Computers & Industrial Engineering*, 50(1–2), 15–34. DOI: 10.1016/j.cie.2005.10.001

Nations, U. (2023). *Sustainable Development Goals*. https://www.un.org/sustainabledevelopment/climate-action/

Nguyen, H. K., & Azreg-Aïnou, M. (2023). Traversable Morris–Thorne–Buchdahl wormholes in quadratic gravity. *The European Physical Journal C*, 83(7), 626. DOI: 10.1140/epjc/s10052-023-11805-3

Ni, B., Guo, Z., Li, J., & Jiang, M. (2020). Improving generalizability of fake news detection methods using propensity score matching. arXiv. Retrieved from http://arxiv.org/abs/2002.00838

Nižetić, S., & Šolić, P. (2020). Internet of Things (IoT): Opportunities, issues and challenges towards a smart and sustainable future. Journal of Cleaner Production, 274. DOI: 10.1016/j.jclepro.2020.122877

Nocedal, J., & Wright, S. J. (2006). *Numerical Optimization*. Springer.

Nti, I. K., Adekoya, A. F., & Weyori, B. A. (2019). A systematic review of fundamental and technical analysis of stock market predictions. *Artificial Intelligence Review*, 53(4), 3007–3057. DOI: 10.1007/s10462-019-09754-z

Ohenhen, P. E. (2024). Sustainable cooling solutions for electronics: A comprehensive review: Investigating the latest techniques and materials, their effectiveness in mechanical applications, and associated environmental benefits. *World Journal of Advanced Research and Reviews*, *21*(1). DOI: 10.30574/wjarr.2024.21.1.0111

Olayinka, E. (2024). Artificial Intelligence in Healthcare Supply Chains: Enhancing Resilience and Reducing Waste. *International Journal of Advance Research, Ideas and Innovations in Technology*, 203.

Orús, R., Mugel, S., & Lizaso, E. (2019). Quantum computing for finance: Overview and prospects. *Reviews in Physics*, 4, 100028. DOI: 10.1016/j.revip.2019.100028

Oyekunle, , E. (2024). Healthcare applications of Augmented Reality (AR) and Virtual Reality (VR) simulation in clinical education. *Journal of Clinical Images and Medical Case Reports*, 1–18.

Papanicolaou & Papantoniou. (2016). Optimum design of textile-reinforced concrete as integrated formwork in slabs. Textile Fibre Compos. Civil Eng., 245–274.

Pare, V., Agnihotri, G., & Krishna, C. (2015). Selection of optimum process parameters in high speed CNC end-milling of composite materials using meta heuristic techniques–a comparative study. *Strojniški vestnik-J.Mechanical Engineering (New York, N.Y.)*, 61(3), 176–186.

Pathak, N., Misra, N. K., Bhoi, B. K., & Kumar, S. (2022). Concept and algorithm of quantum computing during pandemic situation of COVID-19. *Smart Systems: Innovations in ComputingProceedings of SSIC*, 2021, 523–535.

Patil, S. D., & Bhalerao, Y. (2019). Optimization of dynamic properties of hybrid composite shaft with newly developed resin (N.D.R.E.) using grey relational analysis. *International Journal of Structural Integrity*, 11(2), 248–263. DOI: 10.1108/IJSI-07-2019-0073

Patil, S. D., & Bhalerao, Y. (2020). Multi-objective optimization of carbon/glass hybrid composites with newly developed resin (N.D.R.E.) using gray relational analysis. *Multidiscipline Modeling in Materials and Structures*, 16(6), 1709–1729. DOI: 10.1108/MMMS-08-2019-0141

Patil, S. D., Bhalerao, Y., & Takale, A. (2020). Optimization of design variables for carbon/glass hybrid composites laminates using Taguchi Technique. *World Journal of Engineering*, 17(2), 309–323. DOI: 10.1108/WJE-10-2019-0290

Patil, S. D., Hatte, P., Khan, S. N., Desai, A. A., & Yadav, P. H. (2023). Analyzing the Design Parameters and Their Influence on the Tensile Strength of Composite Layers using Taguchi Technique. *Materials Today: Proceedings*, 77, 640–646. DOI: 10.1016/j.matpr.2022.11.276

Peter Efosa Ohenhen. (2024). Low-power processors and advanced cooling systems for sustainable digital health. Sustainable Computing for Healthcare. *World Journal of Advanced Research and Reviews*, 21(1), 957–972.

Phiips. (2024). *Magnetic Resonance - Proactive Energy Management.*https://www.philips.co.in/healthcare/resources/landing/mr-proactive-energy-management

Polasi, P. K. (2023). An IoT-based duplex mode Remote Health Monitoring System. *2023 International Conference on Recent Advances in Electrical, Electronics, Ubiquitous Communication, and Computational Intelligence (RAEEUCCI)*, 1-5. DOI: 10.1109/RAEEUCCI57140.2023.10134141

Pomerleau, R. D. (2017). Fake News Challenge Dataset. Retrieved June 22, 2022, from http://www.fakenewschallenge.org/

Potempa, R., & Porebski, S. (2022). Comparing concepts of quantum and classical neural network models for image classification task. In Progress in Image Processing, Pattern Recognition and Communication Systems: Proceedings of the Conference (CORES, IP&C, ACS)-June 28-30 2021 12 (pp. 61-71). Springer International Publishing. DOI: 10.1007/978-3-030-81523-3_6

Pouncy, J. (2024). *Sustainable Healthcare & AI: The Future of Efficient Healthcare Systems.*https://www.linkedin.com/pulse/sustainable-healthcare-ai-future-efficient-systems-jeremiah-pouncy-xadhf/

Pratiwi, Y. R., Asmara, R. A., & Rahutomo, F. (2017). Study of hoax news detection using naïve Bayes classifier in Indonesian language. *2017 11th International Conference on Information & Communication Technology and System (ICTS),* 73–78. DOI: 10.1109/ICTS.2017.8265649

Preskill, J. (2018). Quantum Computing in the NISQ era and beyond. *Quantum : the Open Journal for Quantum Science*, 2, 79. DOI: 10.22331/q-2018-08-06-79

Puri, M., Solanki, A., Padawer, T., Tipparaju, S. M., Moreno, W. A., & Pathak, Y. (2016). *Introduction to Artificial Neural Network (ANN) as a Predictive Tool for Drug Design, Discovery, Delivery, and Disposition. In Artificial Neural Network for Drug Design, Delivery and Disposition.* Elsevier.

Rahman, M. M., Chowdhury, M. R. H. K., Islam, M. A., Tohfa, M. U., Kader, M. A. L., Ahmed, A. A. A., & Donepudi, P. K. (2020). Relationship between socio-demographic characteristics and job satisfaction: Evidence from private bank employees. *American Journal of Trade and Policy*, 7(2), 65–72. DOI: 10.18034/ajtp.v7i2.492

Rajkumar Buyya, S. I. (2023). Energy-efficiency and sustainability in new generation cloud computing: A vision and directions for integrated management of data centre resources and workloads. *Wiley*, *54*(1).

Rajpurohit, J., Sharma, T. K., & Abraham, A. (2017). Glossary of metaheuristic algorithms. *International Journal of Computer Information Systems and Industrial Management Applications*, 9, 25–25.

Rauch, S. (2024). *Case Studies: The Growing Role of AI and Big Data in Healthcare.* https://www.simplilearn.com/role-of-ai-and-big-data-in-healthcare-article

Read, J., & Le Bihan, B. (2021). The landscape and the multiverse: What's the problem? *Synthese*, 199(3–4), 7749–7771. DOI: 10.1007/s11229-021-03137-0

Rehman, E. (2021). Energy-Efficient IoT e-Health Using Artificial Intelligence Model with Homomorphic Secret Sharing. *Energies*, *14*(19), 6414. DOI: 10.3390/en14196414

Reis, J. C. S., Correia, A., Murai, F., Veloso, A., & Benevenuto, F. (2019). Supervised learning for fake news detection. *IEEE Intelligent Systems*, 34(2), 76–81. DOI: 10.1109/MIS.2019.2899143

Rejeb, A., Rejeb, K., Appolloni, A., Jagtap, S., Iranmanesh, M., Alghamdi, S., Alhasawi, Y., & Kayikci, Y. (2024). Unleashing the power of internet of things and blockchain: A comprehensive analysis and future directions. Internet of Things and Cyber-Physical Systems, 4, 1-18. DOI: 10.1016/j.iotcps.2023.06.003

Ren, Y., & Zhang, J. (2021). Fake news detection on news-oriented heterogeneous information networks through hierarchical graph attention. In *2021 International Joint Conference on Neural Networks (IJCNN)* (pp. 1–8). IEEE. DOI: 10.1109/IJCNN52387.2021.9534362

Rogers, E. M. (2003). *Diffusion of Innovations* (5th ed.). Free Press.

Rubin, V., Conroy, N., Chen, Y., & Cornwell, S. (2016). Fake news or truth? Using satirical cues to detect potentially misleading news. In *Proceedings of the 2016 Workshop on News and Public Opinion* (pp. 7-17). https://doi.org/DOI: 10.18653/v1/W16-0802

Saba, , E. (2020). Secure and energy-efficient framework using Internet of Medical Things for e-healthcare. *Journal of Infection and Public Health*, 1567–1575. PMID: 32682657

Sabri, N. M., Puteh, M., & Mahmood, M. R. (2013). An overview of Gravitational Search Algorithm utilization in optimization problems. 2013 IEEE 3rd International Conference on System Engineering and Technology, 61–66. DOI: 10.1109/ICSEngT.2013.6650144

Sagar D Patil, D.S.Chavan and M.V Kavade, (2012). Investigation of Composite Torsion Shaft for Static Structural Analysis using Finite Element Analysis. *International Journal of Engineering Research & Technology (Ahmedabad)*, 1(7), 1–5.

Sagar D Patil, D.S.Chavan, M.V.Kavade , (2012). Investigation of Composite Torsion Shaft for Torsional Buckling Analysis using Finite Element Analysis. *IOSR Journal of Mechanical and Civil Engineering*, 4(3), 26–31. DOI: 10.9790/1684-0432631

Sagar Dnyandev Patil, Khot, & Hatte. (2024). Multi-objective Optimization and Development of Mathematical Model for Process Parameters of Amaranth Grains using Regression Analysis. Research Square.

Saito, S. (2023). Special theory of relativity for a graded index fibre. *Frontiers in Physics*, 11. DOI: 10.3389/fphy.2023.1225387

Samadi, M., Mousavian, M., & Momtazi, S. (2021). Deep contextualized text representation and learning for fake news detection. *Information Processing & Management*, 58(6), 102723. Advance online publication. DOI: 10.1016/j.ipm.2021.102723

Sansonetti, G., Gasparetti, F., D'Aniello, G., & Micarelli, A. (2020). Unreliable users detection in social media: Deep learning techniques for automatic detection. *IEEE Access : Practical Innovations, Open Solutions*, 8, 213154–213167. DOI: 10.1109/ACCESS.2020.3040604

Sarker, I. H. (2021). Deep Learning: A Comprehensive Overview on Techniques, Taxonomy, Applications and Research Directions. *SN Computer Science*, 2, 420. DOI: 10.1007/s42979-021-00815-1 PMID: 34426802

Sasikumar, K., Arulshri, K., Ponappa, K., & Uthayakumar, M. (2018). A study on kerf characteristics of hybrid aluminium 7075 metal matrix composites machined using abrasive water jet machining technology. *Proceedings of the Institution of Mechanical Engineers. Part B, Journal of Engineering Manufacture*, 232(4), 690–704. DOI: 10.1177/0954405416654085

Schmitt, M. (2023). Automated machine learning: AI-driven decision making in business analytics. *Intelligent Systems with Applications*, 18, 200188. DOI: 10.1016/j.iswa.2023.200188

Serdahely, W. J. (1990). A brief history of time: From the big bang to black holes. *Journal of Near-Death Studies*, 9(2), 123–131. DOI: 10.1007/BF01074212

Shah, A. S., Nasir, H., Fayaz, M., Lajis, A., & Shah, A. (2019). A Review on Energy Consumption Optimization Techniques in IoT Based Smart Building Environments. *Information (Basel)*, 10(3), 108. DOI: 10.3390/info10030108

Sharma, G., Vidalis, S., Mankar, P., Anand, N., Minakshi, N., & Kumar, S. (2024). Automated passive income from stock market using machine learning and big data analytics with security aspects. *Multimedia Tools and Applications*. Advance online publication. DOI: 10.1007/s11042-024-19340-3

Shilane, D., Martikainen, J., Dudoit, S., & Ovaska, S. J. (2008). A general framework for statistical performance comparison of evolutionary computation algorithms. Information Sciences. *International Journal (Toronto, Ont.)*, 178, 2870–2879.

Shi, Y. (2021). *Differential evolution in constrained optimization problems*. Springer Nature Switzerland AG. DOI: 10.1007/978-3-030-74906-8

Shu, K., Sliva, A., Wang, S., Tang, J., & Liu, H. (2017). Fake news detection on social media: A data mining perspective. *SIGKDD Explorations*, 19(1), 22–36. DOI: 10.1145/3137597.3137600

Siemens. (2024). *Sustainability in In Vitro Diagnostics*.https://www.siemens-healthineers.com/en-in/about/sustainability-ehs/in-vitro-diagnostics

Singh, V., Dasgupta, R., Sonagra, D., Raman, K., & Ghosh, I. (2017). Automated fake news detection using linguistic analysis and machine learning. In *Proceedings of the 2017 International Conference on Social Computing, Behavioral Modeling, and Prediction* (pp. 1-3). DOI: 10.13140/RG.2.2.16825.67687

Snoek, J., Larochelle, H., & Adams, R. P. (2012). Practical Bayesian Optimization of Machine Learning Algorithms.

Sood, V., & Chauhan, R. P. (2024). Archives of quantum computing: Research progress and challenges. *Archives of Computational Methods in Engineering*, 31(1), 73–91. DOI: 10.1007/s11831-023-09973-2

Srinivasan, Thirumurugaveerakumar, Raffic, & Babu. (2020). Mono and Multi Response Optimization of End Milling Parameters for AA6061 by Taguchi Based GRA and TOPSIS Methodology. J. Xidian Univers., 14(6).

Srinivasan, S., Thirumurugaveerakumar, S., Nagarajan, N., Mohammed Raffic, N., & Ganesh Babu, K. (2013). A review of optimization techniques in machining of composite Materials. *Materials Today: Proceedings*.

Staff, C.-S. (2020). *VR and the Future of Healthcare*.https://www.cedars-sinai.org/blog/virtual-reality-future-healthcare.html

Sun, , E. (2023). Digital twin in healthcare: Recent updates and challenges. *Digital Health*. Advance online publication. DOI: 10.1177/20552076221149651 PMID: 36636729

Syed, A. S., Sierra-Sosa, D., Kumar, A., & Elmaghraby, A. (2021). IoT in Smart Cities: A Survey of Technologies, Practices and Challenges. *Smart Cities*, 4(2), 429–475. DOI: 10.3390/smartcities4020024

Szpakowski, M. (2020). *Fake news corpus*. Retrieved June 22, 2023, from https://github.com/several27/FakeNewsCorpus

Talbi, E.-G. (2019). *Parallel and distributed metaheuristics for optimization*. Wiley-ISTE., DOI: 10.1002/9781119508653

Tamiloli, N., Venkatesan, J., Murali, G., Kodali, S. P., Sampath Kumar, T., & Arunkumar, M. P. (2019). Optimization of end milling on Al–SiC-fly ash metal matrix composite using Topsis and fuzzy logic. *SN Applied Sciences*, 1(10), 1204. DOI: 10.1007/s42452-019-1191-z

Tanabe, R., & Fukunaga, A. (2022). *Novel variants of evolutionary algorithms and their applications*. Springer Nature Switzerland AG. DOI: 10.1007/978-3-030-87985-7

Tatiana Mallet Machado, T. M. (2023). Literature review of digital twin in healthcare. *Heliyonn - Science DIrect*, 9(9). .DOI: 10.1016/j.heliyon.2023.e19390

Thigale, S. B., Pandey, R. K., Gadekar, P. R., Dhotre, V. A., & Junnarkar, A. A. (2019). Lightweight novel trust based framework for IoT enabled wireless network communications. *Periodicals of Engineering and Natural Sciences*, 7(3), 1126–1137. DOI: 10.21533/pen.v7i3.624

Thippa Reddy, G., Swarna Priya, R. M., & Parimala, M. (2020). A deep neural networks based model for uninterrupted marine environment monitoring. Computer Communications, 157, 64-75. DOI: 10.1016/j.comcom.2020.04.004

Thompson, M. (2021). *The environmental impacts of digital health.* Digital Health-sagepub., DOI: 10.1177/20552076211033421

Thorne, K. S., Braginsky, V., & Ginzburg, V. (1994). Black Holes and Time Warps: Einstein's Outrageous Legacy. *Physics Today*, 47(11), 85–86. DOI: 10.1063/1.2808700

Tien, Wei, Darkwa, Wood, & Calautit. (2022). Machine Learning and Deep Learning Methods for Enhancing Building Energy Efficiency and Indoor Environmental Quality – A Review. Energy and AI, 10. .DOI: 10.1016/j.egyai.2022.100198

Topcu, M. N., & Hirst, W. (2022). *Collective mental time travel: Current research and future directions* (pp. 71–97). DOI: 10.1016/bs.pbr.2022.06.002

Trakas, M. (2023). Journeying to the past: Time travel and mental time travel, how far apart? *Frontiers in Psychology*, 14. Advance online publication. DOI: 10.3389/fpsyg.2023.1260458

Ueda, E. (2024). Climate change and artificial intelligence in healthcare: Review and recommendations towards a sustainable future. *Diagnostic and Interventional Imaging, 105*(11).

Umer, M., Imtiaz, Z., Ullah, S., Mehmood, A., Choi, G. S., & On, B. W. (2020). Fake news stance detection using deep learning architecture (CNN-LSTM). *IEEE Access : Practical Innovations, Open Solutions*, 8, 156695–156706. DOI: 10.1109/ACCESS.2020.3019735

UNEP. (2023). *Emissions Gap Report 2023*.https://www.unep.org/resources/emissions-gap-report-2023

Valdez, F., & Melin, P. (2023). A review on quantum computing and deep learning algorithms and their applications. *Soft Computing*, 27(18), 13217–13236. DOI: 10.1007/s00500-022-07037-4 PMID: 35411203

Valencia-Arias, A., García-Pineda, V., González-Ruiz, J. D., Medina-Valderrama, C. J., & García, R. B. (2023). Machine-Learning Applications in Energy Efficiency: A Bibliometric Approach and Research Agenda. *Designs*, 7(3), 71. DOI: 10.3390/designs7030071

Varntoumian, E. (2021). *European Health Parliament's*.https://www.healthparliament.eu/

Verma, S., Warrier, L., Bolia, B., & Mehta, S. (2022). Past, present, and future of virtual tourism-a literature review. *International Journal of Information Management Data Insights*, 2(2), 100085. DOI: 10.1016/j.jjimei.2022.100085

Vlădu escu, , E. (2023). Environmental Sustainability of Metaverse: Perspectives from Romanian Developers. *Sustainability*, 15(15), 11704.

Voss, S. (2023). *Metaheuristics in renewable energy optimization and resource allocation*. Springer Nature Switzerland AG. DOI: 10.1007/978-3-030-90171-9

Vyas, A. (n.d.). *Robo-advisors as Automatic Personal Financial Advisors: Opportunities and challenges based on recent results and case studies - ProQuest*. https://www.proquest.com/openview/236788025e86a6c976475586ce751cf8/1?pq-origsite=gscholar&cbl=6447394

Wald, R. M. (1984). *General Relativity*. University of Chicago Press. DOI: 10.7208/chicago/9780226870373.001.0001

Wang, W. Y. (2017). "Liar, liar pants on fire": A new benchmark dataset for fake news detection. In *Proceedings of the 55th Annual Meeting of the Association for Computational Linguistics (ACL 2017)* (pp. 422-426).

Wang, W., Wang, S., Fan, W., Liu, Z., & Tang, J. (2020). Global-and-local aware data generation for the class imbalance problem. *Proc. 2020 SIAM Int. Conf. Data Mining, SDM2020*, 307–315. DOI: 10.1137/1.9781611976236.35

Wang, X., Zhang, X., Gong, H., Jiang, J., & Rai, H. M. (2021). A flight control method for unmanned aerial vehicles based on vibration suppression. *IET Collaborative Intelligent Manufacturing*, 3(3), 252–261. DOI: 10.1049/cim2.12027

Wang, Y. (2012). Quantum Computation and Quantum Information. *Statistical Science*, 27(3). DOI: 10.1214/11-STS378

Wei, W., & Wan, X. (2017). Learning to identify ambiguous and misleading news headlines. In *Proceedings of the 26th International Joint Conference on Artificial Intelligence (IJCAI)* (pp. 4172-4178). https://doi.org/DOI: 10.24963/ijcai.2017/583

What is Financial Planning and Analysis (FP&A)? (n.d.). SAP https://www.sap.com/products/financial-management/what-is-financial-planning-and analysis-fpa.html

Wu, L., & Liu, H. (2018). Tracing fake-news footprints: Characterizing social media messages by how they propagate. *WSDM 2018 - Proceedings of the 11th ACM International Conference on Web Search and Data Mining*, 637–645. DOI: 10.1145/3159652.3159677

Wu, D., Huo, J., Zhang, G., & Zhang, W. (2018). Minimization of logistics cost and carbon emissions based on quantum particle swarm optimization. *Sustainability (Basel)*, 10(10), 3791. DOI: 10.3390/su10103791

Xiong, H., Wu, Z., Fan, H., Li, G., & Jiang, G. (2018). Quantum rotation gate in quantum-inspired evolutionary algorithm: A review, analysis and comparison study. *Swarm and Evolutionary Computation*, 42, 43–57. DOI: 10.1016/j.swevo.2018.02.020

Yanagi, Y., Orihara, R., Sei, Y., Tahara, Y., & Ohsuga, A. (2020). Fake news detection with generated comments for news articles. In *2020 IEEE 24th International Conference on Intelligent Engineering Systems (INES)* (pp. 1–4). IEEE. DOI: 10.1109/INES49302.2020.9147195

Yang, X.-S. (2010). Nature-inspried metaheuristic algorithms (2nd ed.). Academic Press.

Yang, X.-S. (2022). *Nature-inspired optimization algorithms: Firefly algorithm and bat algorithm*. Springer Nature Switzerland AG. DOI: 10.1007/978-3-030-19719-3

Yang, X.-S., & Deb, S. (2020). *Hybrid optimization techniques integrating evolutionary and swarm algorithms*. Wiley. DOI: 10.1002/9781119644097

Yao, X., & Xu, Y. (2006). *Recent Advances in Evolutionary Computation*. Springer. DOI: 10.1007/s11390-006-0001-4

Ying, L., Yu, H., Wang, J., Ji, Y., & Qian, S. (2021). Fake news detection via multi-modal topic memory network. *IEEE Access : Practical Innovations, Open Solutions*, 9, 132818–132829. DOI: 10.1109/ACCESS.2021.3113981

Younus, M., Nurmandi, A., & Suswanta, S. (2023). Concept of Time Travel and The Different Theories for Making It Possible and The Implications of Time Travelling. *Journal of Wood Science*, 2(4), 576–582. DOI: 10.58344/jws.v2i4.268

Zanaj, E., Caso, G., De Nardis, L., Mohammadpour, A., Alay, Ö., & Di Benedetto, M.-G. (2021). Energy Efficiency in Short and Wide-Area IoT Technologies—A Survey. *Technologies*, 9(1), 22. DOI: 10.3390/technologies9010022

Zhang, , E. (2023). Blockchain Technology: Security Issues, Healthcare Applications, Challenges and Future Trends. *Electronics (Basel)*, 12(3). Advance online publication. DOI: 10.3390/electronics12030546

Zhang, J., & Li, X. (2020). Adaptive parameter control strategies in evolutionary algorithms. *Evolutionary Computation*, 28(3), 437–460. DOI: 10.1162/evco_a_00259 PMID: 31120773

Zhang, Z., Chen, Y., Wang, H., Fu, Q., Chen, J., & Lu, Y. (2023, June 8). Anomaly detection method for building energy consumption in multivariate time series based on graph attention mechanism. *PLoS One*, 18(6), e0286770. DOI: 10.1371/journal.pone.0286770 PMID: 37289704

Zhao, W., Yan, L., & Zhang, Y. (2018). Geometric-constrained multi-view image matching method based on semi-global optimization. *Geo-Spatial Information Science*, 21(2), 115–126. DOI: 10.1080/10095020.2018.1441754

Zhou, X., Zafarani, R., Shu, K., & Liu, H. (2019). Fake news: Fundamental theories, detection strategies, and challenges. In *Proceedings of the Twelfth ACM International Conference on Web Search and Data Mining* (pp. 836-837). DOI: 10.1145/3289600.3291382

Zikria, Y. B., Afzal, M. K., Kim, S. W., Marin, A., & Guizani, M. (2020). Deep learning for intelligent IoT: Opportunities, challenges and solutions. Computer Communications, 164, 50-53. DOI: 10.1016/j.comcom.2020.08.017

Zubiaga, A., Aker, A., Bontcheva, K., Liakata, M., & Procter, R. (2018). Detection and resolution of rumours in social media: A survey. *ACM Computing Surveys*, 51(2), 1–36. Advance online publication. DOI: 10.1145/3161603

About the Contributors

Hari Mohan Rai holds a Ph.D. from the Indian Institute of Technology, Dhanbad, and currently serves as an Assistant Professor in the Department of Soft Computing at Gachon University, South Korea. Concurrently, he holds the position of Cyber Educator as an Associate Professor in the Department of Cyber Security at the International IT University in Almaty, Kazakhstan. With over a decade of teaching experience, he previously served as an Associate Professor at the Dronacharya Group of Institutions in Greater Noida, India. Dr. Rai's academic journey includes a Bachelor of Engineering in Electronics and Communication Engineering from Vinayaka Mission University and a Master of Engineering in Electrical Engineering (Control System) from Government Engineering College in Jabalpur, where he earned a Gold Medal. His scholarly contributions extend to over 30 research papers published in national and international journals, including over 15 papers in SCI journals. Recognized for his excellence, Dr. Rai received the "Best Teachers Award" from A.K.T.U. of Lucknow, Uttar Pradesh, in 2019. He has actively contributed to conferences as a session chair, co-chair, conference secretary, and publishing chair, and has organized numerous International Conferences and Faculty Development Programs. Dr. Rai holds a prominent role in academia, serving as a member of the editorial board for the BMC Bioinformatics journal by Springer Nature. Additionally, he contributes as a reviewer for reputable publications, including Elsevier Journals, IEE Journals, IET Journals, Wiley Journals, and IETE Journals. Actively engaged in international societies, he is a member of the International Association of Engineers, the Society of Digital Information and Wireless Communications (SDIWC), and the IEEE Professional Member Society (IAENG). Dr. Rai's expertise encompasses bio-signal processing, bio-imaging, control systems, image processing, neural networks, pattern classification, artificial intelligence, and optimization techniques.

AbdulRazaque is an accomplished researcher and educator in the field of Computer Science & Engineering, with extensive expertise in cybersecurity, machine learning, quantum computing, and various other domains. He earned his PhD degree from the University of Bridgeport, USA, and completed his Post Doctorate at the University of Illinois, USA. With over 170 international academic publications, including journals, conferences, and book chapters, Dr. Razaque has made significant contributions to the advancement of knowledge in cybersecurity, biometric authentication, computer networks, and mobile malware detection and infringement. He has authored four academic books on these subjects. Dr. Razaque has held prestigious editorial positions, serving as the Editor-in-Chief for the International Journal for Engineering and Technology (IJET), Singapore, from 2012 to 2015. Additionally, he has been an Editor, Associate Editor, and Member of the Editorial Board for several other journals. As a dedicated researcher, Dr. Razaque has secured significant research funding totaling US$3,548,270.00. He has taught a wide range of courses, including Big Data Analytics, Data Mining, Secure Cloud Computing, Machine Learning, Cryptography for Information Security, and many more. His research interests encompass cybersecurity, machine learning, deep learning, quantum computing, data science, wireless sensor networks, artificial intelligence, cloud computing, and more. Dr. Razaque holds multiple certifications, including Cisco Certified Network Associate (CCNA), Microsoft Certified Professional (MCP), and ISACA Certified Information Security Manager (CISM). Throughout his career, Dr. Razaque has been recognized with numerous awards, including the Google PhD Fellowship, Best Paper Awards at prestigious conferences, and scholarships such as the Commonwealth Fellowship and the Split Merit Scholarship. His outstanding contributions to research and education have earned him international acclaim and accolades from esteemed organizations worldwide.

* * *

Tejaswi Arella, born and raised in India, is a young aspiring engineer with a deep passion for technology. Specifically, she's fascinated by artificial intelligence (AI) and machine learning (ML). Currently, she's pursuing a Bachelor's degree in Technology, majoring in AI and ML. Her focus lies in optimizing AI and ML tools to make them work better and faster. Within the corridors of her academic institution, Tejaswi's enthusiasm for AI and ML shines brightly. Her focus is not merely on understanding these complex technologies but on unlocking their full potential. With a keen eye for optimization, she is deeply engrossed in exploring ways to enhance the efficiency and effectiveness of AI and ML tools. Through her dedication and perseverance, she has already made significant strides in this pursuit, earning commendations from both her professors and peers. Tejaswi's journey is just beginning, but she's determined to make a significant impact in the world of technology. With her passion for AI and ML and her commitment to constant learning and improvement, she's well on her way to achieving her goals.

Prafulla Hatte is working as a Dean Research & Development with MIT Academy of Engineering, Pune, India. He has filed 11 patent applications and published several research papers in various international journals. His research areas include Alternative Fuels, IC Engine, Materials and Engineering Education. He has 8 years of industrial and 22+ years of academic experience.

Manish Khare has been a faculty member at Allahabad Degree College, University of Allahabad, since October 2024. From 2017 to 2024, he worked as an Assistant Professor at Dhirubhai Ambani Institute of Information and Communication Technology (DAIICT), Gandhinagar. He earned his D.Phil. in Computer Science from the University of Allahabad (2015), M. Tech. in Computer Science and Engineering from CDAC Noida (2009), and M.Sc. in Computer Science from the University of Allahabad (2006). Dr. Khare completed his postdoctoral fellowship in Electrical Engineering and Computer Science at Gwangju Institute of Science and Technology (GIST), South Korea (2016–2017). His research focuses on Image Processing, Machine Learning, and FPGA-based Image Processing. A Senior Member of IEEE and active member of IUPRAI and ACM, he has published over 90 research papers and held leadership roles in the IEEE Signal Processing Society Gujarat Chapter.

Chinthakunta Manjunath possesses an experience of 17 years including teaching and research, currently associated with CHRIST (Deemed to be University), Bangalore as Assistant Professor in the Department of Computer Science and Engineering. He is an experienced academic and researcher with a good background in data science area and financial forecasting. Specializes in building comprehensive models for stock market prediction, specifically for the NIFTY50 index. Demonstrates expertise in data analysis, statistical modeling, machine learning, and deep learning models along with a proven record of publishing in peer-reviewed journals. Dr. Chinthakunta Manjunath published a Total 14 research articles which includes 6 International Scopus Journals,6 Scopus Conference proceedings, 2 book chapters and 1 Indian Patent Published. His current research interest focuses on the use of machine learning and deep learning to predict stock market movements in the equity market.

Jayapandian N. has received his PhD from Anna University, Chennai. He has completed M.E.(CSE) from Kongu Engineering College, Erode, Tamilnadu at 2009. He has completed his B.Tech.(IT) from Institute of Road and Transport Technology, Erode, Tamilnadu at 2006. He is active life Member of ISTE. Currently, he is working as Associate Professor in the Department of Computer Science & Engineering at Christ University, Bangalore. In his 11 years of teaching experience and one year of Industry Experience. His research interests are Grid Computing and Cloud Computing. He has published in 4 book chapters, 20 International Journal articles, 60 international and National Conferences.

Poornima Pandian is pursuing her research in the field of Cognitive Radio Networks from the Anna University. She currently serves as an Assistant Professor in the Department of ECE at Sri Sai Ram Engineering College. Her research interests include Wireless Networks, Machine learning techniques, Quantum Computing and Optimization techniques.

Yugha R. is pursuing a PhD degree from Anna University. She has obtained her master's degrees in Computer Science and Engineering from Hindusthan Institute of Science and Technology. She has obtained her bachelor's degree in Information Technology from Sona College of Engineering and Technology. She is currently serving as an Assistant Professor at Sathyabama Institute of Science and Technology in Chennai. Her research interests encompass Wireless Communications, IoT (Internet of Things), and Artificial Intelligence. She has published her research findings in various reputed international journals/ conferences. Her academic journey underscores a strong commitment to advancing these fields through research and teaching.

Pallavi Rajan, born and raised in the vibrant city of Hyderabad, India, is a distinguished student currently advancing her academic journey in Computer Engineering with a specialization in Artificial Intelligence and Machine Learning. From a young age, Pallavi exhibited a keen interest in technology and innovation, which has driven her to excel in her chosen field. Beyond her academic pursuits, Pallavi is a passionate and eloquent public speaker, known for captivating audiences with her articulate and thoughtful presentations. Her love for sports is equally commendable, as she actively participates in various athletic activities, showcasing her commitment to physical fitness and teamwork. Pallavi's leadership qualities shine through her involvement in multiple clubs within her institute, where she holds significant roles in the steering body. Her ability to balance academics, extracurricular activities, and leadership responsibilities is a testament to her exceptional time management and organizational skills. As she continues to explore the realms of artificial intelligence and machine learning, Pallavi aims to contribute significantly to the field, leveraging her knowledge and skills to drive technological advancements. Her dedication, versatility, and enthusiasm make her a remarkable individual poised for a promising future in the ever-evolving world of technology.

Siddharth Rana is an enthusiastic person, profoundly interested to contemplate about the span of the Universe, while putting forward his understanding, crafting Hypothesis, to address the Universe. Siddharth aims to study the nature of Time, specifically in the Quantum Realm, while providing a deeper insight on its nature in the Cosmic Realm. He has exposed himself to the foundations of Quantum Computing to understand the working of the Universe, onto the screen. Siddharth is a passionate Writer and Speaker, conveying deeper understanding about the Universe.

Manmohan Rauthan is working as Head of the department and professor in HNB Garhwal University in computer science and engineering department with 30 years of teaching experience. He has done M.Tech in 1987 from Roorkee University and has done his Ph.D. from Kumaon University in 2013. He has written a several research paper as well as 5 books in computer science. He is a core member of research committees, visiting committees.

Diya Ray is a devoted student currently studying Electronics and Communication. With a keen interest in electronics and robotics, she finds great fascination in exploring new concepts and technologies. she thrives on the challenge of learning and is always eager to expand her knowledge. Her dedication and sincerity drive me to work hard and stay committed to her goals. she believes in pushing boundaries and aspire to make meaningful contributions to the field of electronics and robotics.

David Samuel Azariya S. is working as an Assistant Professor in the Department of Information Technology at Sona College of Technology. He is currently pursuing a Doctorate in Anna University, Chennai, Tamil Nadu, India. He has completed Diploma in Electronics and Communications and Bachelor of Engineering degree in Information Technology and Master of Engineering in Computer and Communication Engineering. He is actively engaged in the research area of data visualization, computer vision, deep learning and IoT. He has published various research papers in Springer and IEEE conferences related to research domain. He is the member of IEI and ISTE professional society.

Chithra Selvaraj received her Bachelor's in Computer Science and Engineering from Bharathiar University ranking Sixth in the University. After completing her Master's in Computer Science and Engineering, she earned her Ph.D. from Anna University, Chennai in 2014. She is a recognized supervisor in Anna University and her areas of research include Computer Networks, Internet of Things, Trust Management Network Security and Cyber Security. She has overall teaching experience of over 20 years in various academic institutions. She has published more than 40 research articles in refereed International journals and conference proceedings. She has published a book titled "Bank of the Future" in 2018, which throws light on the technological risks of banking applications. She is a senior member of IEEE professional body.

Komal Singh is currently serving as a faculty member in the Computer Engineering Department at Pandit Deendayal Energy University while pursuing her PhD at IIIT Vadodara. She holds a Master of Engineering (ME) degree from Monark University and a Bachelor of Engineering (BE) degree from LDRP Institute of Technology and Research, affiliated with KSV University.

Nikhil Kumar Singh is currently serving as an Assistant Professor at Government Engineering College, Gandhinagar, affiliated with Gujarat Technological University (GTU), under the Technical Education Department, Government of Gujarat. He holds a Master's degree from NIT Surat and a B.Tech degree from IERT Allahabad. With over 8 years of teaching experience, he has authored two books and published approximately 20 research papers in reputed journals.

Lingala Thirupathi has 17 years of experience in the Teaching and IT industry. B.Tech, M.Tech. Published 13+ Scopus-indexed national and international journals and 1- SCI indexed journal. He is passionate about advancing the fields of AI, ML, and cyber security. He is committed to sharing his expertise and fostering a collaborative learning environment for the students. He has co-authored 3 textbooks on AI, ML, and Cyber Security.

Sathiyamoorthi V. is currently working as Lecturer in Computer Engineering Department at Government polytechnic college, Dharmapuri, Tamil Nadu, India. He was born on June 21, 1983, at Omalur in Salem District, Tamil Nadu, India. He received his Bachelor of Engineering degree in Information Technology from Periyar University, Salem with First Class. He obtained his Master of Engineering degree in Computer Science and Engineering from Anna University, Chennai with Distinction and secured 30th University Rank. He received his Ph.D degree from Anna University, Chennai in Web Mining. His areas of specialization include Web Usage Mining, Data Structures, Design and Analysis of Algorithm and Operating System. He has published many papers in International Journals and conferences. He has published many books and book chapters in various renowned international publishers. He has also participated in various National level Workshops and Seminars conducted by various reputed institutions.

B. Vasundara, an aspiring engineer and technology enthusiast, was born and raised in Hyderabad, India. From a young age, Vasundara exhibited a keen interest in science and technology, often engaging in activities that fueled her curiosity about how things work. Her early education laid a strong foundation for her analytical and problem-solving skills, which would later become pivotal in her academic pursuits. Vasundara's passion for technology led her to pursue a Bachelor of Technology in Artificial Intelligence and Machine Learning (AIML), She excelled in her coursework, demonstrating a profound understanding of AI and machine learning concepts. She was particularly interested in the applications of AI in healthcare, finance, and education, aiming to leverage technology to create impactful solutions. Her research work often received commendations from her professors and peers, earning her a reputation as a diligent and innovative thinker. Vasundara's dedication to her field extended beyond the classroom, as she actively participated in seminars and workshops, constantly seeking to expand her knowledge.

Neha Verma is currently working as assistant Professor in ECE Dept. of dronacharya college of Engineering. With more than 11 years of work experience, having Industrial exposure, getting 3 patents published and 3 copyrights received, her work in field of projects and prototyping speaks for itself. Her current research work is inclined with advancements required in Smart Farming techniques using Wireless sensor networks, cognitive analysis of received data and Automation of complete process using recent embedded technologies. Her Research work aims to provides a one-stop solution to farmer with ZERO- technical know-how and Sample GIU based Mobile app.

Index

P

Q

R

S

T

www.ingramcontent.com/pod-product-compliance
Lightning Source LLC
LaVergne TN
LVHW081329300926
849161LV00008B/1922